south african poets
on poetry

south african poets on poetry

Interviews from New Coin 1992-2001

edited by Robert Berold

POETRY
Gecko

This book was prepared for publication under the auspices of the Institute of the Study of English in Africa (ISEA), Rhodes University, Grahamstown, South Africa

Published by Gecko Poetry
an imprint of University of Natal Press
Private Bag X01, Scottsville, 3209, South Africa
E-mail: books@nu.ac.za
Website: http://www.unpress.co.za

ISBN 1 86914 031 1

Cover illustration by Tammy Griffin
Cover design by Sumayya Essack
Text design and layout by Paul Wessels and Manoj Sookai
Printed and bound by Interpak Books, Pietermaritzburg

CONTENTS

ROBERT BEROLD

Poets look far and deep for the language that lives and sweats in their poems. The political animal and the innocent, the sceptic and the mystic, the biological and the historical, all inhabit a poet's consciousness. So much the better for us who are trying to decipher our times.

In the 1990s, as the walls of apartheid were finally being cracked open, poets were looking around them to see which direction to walk or run. Their antennae were out, picking up whatever static or clear sounds were coming over the air. Most were optimistic about the new story which they were inventing, even if it was only for themselves. So in one way this book is a record of ten years of a rapidly changing South Africa, jumping perspectives from narrator to narrator.

As editor of the journal *New Coin*, I was fortunate to be in conversation or correspondence with many poets. What they were saying about their values and working methods illuminated much of their writing. In 1992, *New Coin* started publishing interviews. The interviewers asked the standard questions. What did poets need in order to write (live, survive)? What were their literary influences? How did they understand their own aesthetics? How the limited publishing opportunities in South Africa affect them?

A note on how the interviews were edited. Each interview was taped, usually for one and half to two hours, and a verbatim transcript made. The transcript then was edited to about half its original length, with the poet and editor agreeing on what should be cut. I admire the American social documenter Studs Terkel, and tried to follow his method, which downplays the interviewer and retains the oral expressiveness of the spontaneous voice.

The poets spoke openly, articulately, and often, as it turned out, prophetically. It has been a great pleasure to read these interviews again and collect them into a book.

Interviewed by Robert Berold

TATAMKHULU AFRIKA (1920-2002) was born in Egypt and came to South Africa as a young child. He fought in World War II and was taken prisoner. In the 1960s he lived in Cape Town and converted to Islam, founding the armed resistance group Al-Jihaad. He published novels and novellas, and wrote two plays. He died following a road accident shortly after his 82nd birthday and the launch of a new novel.

Books of poems published:
Nine Lives (Carrefour/Hippogriff, 1991)
Dark Rider (Snailpress/Mayibuye, 1992)
Maqabane (Mayibuye Books, 1994)
Flesh and the Flame (Silk Road, 1995)
The Lemon Tree (Snailpress, 1995)
Turning Points (Mayibuye, 1996)
The Angel and other poems (Carapace, 1999)
Mad Old Man under the Morning Star (Snailpress, 2000)
Au Ceux (French translations) (Editions Creathis l'école des filles, 2000)

Your poetry has a tremendous range, some of it introspective, some of it dealing with portraits, with moments of celebration, with place, with political events or events in prison. What links it all, for me, is an ability to observe. Most of us in South Africa don't have very good powers of observation. Things are so difficult and painful around us that we tend to go around with an ideology which we use to filter our surroundings. You have a political commitment but you don't seem to need an ideology to numb the impact of your environment. How do you manage to see the world freshly and clearly without getting cynical or overwhelmed about it?

If you admit to yourself you're all people too, then you have no armour between you and people. Whenever I see a person who is unusual, I write a portrait of the person, a word portrait, so that I can remember that person as I saw him or her. I try to do it as accurately as I can. As I described it to Lionel Abrahams once, I lovingly circle the subject, fleshing it out bit by bit, until it stands before me as complete as I can get it. In that way I see each person freshly, newly, without prejudice, without reservation.

When it comes to writing about nature, I have a hunger. I was brought up on a farm and I love farm life. Sitting here in the city I long for greenery. For water – running water – and birds. I feed the doves out here in the yard. I planted my own little lemon tree and a fig tree in the concrete, so I can have greenery.

I'm pretty ancient by now, in my 72nd year, and well, at this age, one must be prepared to 'shuffle off the mortal coil' at any time. I think that I see things freshly because I realise I may be seeing them for the last time. I do see things more clearly, more indelibly, as I get older.

Why was it that you only started writing poetry a couple of years ago?

Yes, well that is a bit of a myth. I only started writing serious poetry in 1987. But I wrote my first volume of poetry when I was 11. And I sent it in to be reviewed. You could in those days you know – send it into a reviewer's just to be reviewed – for a fee. I only submitted it when I was 17 or so, but I wrote it when I was 11.

What was the response?

He said "Well, one poem is very good, and the others are too personalised – you should rather forget about poetry." So I did. Also at that time (when I was 17) I wrote a novel. That took off very well and was published in England. So I decided I was a prose writer, not a poet. And then the war came. I wrote something in the Prisoner of War camps in indelible pencil and an old copy book which I got from the Red Cross. A psychedelic sort of prose that everybody said was absolutely marvellous stuff and I still think it was very marvellous myself.

Everybody? You mean your fellow prisoners?

Yes, you know in Prisoner of War camps you have all kinds of intellectual guys there, artists and poets and what have you, very professional people. They thought it was great stuff. But then we moved to the other camp and the Germans took it and destroyed it in front of me. That devastated me and I didn't write for years.

When I became a Muslim in the 1960s, I started to write religious poetry . . . but bad stuff, you know. I had no technique whatsoever. Well, that lasted for a long time. Then I was in prison in '87 and when I came out I wanted to express rage. Not faith or 'crook a pinkie' stuff, I wanted now to express fury. I wrote a whole selection called *Tormented* which I submitted to various publishers. They said "Well, it's very encouraging, but it's not good enough." Which rather crushed me, but by that time I'd gained some resilience, because you know, hatred is a very motivating force.

I sent some of it to Douglas Reid Skinner at *Upstream* and he selected a couple of poems. And he wrote to me, he said 'I'll give you a few tips – when you want to stop saying something, put down a full stop, don't carry on and on and on. And stop telling the reader what to think,' he said, 'let them think it out for themselves.' All these kinds of things. I took all these to heart, and then I started to write in a completely different way, and then I took off.

So much for the Tatamkhulu myth . . . in fact you've been writing all your life in various forms.

On and off, yes. But only since '88 when I got some help did I begin to write with any kind of technical soundness.

But still, when you did start writing poetry seriously it seems your voice came out completely developed. You must have had an inner dialogue going for a long time for this to happen.

To be introspective (people equate this with reclusive) is to have a dialogue with one's muse whether you like it or not. But the muse couldn't use me because I didn't have the technique to be used. The message I was getting was garbled.

How did you get it right?

I got it right because people helped me, told me where I was being old-fashioned, or crude, or naive, or whatever, and I rectified it, and the muse found it easier to speak through me. Well now we're becoming real chommies.

Some questions about your life. You were born of Egyptian and Turkish parents, and they came out here when you were a baby.

Yes. They died when I was two years old.

Both of them? At the same time?

Yes, the flu epidemic of that time, remember? This was in the 20s — I was born in 1920. Coming from Egypt I suppose that they were open to infection. One always is, going to a strange country, I believe. I was adopted by a certain family, in the western Transvaal. I was given their name, brought up by them, Christian tradition, English-speaking people, 1820 Settler stock. They used to read a lot. They were serious-minded people, quite intellectual.

Judging from your poems about your childhood it sounds like it wasn't a happy family.

No, my foster mother and father fought like cat and dog. He was a horrible man.

How did you learn you were adopted?

They only told me as I was about to leave school. They said "Well you're going out into the world now and we live in a difficult country" – my foster mother actually told me – "a difficult country where race counts for a lot. Although you don't look the part we'd better tell you that you're not our son and your parents were Asian" – as she put it. In those days, anybody who came from the middle east was Asian, 'coolie.' And so she told me that.

What was your reaction?

It was as though someone had dropped the bottom right out of my world. I felt rootless all of a sudden, lost, absolutely lost. But one gets out of these things when one is young. So I went on, using the same name, but always subconsciously aware of the fact that I was not what I was trying to be. It used to creep out in the oddest ways – the old ancestral blood. Like at school (this was before they told me) we had an art exhibition and I very carefully drew an Egyptian drawing, these one-sided figures of Egyptians. I got a five shilling prize at the agricultural show for that. Even from that early age I loved reading about Egypt.

And after school?

I became an articled clerk in an accounting firm for about 18 months. And then the war broke out. I joined the army to get out of being an articled clerk – man I hated it. I went to see a film at the time with this gung-ho stuff, the Indian frontier, a guy dies there beating a drum etc. I thought "This is for me, there's a war, let's go!"

I graduated at the South African Military College as an instructor in the permanent force, then I volunteered to go up north and went up with the Second South African Division, to Egypt. I was taken prisoner at Tobruk shortly afterwards and landed up in a Prisoner of War camp for three years.

War is the most unsettling experience. When I came back I didn't have any ambitions at all, I just wanted to have a good time. I married and got divorced almost within months, fathered one son and got out of it as quickly as I could. I was too wild at that age, I had no sense of discipline whatsoever. I was forming boys' clubs all over the place, you know, secret societies, getting into debt, launching out in the most insane ventures. I don't drive a car but I was always buying cars and getting somebody else to drive them. Getting into debt, trading them in. I had no sense of responsibility at all. I think that's why I landed up in what is now Namibia, sniffing adventure. Worked there on and off for twenty years, on the copper mines.

You settled down?

No. I didn't have to worry about anything, just had to do my shift. I had a band then. I was the manager of a band at the recreation club, and played on Saturday nights for the boys. That was all I was doing, nothing really constructive at all. It was only when I came to Cape Town in the 60s, when I became Muslim, I began to realise there's a bit more to life than this sort of thing.

How did you become Muslim?

I had been an atheist for quite a long time. I didn't believe in anything. When I came to

4

Cape Town I landed amongst Muslims more by accident than anything else. I couldn't find work for about six months. I knew hell then, I knew what hunger was. The old woman who used to clean the baths and the toilets, we got talking, and we got very friendly and she said "You must come and visit my friends here in District Six." So one Saturday night I very fearfully walked up Hanover Street. It was like walking into a Cairo bazaar, a real lively place it was. I met up with this family and they took me to their hearts in an unbelievable fashion.

I heard the Qur'an being recited. Well, the Qur'an, you know, we Muslims believe is a miracle. Maybe some echo of it from even babyhood reverberated, but immediately I was attracted – I went and bought the Qur'an in English and read it for one whole week and became utterly convinced. So I went to my old friends here and said "I want to become a Muslim" so they rushed me to the Sheikh and made me pronounce the faith, and I was a Muslim on the spot.

Then I began to think seriously about life and living. I concentrated deeply on religious matters – writing religious poetry and so on. Then I started up charitable work. I formed this organisation called Al-Jihaad. I still head it. I began to work in order to earn money to help the poor – people I am now writing about – and helping them, I became myself poor. Now at the age of 72, I have a very small salary, no hope of getting another job. I feel quite happy about it, at least I've wasted my money on a good cause.

How did you go from there to becoming a 'terrorist'?

I started out in the political struggle in the early 80s, under the banner of this religious organisation. Inevitably, working in close collaboration with other activists, I came into contact with ANC members, and into close contact with Umkonto we Sizwe. I was later arrested for terrorism, we needn't get into that. That's where I got my name Tatamkhulu Afrika. It's the only name that means anything to me. It's under that name I flowered politically and also poetically. In any case the name I had before this wasn't even my name at all.

Your prison experience was very important to you, more than the war, it seems.

Tremendously so. I would not have missed it for anything. The war did not have such an effect on me because it was a restricted experience. In a Prisoner of War camp you're only meeting up with a small cross-section of humanity, but in prison you're meeting up with a nation – with your own nation. Coming out of prison you were flowing out into an entire nation of oppressed people, which leads to a much wider and sharper reaction, a much greater absorption into people's suffering and emotions. If I'd never gone to prison I don't think you'd be sitting here talking to me now, because I would not have written anything.

A small thing that happened in prison turned me completely around. Before I was in prison, we used to go to many funerals in the townships and we used to toyi-toyi. And there was one little black guy, a teenager, who was absolutely fascinated by this old man toyi-toyiing with the funeral processions. He'd always come and toyi-toyi with me all the way up to the cemetery, laughing like mad, you know, and slapping me on the back. A real joy to watch. The day we walked into prison, Victor Verster, we kicked up a stir. All the youngsters in prison were leaning out of the upper windows of the cells, watching us come in, us newcomers. And there was this kid, but he was completely changed. All the joy had gone out of him. He put up his hand like this, slowly, but there was no life left in him at all. I went to bed that night thinking of the way he used to be.

These youngsters used to toyi-toyi right through the night. I've never seen such energy – shouting slogans right through the night. And some of them who couldn't take it any more used to scream hysterically. It was awful to listen to this. I think the suffering and the change in these youngsters broke my heart, to use a cliché. If one's heart can break, it broke my heart, and I came out of there enraged.

You talk about being in the black section of the prison. Were you still classified 'white' or had you somehow changed race classification?

I've never been classified 'white.' When I was in Namibia we were not classified at all. When I came down here in the 60s, they wanted to classify me 'white.' I refused. I went into despair because I'd become a Muslim and I wanted to stay in District Six. In those days you were not allowed to stay in District Six as a 'white' person. I went to Helen Suzman and spoke to her about it and she said "I'll help you." I gave her the names of certain people I knew from the days of my childhood. I don't know what she did, whether she actually went and interviewed all these people, I haven't a clue. But she called me in, about six months after that, to her office in Parliament, and told me that the Minister of the Interior had agreed to classify me 'malay.' So I became a 'malay,' although I'd never been a malay in my life. And she said "but now remember, whatever you do, don't become visible, don't take part in politics, for God's sake, lie low." Well of course I didn't heed her, in the early 80s I ignored that completely.

What do you see as the challenge of political poetry in the 1990's?

I've just written a paper for COSAW about this. What I'm saying there is that, after February 1990, it is still necessary to write political poetry. Political poetry in this new phase of the struggle – if you want to use the word 'struggle' – is a protest, not against political dominance but against dominance of wealth, of privilege, residual class barricades, which are very much there. It's become even more necessary, because poverty and privilege are a greater menace to our society now than political dominance.

But we must write poetry which is poetry. It mustn't be sloganising any more. It should never have been sloganising in the first place, unless it was an oral poetry from a political platform. There it played its role, it served its purpose. If we're going to write poetry now, it must be good poetry. That of course is an old theme between the classicists and the new guys. I'm halfway between the two.

I'd like to be read by all people: by whites, privileged whites, people who could do so much to alleviate deprivation in this land and are not doing so; but also to be read by people who are poverty stricken that they might know, understand, that there are people who care. Whether it'll help them in the long run, materially, I don't believe. It might help them spiritually to some extent, and that's about it.

You've said you write your poems in solitude in order to purge yourself, yet you find that you are striking a chord in a large group of people. It's always like that when art comes from deep enough within the artist.

Well in writing to purge oneself – if one is doing it in a universal sense – one is purging others as well if you read it to them. After all, what I am concerned with at the moment – poverty and deprivation – is a universal thing. I myself do not live in the best of circumstances, I understand very well what poverty and deprivation is like. Whether I write in solitude or whether I don't is really not the point. The point is that I know that what I am writing about will register with others who have shared this experience and it will get across to them.

You've spoken about the notion of the muse, the energy that shapes a poem. Is this a mystical experience, an ordinary experience, or both?

Well I believe absolutely that the muse exists, but what the muse is, I mean, who knows? Is it external? Is it internal? I don't think it is really external because if it were external you would not develop a voice of your own. It is something that belongs to you. It will become operative if you encourage it to operate and it'll die if you do not encourage it.

Sometimes one looks at a poem and thinks "Well – did I produce that?" It just seems so unique, so not you, yet it is you. Only it is coming from an aspect of yourself which is alien to your normal self. I know some poets who say 'you must wait for the muse to come to you.' Well it's nice if it does – but it doesn't always come to you that easily. I think that if you want to, you can induce it. I've done that, quite often. Where I want to write and the muse is silent, I'll grapple with it until I produce one line, one line which is musical, which begins to say what I want to say. I'll write it down. I'll dwell on that line until slowly another line is added and another and another – sometimes I don't even know where I am going to. Anybody can be taught the rules of poetry, hey? But unless that person has a very strong muse, and encourages that muse, that person will never write lasting poetry.

Interviewed by Colleen Crawford Cousins

JOAN METELERKAMP was born in Pretoria in 1956 and grew up in KwaZulu-Natal. She now lives in the Southern Cape. She has worked as an actor, teacher, and mother. She has written articles and reviews about South African poetry. She was editor of the poetry journal *New Coin* from 2000 to 2003.

Books of poems published:
Towing the Line (in *Signs*, edited by DR Skinner) (Carrefour, 1992)
Stone No More (Gecko Poetry, 1995)
Into the Day Breaking (Gecko Poetry, 2000)
Floating Islands (Mokoro, 2001)
Requiem (Deep South, 2003)

From your poetry it's clear that your mother and your grandmother allowed you to think of yourself as a free woman, someone with rights. How did these two women ward off or keep at bay the violence surrounding everything in this country?

In my poem "Jeremy Cronin (from inside) calls" there is the image of my mother holding my hand in the veggie garden while a formation of airforce planes flies over in a V. How do they ward off the violence? By investing themselves in their children and their families, and by creating homes and safe places for them.

How did you grow up to differ from them?

The most obvious difference is that I am a woman of the 90s: I experience different possibilities and pressures from those they would have experienced in the 30s and 60s. Perhaps I am less sure of my place than they were, but I have more consciousness of the contradictions that press upon me. I think both feminism and what my mother calls 'that infant science,' psychology, have to do with this. I say this in relation to motherhood and marriage particularly, but also in relation to 'politics' or 'work.' My grandmother was sufficiently 'committed' politically to suffer being listed, together with her husband, for being an SACP member. My mother was a staunch Liberal: though she did nothing overtly 'political' once the Liberal Party was banned. And I don't belong to a political party at all.

Where did you learn about poetry? If there is a South African tradition, what is it for you?

Jeremy Cronin's poems made an enormous impression on me when they came out, not only because of the philosophy informing them but because of the quality of voice. And Serote's use of voice moves me. The South African poetry that I've read and that I like is contemporary poetry. As far as the tradition goes, I haven't done my homework. I've read Ruth Miller backwards but I haven't read William Plomer or Roy Campbell backwards.

My tradition is just my arbitrary fortuitous education, when I was born, where I grew up and so on. My sense of hybrid identity comes from family history as much as anything else – Scots, Dutch, English, Afrikaans. My maternal grandfather's cousin was Eugene Marais, so his were some of the few Afrikaans poems I read with attention. After generations and generations of living in this country I still carry the colonial notion that 'real' culture isn't here. I'd love to go to London just to buy some books!

I went to Maritzburg University, which had a traditional kind of English Department and we read the great tradition in a kind of Leavisite way. Then I went away from English and worked in theatre. I wanted to write. I decided the way to learn about writing – I didn't say this to anyone except myself – was to read, and the way to read was to talk to people about what you read. So I went back, to do English Honours. By the time I came back to do Honours, people were recognising that we lived in Africa. I wish I could do it again, or do it more, or do it differently. I found that kind of dogged attention incredibly valuable – to read a representation of great poems, even if they're not the only great poems. I read Chaucer, I read Eliot and Yeats, I read Shakespeare, Shelley and Keats, Hopkins, Hardy. I read all the men, which is all the tradition that we were exposed to.

When did you start thinking "where are the women"?

Then. I thought: "I've got to start reading women." I started on the novelists. Then I started reading Emily Dickinson seriously, and then I went on to Marianne Moore, Elizabeth Bishop, of course Anne Sexton and Sylvia Plath, and then South African women poets, especially Ruth Miller, because then I was doing my thesis on Ruth Miller . . . And Adrienne Rich. It's very difficult to extend your boundaries. The tradition is helluva eurocentric.

That sense of restriction applies to writing too.

Yes, I have a sense that there's a lot of censorship, self-censorship in South African writing. There are legitimate themes and illegitimate themes. We can write about politics, we can write about art. But if you listen to your inner voices and write about what you care about, the politics is there. You don't have to strive after it; you don't have to write a poem about Boipatong to express the agony of this country.

I agree. My feeling in South Africa is that there are subjects around which major poems are constructed, and they are public subjects. "Jeremy Cronin (from inside) calls" is a kind of major public theme which now holds no interest for me, whereas some of the questions you take up in other poems like "Perfection for me has been shared passion fulfilled" and "In my dreaming," which is a poem about limits, are more interesting. The same with the poem "Dove." I think that's where your voice is, where your voice is more resolved.

I wrote "Jeremy Cronin (from inside) calls" as a response to a public hype rather than from a sense of writing a public poem. When it came out, it was a private poem about a public thing, which was the necessity of violence at that stage, 1984, just before the very worst, before the emergency. I thought that it exposed my fear, and my timidity. It wasn't public. I considered it a gender poem.

Many of your poems raise questions of gender. There's a polarisation in them, between the women and the men – away from the brilliance of men.

That thing about the brilliance of men comes from Adrienne Rich's "Transcendental Etude" where she talks about the necessity of moving out of the realm of men: she talks about moving quietly into the kitchen and piecing the fabric of our lives together. I understand the allure of this, and it's what I want too, and it's what I've done in mothering. I also want to move into the realm of the brilliance of men, but on my own terms. I want to be recognised as a woman and for whom I am. An image comes to me of . . . I want to dance without my shoes on. I want to say "fuck you" at the same time as saying "accept me." And tying it through my experience, through my grandmother and my mother: my mother was a clever woman who never recognised her mind as being her legitimate domain, who gave that up to go farming, which she also wanted. I'm not saying she did it self-sacrificially. She needed that, she needed the emotional sustenance of this close farming family thing with my father. The strong man, the shining man. And what I want to do is to integrate those two sufficiently that I can go into that domain and say "I am who I am" and "recognise me."

Can I read you this wonderful stanza from "Birth poem"?

> Twice I thought I would squeeze a child out
> into the world; twice, at the last moment,
> the men did it for me: They were all there,
> G.P., anaesthetist, obstetrician,
> and paediatrician; and the women,
> accomplices, there, holding the scalpel,
> passing the swabs.

It's the male part of the intellect as being the cutter, the surgeon, someone who operates . . . it's the brilliance of men. It's the rational part of the male mind, and here you're seeing the women as accomplices. It's the men who use the scalpel, it's the women who hold the scalpel.

10

They're holding it for the men to operate. They're saying "here, here's the scalpel, use it." They're neither using it themselves, nor preventing it being used. They're saying "here's this woman who's unable to give birth, cut her open."

One of the central images of the poem is the woman unable to give birth – it's the male part of her who's going to rip or cut open her stomach, to break forth the fruit of her womb through caesarian section.

I was saying the men shouldn't be doing it, I should be.

The women are accomplices, and the men are doing what is actually your task to do. If we take that out of the social realm and into the psychic realm, what is this saying? Isn't it that you are writing with your male voice, whereas you feel it's the female's job?

Yes, what you're pointing to is exactly a radical contradiction in my poems. The male and the female voices, if you want to call them that, aren't in balance. They're not in balance in me so of course they can't be in my poems.

Would this be a theme for you?

It's not a theme, it's a struggle, it's an issue. It ties up with dreams of mine at the moment, of wanting the male to be just the scribe, and the female voice to be the thing that, as you put it, brings forth the fruit. I want that to be where the voice comes from. Not want in the sense of willing it to be so – more like that's where I feel it is.

The emotional house in which you live.

It is. It's funny. I was thinking about it this morning, that maybe the issue of gender is a red herring, but it's actually the burning issue.

Internally . . .

Yes – but amongst feminist academics the notion of female archetypes is very unfashionable – because as soon as you start talking about 'internal' gender issues, feminine archetypes, the accusation is that you are falling into these mythic traps: universalising, being non-specific in relation to material, political realities, whatever.

These 'internal' gender issues relate also to form, to an aesthetic of voice against an aesthetic of text. In reading your work one can hear a voice generating its form as it goes. A text-fixated reader would struggle to find recognisable forms in many of your poems.

The whole question of form really interests me. I wasn't absolutely sure about why I was using syllabic verse, and what its place was, and its limits, and the way in which it limits the voice. But I knew it was about the poetic voice, and freeing the poetic voice.

I must say the emphasis on text at the expense of voice in academe not only pisses me off, I find it philosophically scary. Its emphasis is on absence and loss and substitution rather than on presence and possibility and reality (things as they are, not as metaphors). The metaphor of text, of 'reading' everything, is a post-modern silliness at best and a sickness at worst; and I can only think it is a colonial anxiety which has made it take with such power in South African academe.

One of your forms is the pattern. There is a lovely patterning of "A working holiday at the farm." That is syllabic verse and yet it's patterning, this holiday every day, breaking the day's work, writing about farmers in the sitting room, sitting knitting. The form of this poem is a pattern: sitting room, sitting, knitting, fine freework patterned, patterned, looking up – repetitions and near-rhymes powerful in the way they contain the poem.

The image of the farm for me is safety – the place next to the fire, the hearth if you like. The child's voice. A contained poem, within the home and hearth and the sphere of the child. Ja, playing. I actually was knitting. I was knitting this most bizarre thing, but that's another story. The realm of knitting might have pattern, but it doesn't have judgement, do you know? The judging voices of the brilliant men are not there. I'm just thinking – this way seems to be like Adrienne Rich's quilting, or piecing together . . . but not quite like her way.

What's the difference?

It's more integrated – the two other people there are the men, the workers, who've come in from a day's work. The images of people relaxing after working, women or men. It's a shared place, not saying "this is my domain, that's yours." The other difference is that the men aren't competitive, they're playing with me, they say "horses in a sea green field." So it's not an antagonistic poem at all.

And then you have another form, or another voice, a philosophical, critical and sometimes angry voice, capable of going off on its own, often leaving your sensual voice behind.

Yes, that's true. As I said, it's just a lack of balance in me as much as in my poems. But I think my head also needs to be given its head, so to speak. It also needs to be out of control and be pumping away. The image that comes to me is the one of beating one's head to try and get to something. It's not comfortable for the person who's doing the thumping or perhaps for the person who's reading but it's just another voice all the same.

12

Although the way I see it is that you're trying to find some other way, some other name for this urge towards perfection. Like in the poem "Perfection for me is shared passion fulfilled."

I was grappling with the question of perfection. If you reject perfection in order to turn to the quotidian, where does desire get its image? I mean what do you work towards, what is the impetus for desire? How do you charge the everyday with the god of love, without believing in the capital g for god, or the capital l for love?

The poem is about the search for perfection, for attainable imperfect perfection as opposed to unattainable perfection. I think it's lovely, Mary Magdalene, the love of Christ and the red, red, dress. That sort of longing towards that particular thing which can never be reached and which you say is "dead, dead Christ dead, dead, dead."

I have to say about three times he's dead because I don't believe it in a way. I'm convincing myself: it's dead, it's dead, it's dead, let go. This poem is struggling precisely with that: it's trying to accept, it's trying to see what the place of ideals and myths and symbols is, within a materialist kind of framework. When I wrote this poem I thought: you've just got to look at the everyday and accept that. I still believe that, but I believe that these gods have different shapes and forms and that they are a part of our dreams and our myths, they're not going to save us but they are going to help us – if they are integrated in ourselves – to bring eros into the everyday.

To be helpers rather than terrible avenging angels of unconsciousness.

Yes. But not our saviours. This thing came from a recognition that in South Africa as well as in myself, there was a tendency to look for ideologies, or people, as some kind of salvation. I'm trying to say that those possibilities aren't there.

Yes, we need the saviour, the father, the logos. His name's probably not Nelson Mandela. But in this country it is, and there is some symbolic sense in the fact that he is let out of jail as father, logos figure, saviour, and things do start to change actually.

Well, the interesting thing about Mandela is that he's about as close as you can come to somebody who does his best to live up to the . . .

. . . wise, good, father, you know, and he may well be that person, who knows? The fact is that he holds that. It's good, as long as you don't think it's just him.

Yes, and I suppose what I was struggling with in that poem was exactly that, the problem of concretising it too much, of . . . my lovers are going to save me, I don't have to do it myself. They're going to give me another country, another place, the country of the heart.

A different way which is the right way. Because our way here in South Africa is by definition the wrong way. We've carried such darkness for everybody else, right? We are the wrong way to do everything.

Exactly, exactly. Especially we who are white . . .

So how do you come out of that? Tackle something else? How to live? Amongst the black folk? Amongst the women folk? Is that where all this nurturing, right living, is going on?

You decide that it's just where you are, and you get on with it. The first bit is accepting where you are.

Where you are?

In the suburbs, in the white suburbs. I am. Ja, I accept it.
Mothering in the white suburbs.

And writing poems. For whom?

If I start to think of audience, the judging voices come in thick and fast, from every side, so I daren't. So at the moment the writing's still for myself. Myself holding the poems in my hand – in that sense not only myself. It's myself saying something like "hey look."

In your hand a beautiful shell. No, not a shell, because they're things you've made.

Ja, a basket of fruit. Just saying, "look : fruit of my labour."

Interviewed by Robert Berold

KAREN PRESS was born in Cape Town in 1956 and lives in Sea Point. She is a full-time writer and editor, and has published five children's books, some adult literacy books, and several school textbooks, most of them in mathematics and science. She has translated poems by Antjie Krog and Wopko Jensma. With Ingrid de Kok, she edited *Spring is Rebellious: Arguments about Cultural Freedom* (1990).

Books of poems published:
This Winter Coming (Cinnamon Crocodile, 1986)
Bird Heart Stoning the Sea (Buchu Books, 1990)
The Coffee Shop Poems (Snailpress, 1993)
Echo Location – a guide to Sea Point for residents and visitors (Gecko Poetry, 1998)
Home (Carcanet, 2000)

What poetry do you choose to read for inspiration?

There are times when I go to certain poets and it's like a switch – I just read two lines of them and I'm off – an electric current that gets switched on. They tend to all be people I read in translation, from non-Anglo-Saxon countries. Like Neruda, Vallejo, Akhmatova, sometimes people like Lorca, Brecht. Walcott, whose English is so much richer, more tactile, than English English. Odd anthologies, like a lovely anthology I've got of women's poetry, almost all poetry in translation, they're from Sweden or Lebanon and so on, lots of really interesting styles and forms and vocabularies of images which are just quite unusual. I gravitate towards powerfully imagistic poetry because it provokes energies in me that I find really exciting, although I don't always end up producing something that seems related.

At times in my life I've studied poetry quite intensely in a literary, critical way and some of those then became favourites; friends that you go back to, to use a cliché. The poetry that I first studied really intensely was Afrikaans poetry and I found it wonderful because it was such a powerful learning experience. It set up demands for technical excellence for me that I still struggle to meet. There are certain poems by Uys Krige or Elizabeth Eybers or Ingrid Jonker or Van Wyk Louw, you know the poems you get in school anthologies, that I studied with such intensity that they became very central.

Why did Afrikaans poetry have that effect on you whereas English poetry didn't?

One of the things I really love about Afrikaans is that the vocabulary is so close to a type of tactile reality: the real landscape of this country, the real sounds that people

15

speak here. The words are very three-dimensional and can be very delicate or very full of a type of natural energy depending on what one is talking about; and there's a type of spareness in the poetry. It doesn't tend to be flowery, not the stuff I've read, anyway, though I'm sure there's a lot of crap around.

What I took away from a lot of that poetry was a very tight construction, that sort of archetypal prac-crit-able poem where every word connects to every other word in a very carefully constructed, balanced, thought-through way, and images are very precisely developed through a poem and so on. I got the sense from that poetry that no syllable in a poem was wasted and that everything was chosen and was pruned down to being an essential, cohesive thing. But I think that was 90% the teaching of it . . . somebody else might have taught that poetry in a way that I never looked at it in that manner. I don't tend to read other poetry with that sort of fierce attention unless I'm having to write an essay on it.

English, on the other hand, is not so resonantly written. That is changing slowly as Africa breathes into it, but it's still relentlessly flat, the language of commerce and politics.

. . . and of polite cowardice. I suppose I have a vague sense of always being unfair to South African English poetry because when I think of it, I just think "God, no, I'd rather read a detective story" but obviously there are many poems, individual poems that you read as themselves, and you get drawn into them; the poem has a meaning or you think about it for what it's saying as itself rather than as a representative of a huge body of boring work. And then there are people who are doing interesting things with language, like Joan Metelerkamp for example. Or Ingrid de Kok, who I just read as a really good poet, not as 'South African poetry'. I do skim a lot of avowedly 'political' poetry to see where the poetry and the politics meet, but mostly it's in the usual place of simplistic politics and less than stunning technique, so I don't feel it helps me to take my own work with that political focus much further.

Too often in South African poetry one looks for the poem and finds the author instead. Some authors are saying things elegantly or passionately, but still just saying things, without the consciousness that they're giving birth to something separate from themselves. You seem to have avoided this trap . . .

That's something that I sometimes wonder about . . . how it is that you start with something, an idea or an image or a reality out there, that you want to just put down on paper; and then you find yourself actually working and working at a thing which has become something of itself that you want to make better, that you want to make more real . . . and you're not any more just trying to take a better and better photograph outside, you're trying to shape that object or work with the object that you've put on the page . . . and it is a separate thing, totally.

16

You put an edge to its shaping, its own self-shaping.

Yes, it's a strange thing about South African poetry, especially in the struggle culture: people have been offered or have been forced into an artistic identity which is about reporting – you know, what Ndebele was saying: reporting the reality around you is a replacement for art . . . and there's been a very important role for that, as a type of productive work – cultural work if you like. I suppose it's easier to talk about doing, as well as to do. It's harder to find a language for talking about poetry that doesn't do that.

I have the sense that my reality just is not everybody's reality; there are all these people out there who don't read the sort of stuff that I write, but who do read and write poetry, or read it at least. I don't claim that that poetry is somehow more or less durable. I just don't know what is permanent and what is not, or whether the stuff that is regarded as permanent is better because certain strands of taste and power have combined to perpetuate certain things. I would never conflate what I think is aesthetically good with what a society should or is going to validate. Reality is an agreement between two people; so is good poetry.

Does it bother you that you might sell 200 copies of your book, or that there might only be 50 serious readers of your poetry?

No. I honestly never think about who might or might not buy my books and I don't think my writing is at all to do with who might read the poetry. Nothing I've ever written, and nothing I've ever done with what I've written, has been about trying to get to an audience in a deliberate sense of wanting to write so that people would like what I wrote or even so that people would read what I wrote because the starting point is something you really need to write about. I've arrived at an understanding that the act of writing, even the act of finishing a work that you really feel is your best, is a very different act from publishing. And I've often grappled in a way with what is the satisfactory point of closure in terms of publishing.

For me writing is something you want to make. It's almost like a physical craft. You want to make this object with your hands and when you've made it, then there comes another stage which is thinking about publishing it. It's nice to get a complete product, in a physical sense, and I would like the idea of a book, that somebody took my poems and crafted them into a really beautiful book, as an object. But at another level it has absolutely nothing to do with the poems themselves and I don't expect people to buy my books. It has value and it has pleasure when they do but it's not what the writing of poetry is about at all.

What is the writing of poetry about, for you?

I have a really neat answer which emerged in my own head at a time when I was asking myself that question: that poetry is about having to tame certain things by writing about them. I no longer like that formulation because I don't want to tame things. If you get overwhelmed by certain moments of pain or certain struggles to understand something, or you see something in the world that you can't ignore, you can't for a moment stop looking at it. So the only thing to do about it is to start writing it, to start working it with your hands almost, putting it into a shape that you feel you can move into or move around or carry with you.

I've also tried to think about poetry as a type of scientific exploration: that you don't know what you're going to find and you're not illustrating something, you're not putting into poems stuff that you already know of somewhere else, you're actually on the edge of some sort of understanding all the time and you're pushing it bit by bit further, into a darkness, to things you don't understand. Which is why although the poems have to stand there, have to account for themselves, I wouldn't see any of them as a type of final truth, or even interim truth. They're more in the status of findings, like research findings – if I can say that without it sounding pretentious – but it's a metaphor for a type of exploratory relationship, what I'm looking for.

What you said about taming sounds like what Odysseus Elytis says in "The Little Mariner": 'you must domesticate the idea of existence in you in order to understand it'.

I don't want to believe I'm domesticating something.

I think he means making it your own by writing it.

Perhaps. Or perhaps you're just approaching it enough to see it as itself rather than as some monster that you can't escape from and you can't go close to. It's about engaging with something that's quite wild. I suppose the idea of taming is really just the word that springs to mind because of the wildness that you confront; and it's not a wildness that you necessarily want to eradicate or to dissolve away, but almost that you want to find the resonance of that wildness in yourself, that makes you strong enough to deal with it. I suppose that is a more accurate way of putting it.

In South Africa there are lots of opportunities to do this because there's a lot of wildness around.

Mm, but I suppose I find it very hard to just do the obvious or work with the obvious, and so what I've always found myself doing, like what I'm doing in the work that I'm writing now, is not to do the obvious thing, which is to talk about the South African reality now, the shit that's around, the real, available, visible level of events and people and conflict. My response is more to step at an angle to that, or to step underneath it or something. What I'm really saying is "Here we all are, these human beings, shedding blood like it's going out of fashion" and what that's really saying is

18

that this is like a groundswell, this is an energy, this is a reality that is mysteriously part of how we exist as human beings here . . . not the ANC and the IFP and the DP and democratic fairy stories and teaching people to vote and stuff. It's about something else, maybe something else that's really not useful to talk about because people want to organise themselves in ways so that they can go shopping without getting killed. I mean the newspapers talk about that and all these endless publications from IDASA talk about that and I'm not going to write poems about the same thing. So I suppose I'm coming at an odd, an idiosyncratic angle always to that wildness. What I'm doing is saying "We are these people, who kill each other." I'm almost saying "What the fuck do you expect?" – this is the nature of who we are.

Which is why, I assume, you are not an overtly political poet.

I think my poetry is 'political' in the sense that it accepts politics, power struggles, social oppression, as part of the reality that decides pleasure and pain. But if 'political' means restating party manifestoes in short lines then, no, I suppose I'm not. I'm more involved in the notion of being on the edge of the void, that you're always looking into darkness and you've got your back to the safety of any notion of home, or land. It's very much that sense of being away from safe ground . . . it comes, I think, from growing up at the edge of the sea and just looking out all the time, looking towards the sea and therefore almost having left the land, not being in the middle of a land that holds you. Always being on the edge of falling off the world. That's what the writing is about, that being on the edge and writing out into that space that you could fall into. I don't feel more or less 'safe' than any other single human being. I feel that everybody is alone in the world, I mean everybody really is a lonely little person in the world. Yet we all are these little animals, born from the sea, part of the universe we feel so alone in.

Maybe that's an ultimately democratic notion.

Democratic despair. It's true . . . I don't know where it comes from but that's why the thing that I find almost impossible to work with or to spend any time talking about is this "as a white South African, as a black South African" business. I have no sense of responsibility to any of these constructed identities. People can lay that stuff on you. I'm sure that I get read with a whole lot of labels all over me by people but I have no sense of accountability to anything like that, because I have no sense of being a part of any community that is a public community – in this place or in any other place, and really my sense of my own being here and of other people's being here is as little and as powerful as that space that one person can occupy in the world. All these solitary people, who do construct a lot of identities and communities or allow themselves to be subsumed in that stuff – I'm not looking at them as that, I don't think that's the end of the story.

How does that articulate with your politics?

19

Well at a very intellectual level, or I suppose at a very rational level, the identities within which people define themselves in this country, the racial identities, are constructed things, and they've been constructed for political reasons, they're policies . . . it's not a simple thing. The interface between people's psychological collaboration in identities and the fact that identities are created by social means, is not innate: nobody's innately white or black or coloured or cape coloured or griqua, you know, but those things are real in the sense that people live them, and believe in them and act upon them so I don't pretend for a moment that they don't exist in that daily texture of people's lives. But they are not the only defining moments of reality for people: I think poverty, hunger, loneliness are just as strong. My 'politics,' if you like, is quite hard-edged – some people are starving, some people have three houses and five cars, and there are connections between them. Writing poetry doesn't excuse you from having to understand how power really works in the world you live in. But then you can do more with a political analysis than a sociology textbook would – there's all that mysterious human pain that goes beyond just being "an oppressed member of your class." Needing love, needing a kind of home that the universe doesn't offer you – that lies under everything. How does being forcibly removed from your home, how does desperate hunger affect your capacity to love, your need for emotional food? These are connections I try to explore. That people receive joy from nature – a man who is evicted from his home loses his contact with the sea, as much as his brick and cement shelter – that's something central to being human.

Solitariness is for me the fundamental condition for existence. I can see that it is a very particular angle of vision and that I probably am very far in a corner in relation to the rest of the world but it's absolutely the bedrock of my own sense of self and I project that onto everything. I'm always asking, what does it mean to be alive, to be human, in this solitary state?

How does this world-view affect your style of writing?

I think I'm always trying to state as directly, 'literally,' as I can whatever meaning I'm reaching for. Calling a spade a spade. I always feel I don't have many words, I can't be virtuoso with language. I'm too focused on the 'thing out there' that I'm trying to find in words. A sort of horrified stare, or maybe sometimes a seduced stare – the one becomes the other. What I think I'm doing is examining the way the political and the personal (if you can use such labels) interact, the fact that they are the same thing in a lot of ways.

But then there are also playful poems – this place is *so absurd* sometimes, you can't take it or yourself too seriously. Found poems, poems about cockroaches and coffee shops and the brothels where I live . . . I can get just as obsessed about them as about our capacity for blood-letting.

Speaking to you as a publisher more than a poet, I'd like to ask what possibilities you feel there are for poetry to become more widely read here. My own observation is that people are already starting to search beyond the monolithic political categories which were frozen into their minds by traumatising social engineering. People are looking for other paths, and I think that writers who can bring the different fragments of reality together will have an important healing function. Not only should they be read, but also heard . . . in readings and performances, on the radio and TV: radio in particular is a very powerful way of bringing poetry to people. If enough people want it to happen, there's a possibility that a poetry of depth and colour could finally become part of the lifeblood of this country.

Yes, but it also means that people must be willing to come to poetry without knowing what it's saying. The poetry that people have bad experience of, they could have told you in advance what every single poem was going to be about and if they wanted that, that was great, but if they didn't want that, then they just stopped being interested in poetry. I don't know, but I think that's quite an untested audience: the people who will read a poem the way they like to read an article, you know, where they were actually curious about what somebody was saying about something rather than wanting to have an attitude bolstered by some rhythm, rhetoric, or whatever. It's going to have to be tested by the people who create forums for public culture in that way.

Interviewed by Robert Berold

LESEGO RAMPOLOKENG was born in Orlando West, Soweto, in 1965. He is a
full-time writer and performance poet who has performed in many countries, both solo
and with musicians such as Julian Bahula, Soulemane Toure, Louis Mhlanga, and
Gunther Sommer. He has written a play, *Fanon's Children*, and collaborated on plays
and filmscripts.

Books of poems published:
Horns for Hondo (COSAW, 1990)
End Beginnings (Shifty CD with Kalahari Surfers, 1993)
Talking Rain (COSAW, 1993)
End Beginnings (German translations) (Marino, 1998)
Blue V's (German translations with CD) (Edition Solitude, 1998)
The Bavino Sermons (Gecko Poetry, 1999)
The h.a.l.f. ranthology (CD with various musicians, 2002)

Where you were born, where did you grow up?

I was born in Orlando West, Soweto in 1965, into quite a huge family. I never got to
know my father . . . I was told that he died in some mine or other.

You never met him?

No, I never met him even once. When I was about in my teens, my mother got
married to the person who gave me my name . . . I wasn't Rampolokeng until then.
He saw me through school, he actually sold dagga to get me some kind of education.

When was your first contact with writing?

I started writing at lower primary school, I would play around with nursery rhymes,
although I wouldn't call them that – they had nothing to do with Jack and Jill – just
playing around with ideas about my mangy dog, things like that, with my little cousins
and the other young children. We would create in that kind of way.

In English?

Well, some broken English. In fact, what inspired me, in a very negative way, was just
how people in my family were constantly praising my use of the English language,
then. I think if it hadn't been for that, I would be writing in Tswana or some other such
language but just that I was influenced in that line from a very young age. Every time I
said a stupid sentence in English I would be applauded madly by the whole family.

Your first audience . . .

That was my first audience, and they had their own values . . . glossy, bent. Everything or anything that smacked of ENGLISH and what they saw as sophistication was to be embraced. So if I said something in the English language, that was the glorious thing, for my mother. She wanted me to be I think an EXCEPTIONAL kind of person, for instance she had some very sad notions, some sad ideas, about me playing violin.

At home I was constantly being fed western-inspired values. I was taken to church every Sunday, dressed up in jacket and tie, which was quite a violent introduction into the higher order of things. I started having a relationship with religion that was quite weird, and it was a very scary phase for me . . . up till now I have yet to come into contact with such gruesome images as I encountered in church.

. . . the Catholic church, I take it?

It was a Catholic church, yes. I was being told that I either had to toe the line or be cast into eternal flames . . . I've never in my life really had a positive relationship with authority, or with threats and blackmail if I didn't toe the line . . . I've always felt that I need to have a choice.

What was the line?

Well the line was that I recognise Jesus Christ as my saviour, you know, and that his mother occupies a certain sphere that I would forever owe allegiance to. I couldn't get myself to do so because I felt that if God was there, and was omniscient, he wouldn't need to threaten me to keep his balance. I felt I should have some choice on whether I want to do so or not. It shouldn't be a THIS or DEATH kind of situation.

How old were you at this time?

That was even before I went to school actually, even before I started primary school, because my mother was quite a believer. You know, Soweto has always been, and was much more so in those days, violent . . . I don't mean violence with any political aims or any political backing but just outright criminal conduct. I grew up with that. So having on the one side images of a God feeding on death, and on the other the death that I was encountering in Soweto . . . well this fashioned my outlook on how I was going to view things in the future.

When I went to primary school, at five years of age . . . well even in primary school I was being fed nursery rhymes that really didn't have much of a bearing for me. "Mary had a little lamb" – it didn't have any impact on me, although I joined in, like everybody else. But outside of the classroom I encountered quite a different reality . . .

When the 1976 schools uprising came, you were only eleven years old.

I was a child – I was a baby!

How did the events of '76 affect you personally?

As I said, it was quite a huge family, because my grandmother opened her arms for stray flock, the extended family. There were always more than ten or twelve people in the house. So I had this one cousin, who was involved – although I didn't know the extent of his involvement until much later, around 1977, when it was reported that he had died in a shootout with the South African Defence Force in Komatipoort. But even before that, even before that '76 day, I was constantly doing things I didn't know the reason for. I mean I'd be yanked out of bed in the middle of the night, and I'd have to run certain errands that were quite strange.

How did the violence of '76 differ in your young mind from the criminal violence you were used to?

Well the difference was that instead of me running around in the street as I used to, I can remember one day when I had this huge case of beer on my head, from a bottle store that had burnt down – I didn't drink obviously, and there was no-one in my family who drank at that stage, but because it seemed to be the fashion of the day that everybody'd grab what they could grab, and because I saw people who I took to be my peers doing that, I did that as well. I didn't know what I was doing and for what reason I was doing it. I can remember about fifty children, myself included, in a place called Protea Police Station. And I almost had my genitals restructured, or redefined, by somebody's boot. Fortunately it didn't go beyond that.

How did you make sense of what was going on?

Every night at 8 the whole family used to gather round the radio to listen to these stories: most of them apartheid propaganda. Communists and guerillas were referred to on the radio in Sotho in a much more harsh way than that very negative word: TERR-O-RIST. In SeSotho the word they used, *Baferekanyi*, translates into offsetting the order of things, throwing everything into complete chaos. I at that time had the strange idea that those people being referred to were actually made out of steel. I didn't have any idea that it could be any flesh-and-blood person because of the images that I was being fed on the radio.

And so I was caught between what I was being taught in school and what I was being taught on the radio – which were more or less the same thing – and what was coming from within my family itself because at the same time my cousin was making me listen to Radio Freedom. This person who brought me up, who gave me the name Rampolokeng, was not himself in any way politically inclined or conscious that much.

24

But one of his brothers was politically involved, and one day a bomb that he was putting together somewhere in Pimville exploded and took away one of his legs. This, and this cousin of mine, couldn't help but make me conscious of what was happening.

Poetry helped that consciousness?

Oh yes – not long after things exploded in Soweto, people like Ingoapele Madingoane and all the other groups, Medupe and Dashiki and Lefifi Tladi, started taking to the ghetto streets themselves. I was dragged to some of these and then later I went of my own accord. Their work had a very high impact that was quite different to what I was getting at school – it had a metaphoric way of bringing to life the blood and the gore and the dust of the streets. It had life, I could connect with it. They were talking about the ghetto experience in language that was heightened obviously . . . that very heightening helped to drive their own inner turmoil, their own emotions, and their own experiences in a sharper kind of way. It was something I could understand and something I could relate to. It was out of that experience that I started writing myself – not that I was writing anything remotely creative. What I was doing was to merely echo what they were doing and ape their movements.

So when I started aping these poets it was some kind of a break-out or break-away from how I'd been introduced to English at home and school . . . I was trying to grab or capture what they were themselves capturing, though I wasn't very successful. I'd go anywhere, stand on any platform in the way that the people we had seen doing it . . . like Medupe and all those other people who'd go on stage with drums and horns, and recite. We were just children then and we'd just mess around there, someone would play. I think I was in a sense, saved – if you can refer to it in that way – by all the cultural activity that I was finding myself immersed in.

Then our people got torn and dragged off in different directions . . . some died and some went their various ways. Some just succumbed to what I've referred to as the glitter at the bottom of the gutter. Some got caught up in criminal activity, some were shot or in prison.

And some found solace in poetry – if we can even call it solace – because I think that poetry can actually be the worst form of self-mutilation. I've seen people use poetry to tear their own innards, and their own minds, their own emotions: to bring to the surface their sense of their very existence. And it often comes out as bits and pieces of flesh and blood and bone, until the human being itself is just a series of images: gory and torn and tattered.

Would you say that after the banning of Medupe and other Black Consciousness organisations in 1977, this strong poetic movement became dissipated?

No, in fact instead of being dissipated it got quite focused, and stopped being a series of haphazard explosions and a fashion because by then it was quite fashionable to stand up and chant lines. Some people started taking it much further and much deeper – Chris van Wyk, for instance, Achmat Dangor, Farouk Asvat – those people were trying I think to take it from the level of sloganeering and just plain pamphleteering on to another level, another sphere. Whether they were successful or not is neither here nor there but the important thing was that they were engaged in this activity.

Besides your involvement in this vital poetry movement, what were you reading at that stage that was inspiring you, if anything? Or listening to, for that matter, if it was music?

On Radio Freedom there was a programme in the early evening, where poets in exile – because most of these people were in exile – would recite their poetry or read their poetry. And Soweto being what it is, throughout all those sessions the neighbours would be blasting their radios at full volume. I remember one day, they were playing some jazz on the radio, it was cold, and these people were talking on Radio Freedom, and I was with this cousin of mine. Somehow the lines being read seemed to flow over the music that was coming in through the wall . . . And I think that was a kind of revelation for me. I recognised the merits of those two forms of artistic expression combining, but it didn't actually click in my mind: it just happened I took note of that.

It was some time after that I was introduced to the work of people like Linton Kwesi Johnson, and to an extent Mutabaruka and a fellow called Oku Onuora who were credited with having been among the first dub poets. Of course you can take that back really to The Last Poets in the US, the cultural wing of the Black Panther movement, who were experimenting with the word and music or the word put to music, who would stand on street corners with just drums and microphones and just go for it. Gil Scott-Heron did that piece of his: "The Revolution Will Not Be Televised." This I think signalled the beginning of what would later be referred to as Rap – although Rap has always been pure speech: with or without the music, just speech. People talk, see, they are rapping, I don't mean Rap as it has come to be identified with hip-hop culture.

You were having these thoughts about performance . . . did you try to put them into practice?

I've never been able to play a musical instrument, and I don't really have the inclination to learn. I really don't want to, because I think the human voice can be the world's greatest musical instrument if used properly. What I ended up doing, trying to do, was to have the WORD carry its own musicality within itself, whether or not I was chanting to any accompaniment there would still be music involved. Maybe in the

26

days of the kings and the praise-singers, they would do it with musical accompaniment, often, but even without that there was musicality involved. You just have to listen to traditional Zulu or Sotho music – in essence it's just poetry chanted or half sung and half spoken, it's just that it hasn't been recognised as such because in those languages it hasn't been taken that seriously. But it has been poetry put to music.

What did you do after you left school, about '82?

I went to that bush college in the north . . . which was a waste of my time actually. I think I made it out of there much more ignorant than I was when I first went there. But it put me in contact with certain people with ideas that helped fashion my outlook . . . mostly students in Azaso.

I went there to study law but I found myself being studied BY the law, from every corner. We were thrown into political activity at student level. This political activity and criminal conduct were locked in one, until there really wasn't any difference between the two. This happened because of the split in ideology within the student movement: some people pushing a Black Consciousness line and some people pushing what was called then a progressive line – although I really don't know what was so progressive about it. And some people died, actually . . . violently. Those people were killed by people with the opposite ideology, and I found myself getting more and more involved in that kind of activity until we seemed to have our own home-grown death squad.

What was the function of poetry in this environment?

We in a sense became some kind of PROPAGANDA department, or a pamphleteering and sloganeering wing of the movement. When there were meetings of the student movement in the universities, or rallies or mass meetings on the campus – during the proceedings, in order to shape people's perceptions or push people's outlook in a certain direction, we were expected to stand up and chant some poetry, chant some lines that had some bearing on the things that were being said. Most of it was quite improvised.

At the same time COSATU's cultural work was starting . . . mass meeting poetry came to the fore at this time . . . to put it maybe crudely, poetry moved from being a cultural weapon to being a warm-up to political rallies.

Exactly. In fact, I think that the advent of that came a little later. But you're right that at some stage it became . . . our culture became politically EXPEDIENT – to use that phrase. There was less of the Black Consciousness emphasis on the land and all that went with that. There was a shift towards a much more politically defined vision.

Where did you go after university?

I turned my back on academia – it had failed me, with its completely unfocused vision, politically and otherwise. I went through a stage where I really didn't know whether I was coming or going. I felt I was stagnating: that I was being drowned by everything that was happening around me – because I'd lost faith in my own organisations and in myself as a person. And I think I needed some kind of outlet, which I couldn't find because all doors seemed to have been shut against me and my material or my work wasn't being recognised as really shaped enough to possibly be published. Then I went and did a stint of work at the stock exchange.

The stock exchange? . . . what year was this?

In '87. And in almost exactly the same way as when I was a child, I started walking around in jacket and tie. But instead of heading off to church now, I was heading off to the commercial, economically based and financially-bound RELIGION. This time around – well, the god of Finance held centre stage, and the people there seemed to be moving to a shrine of worship every time they entered that place. And I felt that I was just harking straight back to my early days when I was being taken to the Catholic church and it became quite oppressive to me. After just seven months I threw in the towel – I could not do anything remotely creative with stocks and shares . . .

Then again the cycle began: this time around I was among those people who had to warm up the stage for political statements to be made, the people recognised as the political leaders within our movement had to have the stage cleared – almost like the kings of old when their praise-singers had to go on stage and in a sense sing the praises of the struggle of our land, after which, like the kings, the leaders would enter, take the stage and address the floor. I don't know whether I've moved out of that or not, the problem is I started not being very welcome at these gatherings.

Why was that?

Because I was doing my duty just too well, I think, for comfort. In the old days the praise-singers were traditionally the only people in the nation who could criticise the kings and get away with it. That seemed to me a good tradition, one to be followed. But I found that in the political setup in this country today that doesn't work: if you start introducing criticism then you're supposed to be reactionary, counter-revolutionary – although people don't say counter-revolutionary because the word revolution has itself fallen foul of the politics of this country.

These gatherings you're talking about are recent, post 1990. Were you doing these readings under the COSAW banner? Did you feel you had a home in COSAW? Did this praise-singer role start to irk you?

Well COSAW promised what was in essence a home for writers of all persuasions –

just as long, I think, as their views and visions didn't run counter to the rules of 'positive human conduct', though what's positive has yet to be explained to me. Anyway we gathered in COSAW people who were from Black Consciousness backgrounds, from all sorts of backgrounds I think, well I hope so anyway. COSAW would be contacted to provide people who would read some poetry at these rallies.

You mean like an agency for praise singers?

In a sense, yes. About a year ago I was very disgusted: I was in the COSAW office and someone called me to the telephone, said there was someone who wanted some poet to come recite their work somewhere. It was at a beauty pageant [he laughs] . . . that's the kind of thing that made me reflect on my role in this whole thing, you see. And I was cautioned more than once or twice. Like the time I went to the Sisulu birthday bash.

His 80th birthday?

I don't know if it was 80th, it was possibly. I went there, but I don't know . . . I was, I suspect, expected to chant some praises to my leader – and I must have done something wrong because the next day a very hot-fashioned caution was shuttled to me . . . COSAW was advised to put me on a leash, to put a chain around my neck because I'd conducted myself like a mad dog, they said.

What had you actually done? Which particular poems did you perform?

I don't know, I didn't do anything – I just went up there and recited my work and walked away. I don't actually know which pieces I did. What they said was that that was supposed to have been in honour of one of our tried and tested leaders and not a platform for me to make my Trotskyite statements disguised as poetry. The same response came from someone who wanted to interview me on TV recently – she said I'd have to modify some of my poems because I was seen by quite a few people as being anti-christ, anarchist and reactionary – quite a strange combination to me.

I want to ask you about your work and its changes of emphasis. Horns for Hondo *was a book of anger, vengeance even, which doesn't pause to consider the doubts which come into your recent work . . .*

I was caught in the political environment in this country, and there was no way in which I could lift myself above it. I was born into a particular situation and particular circumstances that were themselves influenced by the political factors in the country. The way I looked at it then was that I couldn't really draw a line between my political and my artistic activities – until it became a fusion of the two: my artistic expression had to be a form of political activity and the other way around – but then the politics couldn't flow so well into the art as the art could flow into the politics.

I was also, of course, from my really young days, completely romantic about our struggle. Everybody looked at the word 'struggle' as though it was a really huge golden thing that we all had agreed upon. We saw only the one struggle in life, and so often neglected the fact that every single moment we live is engagement in struggle or struggles. There are other struggles that are as important as the political one. There is the struggle for all of us to be born and the struggle to grow up. And the struggle not to die.

How do you view the creative struggle?

I've always thought that creative activity springs out of solitude, basically . . . that however much we might be engaged in communal work, at the heart of it is the individual input that actually counts. But I think we've romanticised the notion of what's called people's culture. I could actually say that I have always created out of solitude but that the spirit of communality, that arose out of political activity, actually clouded that . . . I got notions of seeking for solitude in order to create a work of art. And I must admit, yes, not only then, but still now – I suppose it will always be with me – is the realisation that I could only fully create or be able to put out words within me ONLY within solitude and ONLY if I was removed from everybody and anybody else's vision.

Quite a hell of a thing for someone engaged in performance.

Well I do feel sometimes when performing that nobody understands what I'm talking about and that actually I'm being applauded for all the wrong reasons.

I've always tried to come to writing from within myself, not move from the outside in, because I've always believed that before we can embrace our neighbours, before we can reach out to the next person, be it mother or lover or anybody else, we have to take steps within ourselves first, and know ourselves better before we can do anything about extending to the next person.

Which doesn't preclude political commitment . . .

Definitely not. I don't regret that, it was essential. I think it will always be. At the time of writing *Horns for Hondo* the world was itself defined for me in political terms. I don't think that my new book represents a shift from that, or a step forward from that. I carry forward in this book everything that I hold dear, everything that I've tried to define in *Horns for Hondo*. I've only just tried to sharpen it and to go even deeper within myself, and also to go deeper into things and try to find their essence.

I've come to realise holding our scars up is no solution. When somebody can shout to the world that they were being exiled or that they've been imprisoned or that they suffered in this or that way – it means that we actually have some gratitude towards the evils of the world – where we actually owe a lot to apartheid for having made us. All that has actually made me start questioning myself even more, questioning all the values I embraced, and everything I stood for: I've realised that the rot exists at every step of the ladder – at all levels of society.

You see I at some point in my life said I wasn't going to write about flowers. The point is that my mother grows flowers in the backyard, OK – she loves them. And I said I wasn't going to write love songs or love poems. But there are people in my life who I love – I love my son, I love other people as well, I can't put that aside as being secondary now, and seek to define this great and glorified concept that we call THE STRUGGLE. Because it's a struggle for myself to grow up in this world, I walk down the street and see beauty: people in love, people kissing – I can't wish that away.

I see every single human being on this earth as part of a whole: one organic whole – that is actually here for me to participate in. I don't know if you can love that whole because some people are actually just abhorrent – and worth hatred, actually. There are some people that one ought to hate. But whether some of us are capable of that or not is something else.

Your new book Talking Rain *confronts evil, those who deal out death for their own gain, of whom violent people with political power behind them are only one category. Much of the book explores how evil operates in other ways.*

Well I think that we are living in an insane world, that it's very difficult to hold on to sanity. I believe that my writing is informed by the insanity of the world and by my own inner strife and the struggle to come face-to-face with it, to recognise my own insanity and either to bash into the ground or embrace it. I don't think that I should shout from a mountain and claim righteousness. I think I'm as much a part of the rot of the world as anyone. I think that somehow I've also contributed to our putrefaction.

How have you done that?

Well, we're all of us striking up some quite satanic alliances in the pursuit of what was in the past a very noble goal. The steps we take towards certain ends are in themselves as ugly as what we are walking away from or what we are trying to fight against. However glorious and noble the end might be, if one has to put another person into the ground that still doesn't mean the killing of a person is noble in itself. And because we've gone down that road, I think – I don't know, this might be my own paranoia – I think things are bound to get much bleaker, and much more ugly.

I've found people very divided about your poetry. Some love its musicality, its directness and candour, while some say it's an assault, a total barrage, with no space for the reader.

Where I live there is no space. My entire existence is itself an assault on the senses. We're a nation in the grip of psychosis and mass hysteria. I don't think I could come to terms with it by writing poetry fit for lounges and studies. I have a seven year old son – in Soweto he could easily die an unnatural death, doing nothing, just walking down the road, being alive. Not a single night goes past when I don't hear gunshots from my house.

What are your thoughts about the differences or similarities between performance and the printed word?

I've always tried to tread the midline between the word in motion, the word free – I mean without bounds – and the WRITTEN word. I've always tried in a way to marry the two: tried to make poetry that would leave a smudge on the page as it would on the stage. But that has always been difficult and I think it's a near-impossible thing to do. Although of course we could say someone like Allen Ginsberg – that piece of his, *Howl* . . . that's a piece for performance or for chanting: we cannot doubt its impact even if read in print. I've always admired people who do that. You just have to look at the work of Rimbaud . . . it flows, it seems to be made to be read out loud. Or Césaire's *Return To My Native Land* – it seems to be written and structured in a way that it's actually made for performance, and I think it's a kind of inspiration that I've tried to get.

I don't refer to myself as a performance poet, oral poet, dumb poet, deaf poet – I think all those are just unfortunate labels. I'm either a poet or I'm not. But then of course, there seems to be a definite need for labels in this country. The unfortunate thing though, is that if people write some crappy material, because of the deficiencies in our literary criticism and the lack of rules and standards regarding performance, it is easy and simple for people to refer to themselves as oral poets, because they can get away with murder. You just have to chant two lines and you're a poet in this country.

What does it feel like to have become a recording artist?

The day I was approached with the possibility, or the PROSPECT of making a recording, I was quite sceptical about it. I was always saying that the word should be enhanced, although of course I'd been performing with people who were quite untogether – well, musically at least. I've always had the impression that this world is much more ready to dance to any kind of stupid music than to actually apply itself to really listening to the meaning of things. I didn't really want to do it, but I also realised that it could have a much more far-reaching impact. If I thought about Linton Kwesi Johnson or The Last Poets or Grandmaster Flash or any of those others – that was one way, in a way, of broadening one's audience – so I went into it.

But what actually dragged me to the idea that ended up as *End Beginnings* was the ground-breaking work done by Warrick Sony: much more substantial and creative and much more imaginatively put together than anything being upheld as the pillar of South African protest. So I went into that recording. We had disappointments I think – for instance my own voice execution. I'm a poet and I came out quite weak because I had to wrap my words around this music. So it had both negative and positive aspects, but I'm quite glad I did it.

You've been to Europe to perform four times this year, you've had a successful performance at Kippies with Vusi Mahlasela and an excellent backing group. It is wonderful to have done all this, even if, as you say, some of the applause may be for the wrong reasons. South African literature has its creative casualties, many from neglect, some from too much acclaim – who couldn't cope with it. How are you going to deal with this?

I think that there's always a possibility of one being swallowed up by what you refer to as acclaim. But I think I'm much more conscious about myself and my own situation, my own background, and I'm too much in touch with my own vision to let that happen to myself. Although of course positive criticism does do quite a lot to one's ego, I really don't think it's of any importance whether I get recognised for my work or not. What is important to me is that I write, and I write what I feel and in the way I feel it should be written. Whether that pleases the kings and princes of this earth is absolutely of no importance to me.

Interviewed by Robert Berold

KELWYN SOLE was born in Johannesburg in 1951, and has lived in Kanye
(Botswana), Windhoek, and Cape Town. He is associate professor of English at the
University of Cape Town. His numerous articles on South African literature, politics
and culture have been published in books and journals in South Africa and abroad. His
poems have been translated into French, Italian and Spanish.

Books of poems published:
The Blood of Our Silence (Ravan, 1988)
Projections in the Past Tense (Ravan, 1992)
Love That Is Night (Gecko Poetry, 1998)
Mirror and Water Gazing (Gecko Poetry, 2001)

*One critic has suggested that you are "a political poet, but not in the way of so many
other South African political poets". Can you trace your political influences and
development?*

I come from a lower middle class white family in Joburg; a family of Bloedsappe; I
certainly wasn't brought up in a liberal or leftwing household, although I was instilled
with a very strong sense of justice and the uniqueness – let's call it the vulnerable
uniqueness – of all living things . . . every single person killed in this country is a
tragedy for all of us, and it's time we started realising it. From that upbringing I also
inherited a profound distrust, as an outsider, of the disparity between the liberal
sentiments of wealthy whites and their comfortable existences. My distaste for
liberalism is not Oedipal.

But I had to make my own way, politically. I was influenced by a whole lot of
undergraduate enthusiasms – everything from anarchism to Zen Buddhism – as a
university student. You'll remember the types of books doing the rounds in circles of
white youth in the late 1960s and early 1970s – everything from Marcuse to *Soul on
Ice*. In this sort of scenario, where a lot of things were banned and one had to
read what one could find, I first confronted Marxist thought via Cabral and Mao, if I
remember. All of the poststructuralist and culturalist Marxisms that started doing the
rounds on a systematic basis among leftwing people came later, in the mid to late
1970s. It was only the privilege of intellectual space, and the amount of it, that gave
me and others like me the time to do much reading. This changed, for many, during
the 1980s.

I think, looking back on it, that I was lucky to grow up at this time, difficult as it was –
systematic reading allowed me to see the way in which theory needs to be

34

consistent, needs to be rigorous (these are scare-words among those who believe these days that they have done away with 'master narratives' in their lives) and needs to relate to practice. I suppose the latter's what fuelled my attempt to move away from the Joburg suburbs, and work in Botswana and Namibia, for example.

What was your perception of the political practice of socialist governments at the time?

While I was spouting Gramsci with the best of them, it was shortly after I was thrown out of Namibia in 1980 that I started to feel something was wrong in the way in which Marxist theory was being practised, in those countries I had a modicum of knowledge about, as well as among some of the people I knew in the closed circle of the left locally. I began to get very suspicious of Leninism in particular, especially its separation of ends from means, its notions of command socialism, the role given to the vanguard party, the acceptance of the one-party State and other of its damaging platitudes – it was at the time regarded as the only acceptable theory of socialist transformation. Reading Philip Corrigan and Carmen Sirianni finally convinced me that the problems I was seeing weren't just aberrations of my own 'false consciousness'. I currently think that a lot of the problems that crystallised in the fall of Eastern Europe can be laid at the door of Leninist practice – the hardening of arteries of a revolutionary party turned revolting bureaucracy. Djilas was right, all those years ago.

We desperately needed the reassessment of socialism that was forced on us. There was, certainly, a huge failure of a number of the prevailing political practices of socialist countries; practices which, if you think about it, had come to stand in the way of the ideals for which socialism was supposed to stand. However, I'm still a Marxist: I have still found no better way of explaining the imbalances of the world in which we live.

Your poetry has a number of voices in it, there's a lyrical voice, a satirical voice, a polemical voice, a voice concerned with history, etc. How is this? Who is the 'real' Kelwyn Sole?

The thing is, growing up in South Africa has shifted, fractured my personality into a certain shape; and I can do no other than write from that personality. There have been a lot of factors that have helped shape my identity. And although this particular 'shape' belongs to me, I would generalise to say that all of us in this country have been moulded and fractured, in our various ways and as a result of our various circumstances, by the experience of learning to live here. I've never believed that I'm someone with a simple, uniform, consistent 'nature' or 'personality': I am a person with a number of different attitudes, identities, emotional urges, enthusiasms, all intertwined. Often at the same time. These are at play in my poetry – at times in paradoxical and perhaps even contradictory ways. All I have done is try to use them, rather than resolve them before I use them. This pushes me towards a certain type of stance in my poetry . . . to perceive this country – and then write about it – in a way which doesn't remain stuck in some of the dreadful stereotypes that exist in our literature.

This recognition of personal fracture is a useful place for me to begin exploring from: in that it allows me – potentially also, at least – to communicate with differing types of audience.

How much is it possible to consciously find or meet an audience?

I do try and 'see inside' other people and situations, and what they are experiencing and suffering, when I work on a poem, even though I know complete identification or understanding is not finally possible. Yet while recognising these problems, what concerns me first and foremost is where *I* am, as I've said. It's possible to become too uptight about who one's audience is, and try to write to please them. That's death, as far as any poet I respect is concerned. Usually I get on with the process of writing, and let the audience take care of itself; although I'm surprised and pleased when someone tells me they like what I do.

Does this issue of audience influence your stylistic choices in any way?

Yes. I'm not suggesting I'm a sort of polyp with open feelers, indiscriminately tasting everything that floats by. The literary critic in me at times directs me to certain types of utterance, I guess . . . when I started to publish, for example, it was said to me a number of times that I had a 'lyrical gift' – it was meant as a compliment, but I didn't take it as such. I'm dubious of the way the expressive lyric bloats out to include everything into the poetic ambience of a single consciousness. Ja, I know one's eventually stuck in one's own point of view, but for me some of the other forms I experiment with allow edges of the real world out there to jag against me; they teach me more because I have to struggle more to get them to talk. Even with my lyrical poetry, I sometimes try and decentre my first person narrator: you know, undermine his authority with other viewpoints, criticise his point of view, and so on.

Any attempt to write poetry according to a certain style is, to my mind, simultaneously an attempt to define, and maybe transform, human beings. When I choose one style of poetry above another, I'm trying to form and transform people to sympathise with and respond to me in a certain way. So it's my social and psychological conceptions that make me want to speak in different voices and with different styles in my work. I think that the commonly held notion around when I first started writing – that the sign of a 'mature' poet was someone who had found 'his' voice and wrote in a consistently repeated style and with a constant angle of focalisation – was, when all is said and done, not so much a strategy to make writers work at their craft as a straitjacket: I'd be unhappy to be just a lyrical voice, or a satirical voice, or whatever. This way there are different options open to different types of situation and subject matter. At times, indeed, different subject matter calls for variations in form in my work. At times strict use of metre and rhyme makes sense, at times it doesn't. This goes for other techniques of poetry as well.

You have done a lot of experimentation in form and in language (I'm thinking of poems as different as "Akua'ba", "Promised Land" and "Blessing" for example). Do you think readers follow all this, or isn't that the point?

This is one of the ways I do feel lonely. If I'm lucky, a few of my readers might realise what I'm doing and what direction I might be moving in – I'm very restless, formally speaking, in my poetry; but I don't systematise what I'm doing. I follow my nose and explore. I might witness something that I feel cannot be expressed in ways I'm used to using, or read someone who strikes me as someone I could learn from. I remember, in the mid-1980s, as all the poems I'd written over a number of years started to finally coalesce into a book – what was to become *The Blood of Our Silence* – I was really taken, for a year or so, by Philip Levine's poems. For several years I'd had a tape of him reading, a tape Jeremy Cronin had given to me – and all of a sudden it started to make sense in terms of where I was, and what I was trying to express.

Sometimes a literary influence, or fresh perceptions of what I see around me, come together to make something new out of my poetry; at other times these influences and perceptions simply dissipate away. I'm curious at the moment about Charles Simic and the techniques of surrealism, for example . . . but there is no immediate goal attached. It all assists, I guess, in ways I'm not always aware of: it might or might not end in a poem or two, eventually. But the process of enquiry – I would call it the *discipline* – helps. Hopefully, literary influences are tamed by my own needs, have been metabolised thoroughly, by the time they reach the page.

Don't you get irritated when people who regard themselves as knowledgeable about literature are closed to – or ignorant of – the variety of poetic forms available, past the few hidebound notions they're familiar with?

One of the problems in South Africa is that some – although unfortunately too many – of our poetry reviewers, especially newspaper reviewers, are nitwits. What makes it worse is that it's precisely these people who tend to arrogate to themselves knowledge about 'literature', in the grand sense of the word. Mind you, I can't feel too victimised in this respect, personally – reviewers have tended to be reasonable as regards my work, and the criticisms have occasionally made me think very hard. But I've been lucky!

Some recent poets – I think immediately of Donald Parenzee – have really suffered as a result of second-rate criticism. It's upsetting when you see something, a poem or a book, that's really interesting, and would attract attention in a more informed atmosphere – and it's totally ignored. Or taken up for the wrong reasons. Some of the most promising black poets in this country have been destroyed by patronising praise from critics; praise that doesn't engage seriously with their work. Just look at the current size of Mzwakhe's ego.

Could you trace your literary influences?

It's difficult to describe these influences accurately. Rimbaud and Blake have always been with me, not so much as influences but as models of what a poet should risk. I try to read very widely, particularly in poetry, try to read as many different kinds of poetry as possible, try to read and understand different poetic traditions from different countries. This isn't completely a wide open stance: there are certain types of poet, maybe Nemerov and Snodgrass would be examples, whose work I actively avoid: it's so word-crammed, so mannered, it feels like it is activated by the sphincter rather than the imagination, or the heart, or the stomach. There's no room to breathe. In the late 1960s and early 1970s, I also actively avoided the white writers in vogue in journals like *Contrast* and *New Coin,* as they then were – it was an emotional reaction, I guess, and leaves me now with a gap in knowledge I rather regret. I felt that I wanted to avoid my literary 'roots', racially speaking – for me at the time it was a maze with an entrance and no exit.

I've tried not to be too influenced by, and thus too imitative of, particular poets. This has happened from time to time, though, I suppose, especially with poets I really like. I remember being very taken with the Black Mountain School as an undergraduate, especially Olson, and I think traces of that influence will never go completely. Olson's writings about poetry are the only ones which have ever made sense to me, along with Lorca's theory of *duende* . . . Okigbo I read obsessively at the same time. Enzensberger has been important to me subsequently, and Brecht (his techniques of estrangement rather than his verse), and MacDiarmid, and Levine. More recently, there are others, such as Atwood, Amichai and Holub, whom I enjoy thoroughly and who've probably influenced my stuff: I also go back to *Paterson* all the time. Mind you, there are other poets – Edwin Morgan and Tchicaya u Tam'si would be examples — whom I really like, even though I know any attempt to ingest their styles would be a disaster for me.

One learns not only from reading but from teaching as well. I've been amazed how much about the politics of form I've discovered, often without expecting to, from teaching Seventeenth-century English poetry.

I've also learnt some things about form from genres besides poetry. Obviously not directly, but some of the ways these artists have played around with, and manipulated, structure. Zappa and Godard, a long time ago. About ten years ago, jazzmen such as Roscoe Mitchell and Cecil Taylor. I actually believe music and dance are superior forms of expression to literature.

You're one of the few poets in this country – and one of the only male poets — who has written erotic poetry. This has confused some critics, especially those who've expected to find a gulf between the political and the personal. How do you respond to this?

In *Blood of Our Silence*, this problem of erotic expression was a big issue for me. I'd been reading some of the great erotic poets in English – such as Carew and Rochester – and thought about the yawning silence in South African poetry as far as explicit, erotic poetry was concerned. And thought, "Right, let's try that." So in one case in that volume I did what I occasionally do, let the critic in me decide on the type of poem I should write. More and more I think eroticism has to encompass other aspects of the social world outside of that private space of sex as well, even whilst describing it. My feeling these days is that you need to place sexuality in some kind of an historical, even a political, context. Moreover, one doesn't always need to show bodies explicitly to be erotic – the *Gita Govinda* is one of the most erotic poems I've ever read, and it works mainly by suggestion and repetition. I suppose this is an area I want to keep working on – there is something, a way of expressing such intimacy, and of exploring the power relationships in which it seems to become embedded, which I feel I haven't found yet.

So it's a matter of allowing yourself to write poetry out of any and all experience?

It has something to do with what sort of selective processes one is allowed to use. I'd argue that resistance to an openness about sex is typically South African, typically prudish, even perhaps typically macho. Disallowing me, or anyone else, this area limits our artistic choices. All artists select from their raw material: but some South African literati still want a particular kind of selection to take place. They want poetry to be 'elevated', to turn life into some kind of rarefied, distanced world rendered aesthetically spic and span for the page. They want to simply expunge what *they* regard as inappropriate form, or what *they* deem subjects not fit for poetry. Some of these people tried to argue that politics was one such area, for a long time. And now sex. What next – poems which endanger their version of social harmony?

One of the reasons I think William Carlos Williams is such a joyous influence on twentieth century poetry in English is the fact that he is the most democratic, most generous, of writers. He doesn't have to make use of the smarmy 'we's' of Whitman, however. Instead it's in the form of his writing. He mixes prosaic and poetic registers of language. And he selects, but his selections are unusual, at times appearing to be gleaned from trivial subjects or by chance. But it's much more clever than that . . . everything in our life is potential subject matter for him. There's none of this 'elevated consciousness' bullshit.

How do you explain the fact that poetry in South Africa in 1994 has fallen right off the 'culture' agenda?

I think poetry should count itself lucky. Movements and trends in art which are successful are driven, to misuse a quote from the science fiction writer Kim Stanley Robinson, 'at a level below intention'. They are fortuitous and often disorganised. You can influence the direction of a country's art with cultural organisations, to a certain extent, through controlling and directing funding opportunities, but you cannot legislate or plan what *forms* of art and culture will emerge. Creation is a spontaneous process, even if it is dependent on social and economic circumstances and individual preparation and hard work; a process of – combustion? – dependent on contingent factors. Attempts to promote 'official' art tend to go awry, as far as I'm concerned. It's wrily funny that official sanction can end up making heroic symbols out of *very* inappropriate individuals. Look at poor old Mayakovsky! I hope those in this country who have chosen to make a business out of sitting at cultural desks and being fulltime organisers and planners don't get too great a rush of blood to the head about their own power or ability to differentiate or to be prophets. At best they can serve as clerks.

What is so debilitating about the way cultural organisation is conceived of in this country at present is that it is defined only in regional or national terms. It was presumed that a joint antipathy to apartheid was enough to bring artists together, because of geographical proximity, in a sort of 'broad front' manner, or into little suburban and township committees: and it's still assumed that this will help us artistically. I wonder. Perhaps what we need, if we're going to talk about collectivity, is groups of writers cohering out of need and conviction around jointly held interests in form, in the stance of the artist towards society, and so on. I sometimes wonder, especially in the times we're living in, if poetry is ignored because it's not visible enough. Visibility is a big thing in the arts these days.

As a sweeping statement, I wonder if the new South Africa hasn't become mesmerised by a sense of art as easily consumed spectacle; if the spectacle's got a few leopard skins and tutus shoved in for good measure and we can call it 'cross-cultural', even better. From the 'traditional' music shows on television with smoke machines and sequins, to the drum majorettes at political rallies, to the versions of what's culturally or intellectually hip put forward by the Ronges, Mabuza Suttles and Tambos, even to the cultural pages of *The Weekly Mail* . . . look at those pages sometime. The recipe is: blend together some notices about zingy new plays and music in Hillbrow, add some book reviews from *The Guardian*, pop in a bit of postmodernist discourse, gesture towards various minority and oppressed groups, stir and serve . . . it's all on the surface, it's half-baked. There's no debate, no meaningful engagement with culture and art, beyond what nasty things the DAC and the NAI are saying to annoy each other that week.

Where do you think South African poetry could or should go from here?

I am more convinced than ever that we'll need a political poetry in the future: but not of the kind that mouths platitudes of praise, or is satisfied supporting politicians or institutionalised positions. Political art shouldn't be functional to politicians. I can do no better than reiterate the hunch some Black Consciousness writers of the 1970s voiced that, even under an independent majority government in the future, the writer would have to act outside of the privilege and promises of politicians, as a critical voice. That's where I'd like to place myself, particularly as there are lots of ordinary people, both black and white, who have realised that what went on at the World Trade Centre and on SATV has little to do with them – all of this seemingly reasonable and rational language by talking heads wearing suits, Dashikis, Miss Cassidy's, whatever. It's unfortunate that this gap in credibility is assisting the emergence of what I would call lowest common denominator politics, as well as various really reactionary forms of racial and ethnic identification. In this context, poets should aim their expression at people without a political home, maybe even without a home, restless people, those who wish to debate and understand in terms not allowed for in officialese.

When some of our older writers start getting comfy jobs as university professors, as members of parliament, at cultural desks, it's time for younger writers to get into the streets and hidden corners and find out how people are really living. In this regard, it's interesting to me how Zimbabwean literature is evolving, and the number of its young writers who are writing about broken promises, discontent, personal restlessness with what is happening there. I feel an identification with the stance of writers belonging to what Veit-Wild calls the 'second generation' of Zimbabwean writers, even those who are still struggling stylistically, who are articulating this new kind of vision – a vision removed from the nationalistic and didactic concerns of the older generation. When I read Marechera saying, "If you are a writer for a specific nation or a specific race, then fuck you", I become intrigued . . . the middle finger is an underrated tool of poetry. Or Stanley Nyamfukudza noting that he's not interested in teaching people in the old way. Although I do worry about how some of these writers are starting to throw around words like 'universality' and 'truth' . . . it could simply retreat into modernist navel-gazing, if it takes a certain path.

How will we get people to realise how vibrant poetry can be?

One way is cheaper publishing methods, aimed at getting a poet's stuff out there, rather than turning him or her into a successful 'author' with a 'book.' A greater emphasis on performance helps too, of course: although not all poets' work lends itself to that.

Another option is to find ways to widen that book-reading public. I suspect there are a lot more people out there than we realise who would enjoy reading the very exciting poets who are starting to emerge. But they either haven't heard of them or haven't the money to buy them. I don't think people in the main neglect poetry out of sheer disinterest – they just haven't come across what's of relevance to them, or haven't experienced and explored the genre enough to see how exciting it can be.

Literature doesn't lend itself overly much to glitz and glamour. It needs a thoughtful culture to grow; there should be some analysis, not just emotion and display. I once read something by Regis Debray about the Black Panthers which has always stayed with me. He said that their mistake was to merely invert the dominant images of the white world and present these back again as a kind of show. He warned that the world of display is the world of the momentary. To the media, permanence is boredom. To combat this, I'd say you must endure with your vision: become a lasting embarrassment on the landscape.

Interviewed by Robert Berold

MZI MAHOLA was born in the Hogsback area of the Eastern Cape in 1949, and has lived since the age of 13 in Port Elizabeth. He worked for many years at the Port Elizabeth Museum as an environmental educator and now runs a spaza shop from his home in Zwide. He has written a novel about his experiences as an Umkhonto we Sizwe soldier. A selection of his work was published in the 1992 anthology *Essential Things*.

Books of poems published:
Strange Things (Snailpress, 1994)
When Rains Come (Carapace, 2000)

When did you first start writing poetry?

At Healdtown Training College in 1969 a friend opened the door for me into the world of writing. He showed me a poem that he had written, a poem about moths. I read it and I was not impressed, but I did not say anything. Secretly I wrote my own poem because I felt I could write something better. From that initial poem, more were to follow and they were all private; I did not show anybody.

Then I was introduced to a librarian who gave me the name of a masters student at Rhodes University. I went to see him. For the first time I was going to get an evaluation. He read about three. After the third one he said "This is bullshit." I said to myself: "Is this a critic?"

I asked, because I was apprehensive, "Do you think that there is any hope for me as a poet?" And he said, "You must be out of your mind because you wouldn't have written something like this unless you had talent. But you need someone to guide you; to show you the beauty and art in poetry." He introduced me to a kind of romantic poetry and he showed me how I must approach my writing. But I didn't like it – it was not what people were writing about in townships, they were writing what is now called 'protest poetry' although I didn't know the term then. He said I was writing black poetry, something confined within South Africa. He asked me to copy the style he showed me. So I came out with something that was in between because I was trying to mesh two types of writing.

Some years later, after I'd been writing for some time, I met Dimza Pityana, the wife of Barney Pityana. They were going to Gaborone in Botswana; there was going to a black cultural festival there and they wanted an anthology from me. I did not know what to select so I just gave them the whole manuscript and I said "Ask Barney to choose." That was the last time I saw my manuscript because it was confiscated from them by the security police.

When I was taken – I don't know how many times – by the security police, they would show me these poems and say they were going to use them to get me out of my job so that I could cooperate with them. Gradually this caused me to lose interest in writing. Even the youth group I belonged to said that I had better lie low now because this was affecting me mentally. I was a danger amongst their members because anyone who came into contact with me became affected. I stopped writing, for about 11 years. Everybody who was associated with me was also taken in for interrogation.

Why were you being interrogated?

The youth group was open to members of all races and our main objective was to show people that there is nothing wrong with colour and that we can all understand each other. We used to go out and advertise by meeting in places where people of different colours were not accepted. We used to spend weekends on farms where there were strong conservative elements. And then we took on some schools for re-building and supplying books to needy children. We started adult education for farm workers. We gave lessons to unemployed teachers so that we could use them in teaching people. But the farmers were approached by the security police and told they should not allow us to enter there because we were preparing the people for the ultimate revolution. So we had to go to the townships. Even then, they followed us and intimidated people.

What made you start writing again?

I had died spiritually. I still enjoyed reading but I could not write. Then a friend of mine was released from Robben Island. I went to see him on a Sunday and he wanted to know about my writing and I told him "No, I was writing nothing." He did not ask me to write — he just said "You are going to write, because you are not writing for yourself, you are writing for the people. So you are going to write." But I said "No, there is not time, no chance, no interest in writing."

I thought about this for the whole day at work on Monday. "This is a command, he is not asking me, he is telling me." Then I took a piece of paper and a strange thing happened. I started with a title: "I'll take my time." Then I wrote a poem. I left it on the desk, and somebody saw it, a friend of mine, a white guy. He asked if he could have it. I said, "You cannot have it because this is nothing; it is very poor and I am still writing it." But he wanted it. Then he took it away and then he copied it with lettering the kind that goes brown — as if he had put it through fire. And it looked beautiful. Another friend asked me for it, so I gave it to him. That's how I started writing again.

In 1989 a lady at the museum showed me entry forms for the Sanlam Literary Award. She said, "Try it – you never know." I tried it, and I was surprised by the results of that competition. One of my poems was published in the anthology *Soundings*. Then I started corresponding and sending poems to *New Coin* and *Contrast*. I attended some of the New Coin workshops at the Grahamstown Festival.

I had a poem called "The Dassie Hunter". In the workshop you [the interviewer was running the workshop] made a comment that this was a narrative poem. It was as if you had opened a big door. All along I had tried to imitate other writers like lyric poets and I would say they write beautifully but I cannot produce what they are producing. Before we parted I said "How do I encourage this?" and you said "Read more and more narrative poetry." I knew there were so many stories I wanted to tell but I had not written them. I contemplated putting down my experiences of childhood in the Hogsback area. When we met again I had about eight poems. I felt my objective starting to take shape now.

Do you remember what you were reading then?

Langston Hughes, John Eppel, Tatamkhulu Afrika and the old Xhosa writers like Jolobe, Mqhayi and others. I have an anthology of those writers.

You have a straightforward, simple style. Is that a deliberate thing?

It is very deliberate. When I write something I always want to be simple. I don't believe in using flashy terms. Even when I talk with people I never use words that are going to obscure my meaning. I like to be simple.

You now have a book published but how many people are reading it? Is the size of your readership an issue for you?

Yes, it is an issue. I know that this book is not necessarily going to be read by the masses. It is popular with some white readers because of its emphasis on our culture. But my aim was to have the book read so that our people could think again where they are going wrong and where they could restore the traditions that are not destructive.

Are you always driven to write a poem, or do you sometimes have to force yourself to write?

I only write when a poem comes, because I do not want to force it. You have got to have strong feeling for what you are doing. Now if I take a pen and paper and start scratching my head, what I'm going to write is going to be a parody because there will be no feeling in it. Maybe I still have to train myself because some writers can actually train themselves to write.

Do you write in Xhosa as well?

I have been asked that question many times. I tried in Xhosa but I did not find the passion. I always loved the old Xhosa writers, so when I started writing, I wanted to emulate them. When you read good quality Xhosa, it really absorbs you. But I wasn't happy with the results. Maybe it's because when I started reading I was not reading in Xhosa, I was reading in English. Moving away from Hogsback took away a lot of traditional influences. My sister introduced me to English because she had that culture of reading, she had a group and they would always go to bookshops and get books by the traditional English writers. It was through reading English that I started to appreciate quality writings.

What was it about the Xhosa writers that you admired so much?

In describing things they would take from nature. It opens your eyes and you are more appreciative of what they are observing. Contemporary writers do not have that talent; they are so academic and it kills poetry.

Did you come across many storytellers and imbongis when you lived in the rural areas?

Yes, my grandmother was a good storyteller and we used to listen to her. She was a Swati. She met my grandfather in Johannesburg then he went to live in Alice. Even at school we used to be asked to tell stories – one by one – and you had to come up with a story and tell the whole class. And if you did not have any story to tell, you had to make your own stories from what you heard from others. So in a way it was training you to be creative. We learnt that you must entertain when you tell a story, you don't just impart information or knowledge.

Do they still do this in the schools now?

It doesn't happen any more. I have been to many schools because of my job and I ask children "Do your mother or grandmother tell you stories?" but they don't know anything about it. In Lushington, where I grew up, every household had a storyteller. So if there was a feast one person would call a narrative song and everybody would join in. It just came out spontaneously. If she was a storyteller (it was usually women), she would just stand up and start with a small group. Then the group enlarged because the narrator attracts other people. The body language is so interesting that people who are far away come closer.

Your poems describe how the world of your childhood village was broken up by bantustan policies. Were you aware of the political implications of this?

Village life started breaking when Ciskei took over, because the white farmers were bought out. It left smallholders helpless, reliant on white farmers for transport, harvesting and machinery. Even the train that used to come to carry the wool and tobacco for the market was discontinued. The agricultural economy was destroyed – it became just a means of subsistence. So people started leaving for bigger cities where they could find work.

I was about eleven or twelve years old during the time of the Republic. Now there were strange sitings, like a Falcon jet would fly over Lushington. That area is so remote even a single plane flying over would make a noise because of the mountains. There were explanations or analyses by the rural people. They would say a war is going to break out. And then there was a change of currency because up to then we had been using the British currency system. And we were given little flags to replace the Union Jacks. All these things were associated with the coming war and the elders would say the boers or Afrikaners are going to be the main protagonists, that the English would help us against them. So they were dividing the white communities in their minds. Maybe because those farmers who were very hard on the workers were Afrikaners.

Now, these things were new to me. I did not know anything about that. So I was learning strange things. Then I started asking questions but who was there to give out the correct answers? We were confusing ourselves. If a guy from King William's Town would come home, he would portray himself as a know-all and we would believe him, we would be so gullible.

I grew with those kinds of misconceptions. I always really believed a government was somebody with a very big tummy. You were not supposed to throw stones at birds sitting on the telephone lines because we were going to disturb *rhulumente*. We were not supposed to graze our cattle in certain areas because that area belonged to *rhulumente*. Everything belonged to *rhulumente*. I thought of rhulumente as an individual who owned everything and he was so powerful that everyone cringed at the mention of his name; whereas with God it was not so horrible.

One Sunday, I cannot remember when, we were assembled near the kraal. Then we saw these horses and then I cannot even say today what it was, there was some mirror affecting our eyes, being shone at the community. What was it? I never knew, even today. One of them alighted and they were coming to our kraal. All the males in the homestead ran away. They knew that if a man had not paid his tax, he would be taken in a bakkie to Seymour to pay it. But my grandpa didn't run away. He was a respected man in the area, a retired teacher and a lay preacher. I didn't know what they were talking about; I didn't understand the language. I only heard that it was the *rhulumente*.

How did your political understanding develop from this point?

When I left Alice I was only about twelve years with all those misconceptions. Then I came to PE to live with my parents. When I came to PE, things were totally different. Where I had come from, my surname commanded respect all over. If a person met me and I told them my name they'd say, "Oh, are you the grandson of Mr Mahola, the teacher?" When I came to PE, it hurt because my name didn't mean a thing to people; there were important names in PE and they were commanding more respect. I wondered what my father's role was because he was respected in Alice as a soldier in the Second World War, yet here he was not known. The world is so big, you could not expect people to know everyone. So in a way I just disappeared: the name Mahola didn't mean anything.

New Brighton, where I grew up, was the centre of the stalwarts of the ANC; Ray Mhlaba lived in the back of our street. A block down, at No.39, lived Govan Mbeki. If I was sent there in the evening by my mother, I would find the house in darkness. This was very weird to me. Inside people were wearing balaclavas, big hats, and using candlelight. It was a strange thing and I never felt comfortable. The owner of that house was an old woman, we never saw her smiling or laughing, she was very quiet. When members of the ANC were arrested, there was that sadness over the community and people were talking about the liberation of the black people by the ANC.

I always identified myself with the ANC. I went to Alice to do my high school education at Lovedale then again we were transferred to Healdtown and for the first time I was introduced to politics. I was about nineteen then. A guy from Durban gave me a copy of *The Outlook* with a story of Toivo ja Toivo, the leader of Swapo, how he was arrested, how he started Swapo, how he was detained in Pretoria. It was a painful story, written in the first person. And I read it and had a strange feeling in me; I became so emotional. I wasn't aware that the guy who gave me this was observing me. When I'd finished it, he asked me, "If you were given a machine gun, what would you do?" The answer was easy, "I would just march out and shoot down every white person I met on the street." His plan was to form a secret group called the High Command and no-one was to know anything about it. It was about 5 or 7 people. We started planning and sharing literature. At the end of the year, we had to go back to our homes in the towns but we kept meeting.

Were you ever attracted to the Black Consciousness movement?

Although at the time I did not know it, my own aspiration was for all people who suffer to be together. But one time I was in the car with someone and he challenged me for my stand for being a member of a non-racial youth group. He said, "Say you've got a homestead, now here comes a lonesome person who wants to lodge. Then you give him a place and then you go to him and say, I want you to overpower me, so I'm going to show you how you can own this homestead. You think the white people can teach you to overpower them so that you are in charge tomorrow? No, you are missing the whole thing. You don't belong there, you must go to the BC." But I never went to the BC. Maybe the ANC appealed to me long before the BC so in a way I stayed with it.

In 1985 I became more active. I joined a cell, and the ANC sent me out to Lesotho to be politically trained. This was a very good experience although I nearly got nabbed when I went back. Then we started communicating with the outside body and things were really developing. We learned how to publish and distribute pamphlets overnight. All our operations were very clean. We never made a slip. Even after one of us was arrested, through his arrogance, he never exposed us. So we replaced him with somebody else and we continued. We were printing pamphlets and distributing them – and we could see the results of our publication were very immediate. The way we used to distribute was very interesting. We would plan a route on the kwela-kwela (taxi). You got on with plastic bags with pamphlets inside. Now when you leave you give them to the conductor, saying he must give to everybody. Then you take the next kwela-kwela until you've finished your route. Soon the whole township would know.

We were also trained on how to make petrol bombs and we used iron filings and sunlight soap so that the flame didn't burn out quickly. I used to get some strange inflammable liquids so that the flame would give a bright red colour or blue colour and if it hit the bus – hey! – it made a beautiful scene.

How are you involved in the ANC now?

No, I am not involved now, I'm just a supporter because I'm busy now. I've got nothing against supporting and I go to meetings and I am still a member.

Your recent poem "Forget the Past – Forget Yourselves" warns black people that they should not be gullible. As I read the poem, it says that they have been betrayed many times and they should not, just because there is a majority government, assume that they are not going to be betrayed again. They should be learning from all the lessons of the past.

There have been different perceptions, from euphoria and high aspirations among blacks to fear and apprehension among whites. Whites think that blacks have been promised things that will never be delivered, so they fear that blacks are going to rush and grab companies, cars, houses, because they'll be disappointed that they did not get what they were expecting. Many black people thought something like this too, that after the elections there was going to be a free-for-all.

What I tried to portray in that poem was that people must come to reality. They must know that statements that were made, were made to garner support before the elections, because every party wanted his party in power, everybody wanted his party to win. I was trying to warn them that there are going to be hardships, because the country has been milked bone dry. To many it would be as if they have been betrayed, they won't understand that it took the nationalist government about 45 years to fail – so how long is it going to take the new government to amend those failures? It is going to take a longer time still.

But people will not understand that. You will find that there will be a high rate of crime and those organisations who didn't win the elections will use people to make South Africa ungovernable or discredit the ANC for not delivering.

How do you feel about post-elections South Africa?

The unemployed are disillusioned. They think the RDP is going to address their needs. But the RDP is not going to feed them, so it means that they are still going to be disappointed. Then the employed are finding that there is no increase in their wages so they are using labour unrest to get more. Industrial unrest is sending wrong messages to the unemployed – that nothing has changed. Such misconceptions are good for the enemies of democracy and bad for the ANC.

Then again, there are those who are still working for the community structures. They are trying their best to convince the people that the RDP is coming but many of them have lost interest so there is a break of communication. People do not understand. After the elections, there were no more rallies where people could tell you what is going on. The illiterate people do not know what is going on.

You would think that there would be more rallies after the elections.

Exactly. But those who were left out, lost that interest. It is not a liberation movement, it is a government now. We were told that it is going to be government from the bottom up but now this is going to be top-down. People are tired now. The toyi-toyiing is over. But the street-committees still are a tool that can be used. When street-committees call for a meeting, people attend because their problems can be addressed. And their main problem is the criminal element, the 'hungry wolf' that I warned of in my poem "The End of an Era".

How do you go about your work in environmental education?

Many people have a misconception. You are coming from a white institution and you are going to talk about nature conservation. My approach is different. I don't talk about the environment. I bring objects and animals, dead or alive, and children try to identify these things. Once I have got my audience interested, I always try to leave them and let them express themselves. I ask them which group, mammals or reptiles, would they like to keep or have at home. They always say mammals, because they are more familiar with them. This gives you an idea why reptiles are feared. They are

50

neglected because of misconceptions; nobody knows their behaviour, because we have been taught since childhood that they can kill you if you meet them.

I become a storyteller. I tell them all the stories that we have been told by our parents and even as far back as our ancestors. Their response is so positive it is easy for me to convince them of the confusion we make. They trust me and believe me. When they meet a tortoise crossing the road their role is to take it across because the next motorist is going to run it over. They understand that if they don't do that, sooner or later we will be telling the children that there used to be tortoises and we will only be able to show a picture. I have to present that in a very story-telling fashion so that for the first time they are listening to a story now, I am teaching them but I am telling a story.

Is there a tradition to kill snakes?

Yes. In our tradition, a snake is something that you must distance yourself away from. But not always. There is a custom of the mole snake, we call it *inkwakwa*. Now that snake is viewed as an ancestor of the Jola clan. They are not supposed to kill it if it comes inside the house. They must just ignore it. And when there is a newborn in the family, if they find it in bed with the child, they are not supposed to kill it, otherwise something serious will happen to the one who kills it.

Now what I am saying is that people should not kill snakes, even if the tradition says so. I explain that often the snake cannot even see you. Snakes cannot see at a distance, they are short sighted. They are literally deaf, because they have no ears. They use their body to feel the vibrations of the earth. We are so scared of snakes because we think they are very fast — but they are not very fast. You don't have to jump and run away because they do not chase you. I explain that snakes are helpful because they get rid of rodents. Every animal has a purpose.

With the creche children, who are innocent, I tell them these things. Then I assure them that I will not harm them – but they must promise me one thing: not to run away, not to scream, just to look at me. Then I take out a live snake. I tell them first. After playing with it, I invite them to come and touch it. One volunteers, then they all want to come and touch it. At primary school, a trickle will come and volunteer. At high school, even if one comes to touch it you will be lucky.

The more we expand, the more we push other species out and drive them to extinction. Until people start accepting this as a problem, it will have very little effect in addressing nature conservation. I was reading another book the other day. In about 1920, we had less than 7 million people in South Africa. Now we are close to 35 million. How are we going to address the holding capacity of the country? If we see it not as a political issue but a life and death issue, then we have a chance.

From your writings it is obvious that you think traditional knowledge should be introduced back to African culture. Why do you feel so strongly about that?

Tradition is something that really disciplines. In the rural areas each home had its own system of educating the children. The community was also involved in each and every individual. Look at the social purpose of stick fighting – it was not just a sport. From the age of seven a boy was sent out to look after the cattle. Then he met with boys of his age. As long as he could withstand them, he belonged to that age group. He commands respect from the lower group and he bore allegiance to the other groups. When they met at ceremonies you never found discipline problems between these groups. They grew up from childhood knowing that they could not sit with that group. It is something that you just cannot get rid of, it is something in your system. And there was order and discipline but today you find that young boys attack old people. That was never seen before.

How would you go about restoring traditions?

I don't see a chance of restoring them because we have gone so far from our traditions and people want an easy life now. We are isolated now and each home is on its own. In the past you could discipline, even punish, a child and nobody would complain, because you were doing the proper thing, you were training a person's child and you had the support of the community. But today you would be taken to court for child molesting.

Even at school, there are no boundaries, there is no difference between teacher and child because of the political changes that have changed the attitudes of parents towards children. How long it is going to take us to go back? I don't see it, really.

So that means you are quite pessimistic about the future.

Yes, very pessimistic towards the future. That is where the contradiction lies, because we have money and we are educated, but education is taking us away from our traditions. We do not want to be seen with those customs. But no nation can have a future without customs. We are going to lose out.

Interviewed by Robert Berold

PETER HORN was born in 1934 in Teplitz-Schönau in Czechia. He retired
recently as professor of German literature at the University of Cape Town.
Besides poems, he has published short stories, essays, academic articles and
reviews.

Books of poems published:
Voices from the Gallows Tree (Ophir, 1969)
Walking through our sleep (Ravan,1974)
Silence in Jail (Scribe Press,1979)
The Civil War Cantos (Scribe Press,1987)
Poems 1964-1990 (Ravan,1991)
An Axe in the Ice (COSAW Publishing,1992)
Derrière le vernis du soleil, poèmes 1964-1989 (French translations)
     (EuropePoesie, 1993)
The Rivers That Connect Us to the Past (Mayibuye,1996)

As a young poet growing up in Germany, what were your influences?

At school I was made quite familiar with the essential German literature from the
Middle Ages to about 1920 or so. It stopped there, because there was a great
reluctance by our teachers to deal with the Weimar Republic and with the Nazi
empire. A lot of our teachers came out of that period, they wanted to forget it: the
kind of amnesia symptoms which we get here in South Africa at the moment too.
Nobody was a Nazi in Germany after 1945. We discovered Kafka at school, and our
matric class suggested it as possible reading material, but we were answered no, no,
we are not ready for that yet.

How did you learn about more contemporary German literature?

When I came to South Africa with my parents in 1955. There was a tiny German
department at the University of the Witwatersrand. The head of the department
introduced me to a lot of 20th century exile literature, because he himself was an
exiled Jew. He knew Thomas Mann, had corresponded with him. He knew about
Brecht. So he introduced me to what I hadn't had at school.

Most of the German writers had some kind of contact with other European literature.
Brecht for example at an early stage loved Verlaine and translated and plagiarised a
lot of Verlaine . . . so there was always this sort of openness to European literature.
When I did my PhD I got to know a lot of the contemporary Russian writers, so that's
sort of my background, and that was the idiom in which I started to write.

Did you publish poetry while you were studying?

A few of my early German poems were published in German literary magazines, but very soon I found out that I was regarded as something exotic. If you write in a language which you don't continually hear around you, the language loses its freshness. Interestingly, in 1980 I did an anthology of South African poetry in German translation, and the editor in Germany said "Very interesting, your German verse translation sounds very 1950ish." That was the time when I left the country.

I hadn't known a word of English before I came to South Africa, so my very first attempts at writing in English were somewhat flawed. I started to write in English in 1964 when I was at the University of South Africa, and met Walter Saunders, Michael McNamara and Walter Battiss. We were then the core group out of which *Ophir* grew a year or so later.

What were your politics then?

I was writing about the modern urban experience of alienation, of loss of roots. "Voices from the Gallows Tree" was one of the earliest things I wrote, and that experience was very much the sort of modern experience, which was my only experience, both in Europe and in Johannesburg and Pretoria. I was vaguely liberal politically. I remember going to the Treason Trial, out of interest, but I don't think I really knew what was going on. I remember marching through Johannesburg in a student demonstration – I couldn't tell you what the demonstration was about. That's the kind of political innocence I had at the time. I was vaguely against apartheid, but that was about it.

It was in 1966, when I came down to teach at Zululand, that this began to change. The University of Zululand, in contrast to Wits, and even to UNISA, was one of those apartheid bush-colleges. 95% of the staff were white Afrikaans males, a lot of them in the semi-political organisations of Afrikanerdom, like the Rapportryers and the Broederbond: the usual setup. I felt very strongly that I was being hemmed in by this extreme narrowness. I became painfully aware of the poverty in rural Zululand, and that changed me a lot, it's when I started to write politically.

The other big influence was in 1970, being back in Germany for the first time on a study grant. It was right in the middle of the student revolution. That is when I became aware of Marxist thought in a more than superficial way. When I returned from Germany my whole outlook, both as an academic and a poet was changed quite fundamentally.

. . . leading to confrontation at the University?

In 1973 I wrote a poem called "To My Friends Overseas," and it appeared in *Ophir*.

54

One of my Zululand colleagues had been up to UNISA and had been shown this poem, it had caused quite a stir at UNISA as well. And he came back and said: you're writing about the University of Zululand, aren't you? He was referring to a line about student spies amongst the professors . . . student spies playing James Bond, and so on. This was quite a common thing at the University of Zululand – the university was full of student spies. One of my colleagues in the philosophy department organised a study circle on Marxism and everybody knew that he was a spy – this whole study circle was to flush out any communists amongst the students. I was threatened with dismissal.

When I came to Cape Town, I became even more politically involved, through a cultural organisation called the South Peninsula Education Fellowship, which was a front for a political organisation. We met regularly at a venue next to the Newlands cricket grounds. We did things like show films about the Spanish civil war, we had a lecture on Picasso's Guernica. This was in 1974. It was later that I found out it was one of those crypto-Trotskyite Western Cape organisations. This was before the UDF time, there was very little open political movement. There was a lot of Trotskyite-Marxist debate going on. The Fellowship was the place where I read "The Plumstead Elegies" for the first time.

That poem must have been a rare statement of public defiance at that time.

Yes, I also performed "The Plumstead Elegies" at the university, to an astonishing crowd – about 300, 400 students. That was the second time I was threatened with being dismissed – by the professor of Afrikaans who had heard about this from his son. He cornered me as I came up the stairs and said "If you do something like that again, I will see to it that you are deported from this country." I took this very seriously, because Van der Merwe Scholtz had very close connections to Vorster, and knew him personally.

During that time, "The Plumstead Elegies" was published as a student publication, and was immediately banned, like practically everything else I published in English in South Africa between 1975 and 1989. The mere appearance of my name at that time was sufficient to ban a journal or a student newspaper. Behind this was a guy called Professor Murray, a retired professor of Philosophy at UCT and a member of the Censorship Board. After 1974 it became extremely difficult for me to publish my poetry until my collected volume came out in 1993. But I did publish in cheap photocopied booklets.

Surely one of the effects of this constant banning is that oral performance becomes a primary form of publishing. That must have transformed your view of poetry.

I think even before that. When I met Walter Saunders, we were always of the opinion that poetry, like music, was something to be heard, to be performed. That you had the script, the score . . . which you had to translate into a performance.

When it came to political poetry I was addressing an overwhelmingly illiterate audience in a language which was at best their second language, and therefore the performance became even more important. It had to be performed in such a way that it could carry across what we were trying to say. People need to hear poetry to understand the complex rhythms and counter rhythms which are involved in performing a poem. What is called free rhythm really isn't any more free than if it were rhymed.

My experience was that astonishingly complex things would get across to people who had had very little experience, if any, of poetry before. In the 80s when I was reading in front of large masses, they immediately picked up important ideas contained in the poetry. And my poetry wasn't as easy, I would say, as some of the poets who came out of the *imbongi* tradition who were much closer to the audiences. So, yes, performance was actually one of the few ways in which I could reach people during that time. The funny thing was that we found out that you could actually read from a book that was banned. The act of reading from the book was not an offence. Possessing the book was, so there was this funny contradiction.

"The Plumstead Elegies" takes its title from Rilke's "Duino Elegies," and there are echoes of Rilke throughout. Yet, Rilke isn't anyone's idea of a revolutionary poet.

On the one hand he is a very great poet, and on the other I have the greatest difficulties with his politics, as I have with T.S. Eliot's politics, or with Yeats's politics. "The Duino Elegies", in a way, give an image of modern alienated urban life which Rilke, from a conservative point, rejected.

What I wanted to do was an exercise in what Brecht had sometimes done. You take an old text, and you read it against its grain, and you point out the problems, the sticking points in it, so you get a complex text of affirmations and contradictions. You affirm some of the beauty of the original text, and you contradict its politics. I think that is what is happening all the time in "The Plumstead Elegies". It's reading Rilke against Rilke, as it were.

Your performance audience wouldn't know the references to Rilke, but I suppose it didn't really matter.

No, it didn't, because they would see how some of the sentences are directed against that kind of aesthetics. Brecht once said that you can take a camera and make the most wonderful picture of poverty, but you are aestheticising poverty by doing that. You have to look at your aesthetics and see, by making something beautiful, if you are condoning its existence. That tension is there, between the desire of the poet to write beautiful poetry, and the political commitment and consciousness of the poet who says: can I do this? Can I create beauty out of the suffering and misery of people?

If you read "The Duino Elegies" carefully, you will see in it a conservative anti-capitalism. Not from the point of view that it exploits workers, but that it destroys the modern world. So there is a sadness about the destruction of the beauty which he sees in the past.

. . . the same as Ezra Pound . . .

Ja, exactly. There are differences between Pound and Eliot or Yeats but politically, aesthetically, they are very similar. I could just as well have taken Ezra Pound. In fact "The Civil War Cantos" are an allusion to Ezra Pound's Cantos.

So in your mind you solved a problem, which was how to deal with the burden of that tradition, and to communicate it to an audience who was not involved with it.

Yes . . . if you read "The Civil War Cantos" carefully you will find allusions to people like Brecht and Pablo Neruda. The style changes, and it changes under the demands of the political situation in the 80s. From very early on, from the formation of the UDF in 1982. Even in 1980, I was invited by the students of the University of the Western Cape, they had a three day strike, and I was one of the main speakers there and reading poetry, and it became a demand to try and say things as simply as you possibly could without becoming non-poetic.

What does non-poetic or poetic mean in this context?

To say things in a way that is memorable. A distinct voice, but saying things in a way that people could understand them, identify with them, come to grips with them. It's no use standing in front of 10 000 people, and only two of them know what you're talking about. Under that kind of imperative the language becomes simpler, more direct. The simplicity I was aiming for was the kind of simplicity which Brecht has in his poems, not artless but formulated in such a way that it sticks in your mind. My feeling was that I had succeeded, because people were asking for certain poems to be read again and again. And they seemed to understand that this poetry was about us here, now.

By that time I had already taken up a lot of South African influences, I think essentially it was the black writers mostly who I had met at the Poetry Conference in 1974 in Cape Town – you know – Serote, Sepamla. It was quite an intense interaction. As I was appearing on struggle platforms I more and more came across this phenomenon of the people's poet, the *imbongi*. I never pretended that I was a people's poet, but that kind of language I began to hear, to take it in.

Can one find an aesthetic, a frame of reference in which South African poetry can be put alongside the European 20th century poetry? I've noticed that in your recently published book of essays, you concentrate on oral or performing poetry as the South African poetry.

I think there are two things – or three things really – that make great poetry. One is having something to say, you know – the Campbell idea of "here's the bridle but where's the bloody horse . . . " That's what I feel about a lot of South African poetry: it has form, but it hasn't got any kind of content. It sort of blinds itself to what goes on around itself. The strength of a lot of struggle poetry and oral poetry is that it takes all that in. You know – the real passions, the real questions, the real problems of South Africa.

The second thing – and that's my European background I think – is looking for a very individualised voice. But I realise that not all cultures work like that. The individualism of Europe is in fact a very isolated phenomenon if you look at the world as a whole. In most traditional cultures an individual pronouncing his or her ideas is something quite extraordinary. Brecht once said the Chinese are proud if they write a book which contains 10% new ideas. They're quite prepared for the 90% to be taken over. 90% of what you say comes from somewhere anyway, whether you know it or not, whether you're aware of it or not. If you're an academic you footnote it and demonstrate where you've taken your quotes from, if you're a poet you don't necessarily do that.

I feel that the poet needs to have a very distinct voice. That doesn't mean to say that all his ideas are new, but that you can immediately recognise his voice in the poem. Even if I've never seen it before, I immediately recognise that this is a Jeremy Cronin poem, or that this is a Serote poem, or that this is a Sepamla poem. So that is the second element of good poetry, to develop this distinct voice which in a way is like the distinct melody and rhythm which you find in a certain music or in a certain musician.

The third thing is the form, and there again we must break loose from preconceptions of what form is. You know – if you know form only through having studied English poetry then you have, I think, a very insular understanding of what poetry can be or cannot be. One needs to understand that Japanese Haiku works in a quite different way from a European romantic poem. And because I began to understand that, I began to understand that the *imbongi* and the struggle poetry derived from a kind of poetics quite different from European poetry. One needs to approach it and analyse it in a different way.

Surely South Africa needs a new kind of literary criticism, one which will be able to assess oral poetry? Better still, an aesthetics which can encompass both written and oral poetry in one context?

I think that will be very difficult. Sizwe Satyo, the Professor of African Language and Literature here at UCT, is quite an expert on the Xhosa *iimbongi*, and I spent an afternoon with him looking at video recordings which he had taken at an imbongi festival in Alice at the university there. He pointed out to me the strengths and weaknesses of individual performers. For the traditional imbongi, and probably for most of the people who have grown up in that tradition, there is a very clear concept of what is good and what is bad.

I don't think that I could judge a Japanese Haiku even if I knew the language — it's not sufficient to know the language, you also need to grow up in that culture and acquire its norms, its judgments, and begin to be able to take a position towards those norms and judgments. Otherwise you will be saying things which to a Xhosa speaker are totally irrelevant, and you will be missing things which to the Xhosa speaker are very important. In the same way you don't have to agree with what Mzwakhe says, but you have to understand in which context his poetry functions, and you have to understand what are the important questions it revolves around, both politically and aesthetically, in order to judge it.

Walter Saunders and I worked together with Qangule who used to be a lecturer in African languages at the University of South Africa and he translated for us about 12 Xhosa poems, and I then got a copy of his PhD thesis on Mhqayi which I treasure very much, it gave me an insight into Xhosa poetry which I would not otherwise have had. I think unless we come to see South African culture as a rich diversity, of which you really need to know the whole spectrum, there will be a lot of prejudices about other cultures . . . of the kind which are very often found in newspaper reviews of poetry which start off practically knowing nothing.

How do you see this process transforming South African poetry in English?

People at the forefront of writing in South Africa are experiencing being in a multi-faceted, multi-cultural society, and one of the great problems for a South African writer is to be locked up in his own section. You don't necessarily have to agree with other traditions, other cultural preconceptions, in order to live together with them and be enriched by them.

The greatest mistake which South African writers in English have made, in my opinion, is that they thought they had to write as if they were living in Britain or in America, which meant that they were presenting back to the world a second-hand product. This obviously didn't create a stir of interest in those countries, because they said: that kind of thing we can do better, we have in fact already done better. Naipaul's or Salman Rushdie's contribution to world literature is in a way extremely parochial because they grew out of their experiences where they came from – you know – East Africa or India or Jamaica or wherever, and they present that experience. Thomas Mann's *Buddenbrooks* is his most successful work in the sense of reception, because he describes this sort of bourgeois life of people in a small north German town which he really knew. Anybody who succeeds to capture South Africa in that way would be a very South African writer. I think that various people are doing this, at least in fiction. Nadine Gordimer has grasped this, Brink has grasped this, and in a very different way, Coetzee has grasped this.

In the end you read poetry to open your mind, and opening up your mind may be meeting someone who thinks in a completely different way, acts in a completely different way. I think what will happen now is that we will probably be able to experiment far more with this interplay between our European past and our African past, and very interesting hybrids can arise in the South African situation between those two ways of thinking and experiencing.

Can you give an example of what for you is a successful hybrid?

Some of the things which Serote was doing, what he was doing in the 80s. Where he became weak in *Third World Express* was that he became too influenced by attempting to go back to his African roots. I think that made his poetry more superficial. In the 80s there was this real tension between speaking to a European audience because he was writing in English, he was publishing in books that were read mainly by white people, and that tension brought out what is most interesting about Serote. Whereas now there's a flatness in the latest work, because this tension is no longer there.

You've been running writers' workshops informally, and also you've been involved with COSAW in the Western Cape. What has that meant for you?

It was an incredible enrichment to meet some really interesting writers, whom I would never have met in the same way otherwise. It was a way of going across boundaries which I think few white South Africans had during that time. That for me was very important.

Look, my feeling is that you can't teach anybody to write who can't write. What you can do is to encourage, to nurture, to criticise, to bring out the best in people who are potentially good writers. The Lansdowne Local meets every last Friday of the month at my house. We've met some excellent young writers. The interaction with them has enriched me but I hope it's also enriched them. People like Rustum Kozain, and this young writer from Khayelitsha, Simeon Kanunu, who writes these wonderfully crazy poems. His English isn't all that good, so we work with him on his English. He also writes in Xhosa.

Since the elections there are so few platforms for oral poetry. How are oral poets functioning without their audience?

Well since the collapse of COSAW, and since there are no longer these big rallies, a lot of them are totally disoriented. I don't think we are going to see the great rallies with poetry and music which we had in the 80s anymore . . . that was very much a sort of UDF thing, and it's not going to reappear.

What I think we should be working towards is to create cultural centres in communities. We have one for example here in Manenberg, really a wonderful institution where they have created the space for all sorts of things to happen. For people to learn how to play the guitar, to dance, to paint and they invite poets . . . we have poetry evenings. At the moment it's a bit difficult, because Manenberg from time to time is in the centre of one of our Western Cape gang wars, but you know the place is there. It's the sort of place that we need to fight for in all communities, where people themselves decide and say, we want to listen to a poet, or we want this play to come to our community, or we want to have a jazz group come and play here. In this way people begin to understand that culture is a necessary part of their life, and that is something which you know has been destroyed again and again and again.

There have been moments in the history of this country like that. Sophiatown was a lively place. It had its dark side, and it had its gangsters and everything and it wasn't as beautiful as some people believe it was. It had a vibrancy which was incredible. There was a time when the area around here – Athlone for example – was seething with writers and cultural activities. That is the kind of thing you need to encourage. You need to be able to get people together. COSAW to a certain extent performed that function.

The question is whether our new dispensation will have money for that kind of cultural activity, because culture needs to be nurtured. It does happen to a certain extent on its own, but in order to meet its audience you need a kind of facilitator in between. Unless you have people who make it happen, it doesn't happen.

But it must happen at a very local level, and vigorously, otherwise we are inviting the mass media to take over and put across a false culture.

It's very important. It's important that Worcester and Paarl and Atlantis have their own cultural centre — their library, their place where they can go and see a good film, the place where they can invite a music group. It's important that whoever organises that centre is in close touch with the community and sort of translates what the community wants. Translates, because the community very often doesn't know what they want, because they don't know what is around. You need someone to introduce the artist to the community, and the community to the artist. I made a very strong plea for COSAW to become this kind of organisation.

How can poetry be popularised?

I have one experience which makes me very hopeful. For a long time, wherever there was an opportunity, I have accepted invitations to go to schools, and I've been in black schools and white schools and coloured schools in the Western Cape, and it's always been a wonderful experience, because there you meet young people who are genuinely interested. And you read to them and the discussion is lively, and they really want to know and so on. While I admit that amongst adults poetry is not that important, I think that particularly between 15 and 25, poetry is a very important experience. That is one direction I would go in to make poetry more popular, and if you can convince teachers that they shouldn't teach poetry as if it was some kind of punishment, then you could do a lot to change people's attitudes to poetry.

I noticed that in "An Axe in the Ice" there's an emergence of humour in your work, picking up on your earlier poem which depicts the poet as clown. Is this where you see your work going?

If you are in the struggle and people are killed around you, the only humour is a kind of very black humour. What I see now are all these wonderful contradictions in our society, like the Nats actually claiming to have brought about the new South Africa, and people like Yengeni no longer sitting in prison but in parliament, that kind of total shift. It's confusing . . . confusing to the people involved, they're suddenly sitting in mansions in upper-Newlands and Constantia.

What I'm concerned with at the moment is this confrontation with the humanness of people with all their weaknesses. Humour really is about laughing at yourself, and to laugh about others in the sense of recognising the limitations which you have. If there was an element of humour in my previous poetry it was satire rather than humour. I don't think that satire is entirely absent from what I'm writing now, but I think the satire has become less aggressive, because things are changing, and things are confusing as they're changing, changing fast. In my book of short stories, which I am told will be published soon by COSAW, there are quite a number where in a humorous way I'm pointing out not only the failings and shortcomings any longer of the old regime, but of us all as we are now.

It's important to be irreverent, critical, because otherwise we're breeding the conditions for censorship again.

I agree. I think that some of my friends really have a problem with that. They are defending the ANC even when it is indefensible, and they can't see that you are defending the cause if you prevent the ANC from making silly mistakes, by being irreverent about these mistakes. There is something like N.P. van Wyk Louw in his relationship to the Nationalists spoke about – "lojale verset" – loyal kind of criticism of your own party. I'm not saying now that the ANC is in government I am suddenly against them after I fought for them for 20 years, but I am also not saying that I am going to be silent as a writer about every mistake they are going to make. They already have made mistakes.

Interviewed by Robert Berold

ARI SITAS was born in 1952 in Limassol, Cyprus, and grew up in Johannesburg.
He was a co-founder of the Junction Avenue Theatre Company in the 1970s. In
the 1980s, he worked with COSATU-linked performance groups in Durban. He has
written plays, an opera libretto, and a novella. He is a professor of Sociology at the
University of Natal. A selection of his work was published in the 1992 anthology
Essential Things.

Books of poems published:
Tropical Scars (COSAW, 1989)
Slave Trades (Deep South, 2000)

*Your writing has come a particular route – starting with workshop-written theatre in
Johannesburg, then, as a trade union activist in Durban in the 1980s, becoming a
poet within the labour movement. What was it about moving to Durban which drove
you towards poetry?*

I was privileged to be made aware of Durban through the labour movement in the
early 80s. Downtown in Gale Street, where the offices were – they were dingy little
offices – that's where a lot of the life of the labour movement was, that's where I
would hear stories, make plays and be involved in running workshops afterwards. And
being new in town I wanted to know much more, search for more, find out about this
place. From that office I, we, went out and 'discovered' the Dalton hostel, the Dunlop
factory, the black side of the inner city towards the harbour, the industrial areas and
from there all of a sudden Umlazi opened out; and from that activity at the heart of
town you were called out to Pinetown, not the white side of Pinetown. So a whole
world opened up. I got very familiar with all that side of town, and also I became
familiar with the underside of this harbour town, this beach town. There were all these
forms of life, moving, shaking, dealing, wheeling.

It was very difficult to make all this correspond to my other life, as a lecturer at the
University, teaching a broadly white student body with a sprinkling of 'Indians'. All this
made me divide my life in two neat slices. During the day, of course, I would be doing
all the affirmative things: organising projects, organising people, making plays,
looking after some of the needs of the cultural movement that was beginning to
grow, hanging around with very creative people on that side of town.

When I really started writing, it was during very private moments, about issues that
upset me during the day, arguments going through my head, debates I was having

with all kinds of imaginary and real people, stuff that I needed to pour out like a private therapy session. So the poetry was never affirmative, but very reflexive, reflective, surrealist – surreal I suppose because I had to move through so many emotions in a week, in a day, rather than a learned surrealism steeped in Breton, Césaire and others . . . Once the first lot was written I realised that I was talking to people, seeking their attention, so that however private it was, it had public pretensions. So my poetry started having that other voice, started introducing the doubts, asking the questions – myself, where I was going, what people were saying that was really upsetting me.

Your poetry engages passionately with physicality, texture, a sense of place.

The sense of place was unavoidable, because I did not seek to play with ideas, or metaphors or concepts. I was encountering something, I was learning from something very literal, something very tactile, very 'scratchy-scrapy.'

Being in the labour movement created the urge in me to discover, to be able to name objects, and to learn how to talk about them, and that's how I started learning more and more through the description of objects and just accumulating nouns, I suppose, as opposed to verbs, and increasingly beginning to utilise these into the communication, English, Zulu, it didn't matter, that was happening between myself and a primarily black working class audience.

Also, I came from a socialisation that I suppose was more musical, bodily, gestural, touching . . . If I have ever felt repression as opposed to 'oppression,' it's the repression that tried to limit me socially in terms of these non-Anglo things. Growing up first in Cyprus, then in Johannesburg, (in fact, Hillbrow) I had my fill of physicality.

From which you escaped into books, through the 'book ladder to the top', as you put it in "Our Little Tropical Scars":
> 'eager to make a book ladder to the top and
> page by page to climb there'

You climb the book ladder to the top and then you realise from that hill, hey dammit, what is this? – total alienation. The moment of victory, of arrival, is also one of total alienation. There is a new kind of violence up there. And there you are: you have violated what you had in order to arrive somewhere else, where you do not belong.

Nevertheless, your reading confirmed your sense of self, so it was not entirely alienating.

The poetry which moved me and influenced me had always been textured by landscape, feelings, sea, movement, music. A lot of the Greek poetry I had been schooled in was about settings, landscapes, rocks, people dancing, culture – Elytis,

64

Gatsos, Ritsos, Sikelianos and to a lesser extent Seferis. French poetry too, so violent and maudlin since Baudelaire, has been very much about that – down there away from 'exalted' 'bourgeois' feelings. The American poetry I grew towards in the 1960s was also a rhythmical celebration of the body as opposed to the mind. And in South Africa a lot of the African poets I listened to had the kind of influence that just boiled and boiled away. The poems in *Tropical Scars* were like little explosions – bang! – in those margins of time; and then came the hard work of trying to discipline them, give them the musical form they were demanding . . . I never start with a clear vision of a total structure and work towards its completion, I start with inarticulate sounds, snatches, and then I just start organising its timbre.

Finding yourself a poet within an active labour movement must have given you an immediate sense of audience.

I knew that I had an audience, so I tried to communicate in different ways with them. At the same time there was always this doubt that I was a fraud, that I had said everything I ever had to say, and now I was just embellishing things here and there, finding new ways to tell the same old boring shit. I think the publication of *Tropical Scars* was a great boost. Ironically also it was crippling, because it sold well, it sold fast, it was riding on a wave, it was launched at the right time at the right venues, a lot of people bought it as a memento, not to read it. It got a positive glib type of response that was good for the ego but then I started saying "where am I at? where am I at? now I am doing this second rate stuff."

I started working on song-like structures, said OK, damn that, there is an audience out there, let me try all sorts of musical forms then which are already there in the first cycle. So I spent a lot of time writing poem-songs . . . Initially it was jazzy things, poking in a light way, but as the violence increased around here so it became more and more difficult to do that sort of stuff. There was all this counting of bodies, the dehumanisation . . . I think that I was very lost during that time.

You lost your mass audience too?

It was great having a mass audience but that audience was not interested in what I was saying, they were not listening carefully anymore, or how I was saying it, and in which context I was saying it. The mass rallies were getting bigger and bigger and I said, uh-uh, I'm not doing it any more. Then it was the smaller venues like the restaurant pub type of thing, someone would be putting on a fundraising thing and say – won't you come and do something? That was killing as well, it was a more intimate audience but they were too poep-dronk to really care. So I said, next time we'll play rock'n'roll, that's fun, appropriate things for appropriate times: 1-2-3, jive baby, jive, mangos and spikes. Then there were the poetry circles that were as stifling as anything else with their weird patronage systems, people becoming dependent on the patriarchy and matriarchy existing around them and rather unprepared about the frightening changes all around them. If there is one thing that I have never learnt it is to find meaning through patronage-systems.

What have you written since Tropical Scars?

William Zungu – A Christmas Story was published by Buchu Books, then COSAW thought that there weren't enough poems in *Songs, Shoeshine & Piano* to warrant a book-length book, so COSAW included it in *Essential Things*. Then the other book, a novella, *Etopia*, is instructional, it was written for labour and community education programmes, a kind of futuristic novel describing the processes and structures of the 'good life' in the year 2020. New poems have appeared here and there. There is one that *Botsotso* has published recently, a cluster of lyrics for maskanda guitar. I collaborated with Mi Hlatswayo on this and had him pen the maskanda chorales in Zulu. There are a few plays here and there and a libretto for an opera, *Dead Fish and Dreams of Love Again*.

How does one find a workable aesthetics or poetics when you are so surrounded by violence?

As I was saying, my 'alienation' from many people increased once the violence escalated. I knew many of the people who were being killed. I would be involved in all that side of the world and come out of it, go to work. It didn't make any sense. Cultural workers were being killed, I had to meet with their bereaved children. I had to convince them that those lives were not cheap, those feelings were very real, what people believed in was very serious. And the more that was happening the more tense the poetry got, in trying to shock people into the realisation that there was a civil war happening here.

I learnt a hell of a lot too from some of the social photographers here, Badsha, Raijgapaul, Nunn, Peter, Mayet, who were documenting people's lives, who were saying "Come and look at this", "Come and look at that." They too were undergoing major artistic and existential crises around the violence. They could not make aesthetic statements out of the ugliness and grief any more. A phrase like 'working class struggle' was never an abstraction, there were hundreds of faces, contexts, experiences. And I could never just believe in abstract ideas, you know. I found myself linked to a combination between ideas and real constituencies, real people, real reciprocities, and that I think made me painfully richer at that time but made my integration into my professional class very difficult and very, very unsettling.

How did you get onto the track of Slave Trades?

I was getting caught up in the kind of 'revenge against my world' type of mood. One of the plays that I wrote about the violence, *Charred Loving*, has been hated by everyone who read it, not because it wasn't 'good', but because it did things the way it did, it was too close to the actual violence and the blood to really allow people to absorb it. As I said in one of my poems, "The Monkee Tree," in Natal, the healing of wounds had been proclaimed, there's peace, there has to be peace, it's been proclaimed – and one forgot the nightmares or tried to forget, and sweep them under the carpet. But the ghosts of the past were, are, still howling at us.

I needed a new space which would not be bound by any people, any particular people I knew in order to explore some of the more problematic phantoms that whizzed about in my brain; and that's where Ethiopia became both a metaphor and a reality. It allowed me to write about very painful issues, about liberation that's not a liberation, a golden past that's not a golden past. I felt that it allowed me to go wild in all kinds of ways, and in ways I could not explore before.

It opens out to something much bigger than anything you've done before . . .

I'm trying to deal with all kinds of discomfort in myself, all kinds of roots, traditions, history, destiny, religion, atheism, men, women, many voices speaking, to see whether it would be possible to really create multiple voices that create tensions and say something that is about all the times we've lost, also the times that we might get, the real rootlessness that exists now, the horizon shrinking. *Slave Trades* was born through all kinds of real and metaphorical slaveries, of ownership, of possession, of mastery, of servitude, mental, manual, patriarchal, historical. I'm still drowning in that project so there's lots of flashes of it coming here and there.

Why did you set it in Ethiopia?

When I was doing the futuristic novella, I used a liberation song which goes, "S'pume Etopiya/ sihamba ngomoya/thina solala/emakhaya" – "We are flying through Ethiopia/ We are flying faster than the wind/ We are sleeping home tonight". It started reminding me how Ethiopia was one of the images of redemption in the resistance to colonisation. It was a similar kind of impulse that started the Shembe Church here. In African Christianity, Ethiopia was Jerusalem on earth, and Nazareth was going to be built here by Shembe, it became part of the so-called Ethiopian resistance to Christianity. It fed into all kinds of things all over the world, but specifically here Ethiopia had a very particular ring to it, both as past and Utopia. In South African languages, certainly in Zulu for the last century, Ethiopianism was equated with sedition. But if you look at it, if you go to the US, you go to Jamaica you go everywhere, it was that defeat of Italians in 1896 by a Black Christian nation. That started me thinking.

How is it that Arthur Rimbaud is one of the main characters in the poem?

Rimbaud was a big influence on me and a friend when we were very much younger, in our Bohemian days in Joburg. Poems like "The Drunken Boat" and "Season in Hell" were defining influences. But then I kept on coming across appalling, disgusting erudite books that have been written about Rimbaud's life in Africa; disgusting in the portrayal of Africa, the portrayal of the other through this genius who runs aground, who bought himself guns there, who might or might not have been involved with the slave trade, who – and this is irritating for someone who was born in Cyprus – he went to Cyprus, and wrote those appalling letters about the people and what was happening there. It's rumoured that he killed a workman there. He helped build the Colonial Governor's house there, remember we are talking of the *colonial* governor's house, and moves on in the literature, goes and buys a wife in Abyssinia and then decides he's not into it and just chucks her out, and so on; and one is reading all that, that stuff that makes your hair stand on end, written as though Africa was just part of nature through which this genius crashes. Nothing is said about the total insensitivity betrayed in his actions. What we need is the other story from the other side, so I started an excavation the other way around.

Then also, his ambiguous sexuality – they are not tackling this when they are writing about him either. And this woman who was just taken, paid for, taken out of context, family, clan, taken across to Aden. He tried to make her a French woman, she was beautiful, she was a good mate, then because she didn't fit his narrative, putting money around her neck and sending her across the water back home. The catastrophe of that woman, what happens to her afterwards, what made her to go over in the first place, her resistance to becoming Frenchified, none of that's there in the literature, she doesn't matter.

Then there is the whole Greek connection, my discovery of it in Cyprus, the connections that existed between Cyprus, Ethiopia, Sudan and other places in pre-colonial times, as part of the Ottoman Empire, as part of trading, as part of being the innkeepers there; which might in a sense give me the textual freedom to go and search for roots as well. So the poem metaphorically looks at my predicament, the exploration of my roots, where are my roots? where are everybody's roots? But the thing is, the more you go back into history to find roots and ground, what you find is violence, slavery, killing. We cannot find the Patriarch's estate, the garden, described by Mahfouz in *Children of Gebelawi*.

At the same time I'm challenging the easy certainty of the past tradition, ethnicity, what happens is all of a sudden – when you think you've found comfort and belonging, it turns to its opposite – that creates the turbulence in the text.

What gives it its power I think, is that you've thought it through, you've thought about how these things fit together, while at the same time you're letting go of your imagination as well, so both an unconscious and a conscious process come together.

Look, without sounding too arrogant I feel very happy about some of the pieces in *Slave Trades*. I look at them and I say, phew! you know, but that is based on hindsight. I was taking risks, and looking at it and even feeling I risk being misinterpreted here, and saying, well, damn that, it hangs together well, it captures something. The idea of slavery, at all kinds of levels, all of a sudden opens up – not the obvious ones but the kind of man/man, woman/woman, man/woman, woman/man, priest/subject, dominant idea/subordinate idea, servants against other subordinates, you know that just released all kinds of shit.

I am also saying that we're not driftwood, you know, we come from a long way back. At the same time wherever you scratch you don't find paradise, you don't find that golden past from which the fall has happened, the more truthful you are you find, power, power, power, that's what I find very frustrating at the same time. That's the struggle that's happening: I want to be absolutely positive about something but then I can't. All the past is basically an act of rape and plunder.

In Enid Starkie's book about Rimbaud, there's a description of Rimbaud's last days when he went back to France and his sister was looking after him and his mind was rambling, he decorated his room with all this African stuff . . .

Look, he was possessed by the place, he was, despite the letters he was writing, slowly sinking into something there. They thought that he might have converted to Islam, the relationship with his manservant, all these 'facts' are opening up all sorts of possibilities. He wasn't just a colonist. But some of his attitudes, his stinginess and his whole bearing and the fact that he wasn't killed, basically because he was being protected by the various chiefs and notables there, because he was running guns. A small incident . . . he had these hides at his warehouse and the dogs fouled them up so he poisoned Harar's dogs, he killed a thousand dogs! Now the dogs were the ablution of the town in those days, nobody owned those dogs in a literal sense, they would go about and people would sweep their stuff out and the dogs would clear the streets . . . But you know the total arrogance of some shmuck like him, he just decides to poison them, you know you look at that attitude that comes from him and you say well he is just a shit. But he wasn't as racist as the French colonists, he intermingled, he had black lovers, he dealt guns against the interests of the Europeans.

Maybe he was a modern white African, a post-colonial prototype?

Yes, but he was a shit. Where's the genius? There's nothing profound about his existence in Ethiopia. And the fact that he is hardly recorded in a culture that has left lots of histories, he was no great shakes there. Even the house that is now paraded in Harar as his, is the wrong one, an invention for French tourists.

Coming back to what you've called his ambiguous sexuality, how do you explore issues of sexuality in historical and colonial contexts?

Ja, that's the hardest work. I find myself a lot of the time writing something and then inverting it, recorrecting it, in order to be able to estrange it from my immediate experience, in order to give a voice its own dignity there and try and dig and dig and dig and find what that sexuality would have meant from a different angle. The themes are very liberating but the danger is that there is just a monologue, an autobiographical monologue that comes out. And I think I'm discovering that in my subconscious, (not so much my unconscious), there are other voices, too, you know, in an interesting way I'm sort of undermining myself and letting those speak, and trying to see how the voices could take within a different kind of character. I find that very hard. That's why I get lost, it takes time for me now to say OK now, this is an authentic feeling, a feeling which is usefully different from this other authentic feeling.

Differentiation of these voices . . .

Everybody has different voices within themselves at various levels of dominance, at various levels of one's life. I've had to really really work hard to approximate the possible feelings and images that go with those feelings. It is very difficult, for example, to work from the bisexual feelings within an historical context, so that it fits in to the time, 1881. How did the sexes meet then? how did the men meet? how did the women meet? what were the possibilities of interaction? who were these women who were available? who were the men who made themselves available, given religion, given mysticism, given taboos, given prohibitions?

And realising what a hard time ideologues and the clergy and the political order had, and the family and the patriarchs and the matriarchs, what a difficult time they had to keep the balance – in every historical period – because anything that might be an aberration could really create all kinds of chaos. So, in exploring sexuality and transgression, at the same time you explore how things hold together, and you explore the repressions that hold things together now. How authentic historically they are, or not, I don't know, because no text has been written covering those issues, the most dangerous ones. Those are acts of imagination that you hang around real history.

It's quite a task to set yourself.

It is, but I never knew when I started. All of a sudden I realised how difficult the task was. Until then the work was easy. It was one energy that went through to many voices. How do you take another step that doesn't exactly repeat the cycle?

What do you imagine is the relevance of this kind of writing?

We are at a time when new kinds of tribalisms are being remembered and reinvented, that have to do with the past, the pre-colonial, the post-colonial, that's the new language of postmodernism. My struggle is against these new tribalisms – they're false.

70

If you look at pre-colonial African belief systems, they were incredibly universal and tolerant provided you entered their sphere. There was no inequality embedded in either discourse or transcendental deliverance. They all called to believers to pray for people who were an aberration. Sometimes they killed them, but if one looked at the aristocratic and repressive regimes that animated them, these systems of belief were very democratic, if not in this lifetime at least in the next one, and addressed everybody as an equal.

Women as well?

Yes. Differently. Women were controlled: sexuality, oppression, taboos, men controlling women, selling them, slaves, selling them, buying women, bride wealth, but at the same time women are the central 'cultural workers' that create society, the essential pillars. If you look at religion, they are assigned roles the wonderful roles to raise these boys to go out as fodder . . . All the contradictions that were then, are still with us now. If one looks at the ways of tradition and women that is being invoked now, they are being invoked for repressive reactionary reasons.

Then my own roots, Who am I? Where am I? Where am I going? And I feel very rooted, but ambiguously so, as somebody who was born into a Greek culture which has been elevated into a myth of origins for Europe. I feel quite uncomfortable with that. You know the whole Hellenistic period was quite barbarian, quite savage. It was not only Reason and Philosophy it was also about untrammelled sexuality, about taboos, transgression, violence, all kinds of other unhellenic shit, and all kinds of beliefs that link it to the Middle East to Egypt and beyond, so I don't feel European in any sense. Having grown up in Cyprus, under British colonialism then, it doesn't make sense. At the same time being in Africa, being in South Africa, what sense do I make of that?

It seems as if you use music to make sense of a lot of it.

Music's got a lot to do with it. I'm at a type of a crosspoint between three major influences: a very rhythmic type of influence; then a very byzantine, eastern, long, mournful, sorrowful voice, that bemoans a situation, an ancient blues that is quite different from the blues. And then what jazz has done to us – taught us how close language is, and poetry is, to music, how the interaction between instruments is the beginning of an articulation which gives shape to words, to poetry. These influences discipline all the material back into some structure. It's not very clear in the structure of the poem as such but I can feel it as an organising principle: theme, improvise, improvise, improvise, come back, theme, improvise, improvise, improvise – so that gives it shape.

A cyclical arrangement . . .

Yes. Each one of the cycles has got some dominant characterisations beyond its story-line dominant characterisations that come to that, so for instance in the second cycle there is an element of the wanderer who travels around a lot, and through that wanderer you see the land described before, in new ways, you come back to the theme, there are themes from the first cycle drawn into it.

Next year you're going to actually visit Ethiopia. What do you hope to find?

To be really imaginative you have to step out of your own imagination first and try and understand other contexts. Every culture has its Odysseus, and each Odysseus sees you as an 'other'. The Troglodytes have also got their Odysseus and also have the vote and their own lives and aspirations too . . . They are not those creatures that Odysseus tricks and uses as he goes on exploring. Once you are there, in that reality we need be like the Laistrygonians, what is demanded of us these days is to understand the Laistrygonians.

Ethiopia has these resonances, it's like Africa's Utopia and it allows me to be fanciful within limits. I need to get there because I have to understand Ethiopia, I have to see how things are done, I need to see gestures of people, I need to see whether they move their arms like I do, I need to see how they relate to authority or to eyes, movement, goods, landscapes, colour, sun, night, all these things . . . to make sure I am not constructing the other like in old ways, making the other strange and foreign. Then to let the imagination regroup itself and correct things if need be.

I don't know if *Slave Trades* will finally achieve what it sets out to do, communicate in a serious way. It's a battle, in the most difficult of battlefields, the one of language. I hope it completes itself, finds the words and the colours and imagery to create a world that is coherent and at the same time expresses its multiple feelings properly. And if you can dance to it, all the better.

Interviewed by Robert Berold

DENIS HIRSON is the author of a prose memoir *The House Next Door to Africa* and was editor, with Martin Trump, of *The Heinemann Book of South African Short Stories*. He has translated a selection of Breyten Breytenbach's poems *In Africa even the flies are happy*. He was interviewed while compiling an anthology of South African poetry from 1960 to 1996, subsequently published by Northwestern University Press and David Philip as *The Lava of this Land*. In 2001 he edited a French translation of this anthology, published as *Poèmes d'Afrique du Sud*.

Can one talk about South African 'poetry' rather than South African 'poetries'? Because after all, South Africa has never had a single literature, it has had 'literatures.'

It has had fragmented bits of literature, islands if you like. It's had oral traditions originally coming out of the rural areas. It's had an urban European based tradition. It's had a scattering of different approaches to poetry, echoing the shattered political and social realities of the country. Nevertheless there might be a constellation of poetry developing which could begin to be called at least a nascent South African tradition or lineage.

How would you articulate it?

I would say firstly that it's not about the world 'out there.' In *White Writing* J M Coetzee talks about the development of English poetry in South Africa from Pringle to Clouts as a movement from the perception of Africa as a shadow of Europe to a search for 'an interior Africa'. I would say that the kind of poetry I'm speaking about does not describe the world outside the window. It describes a direct fusion between perception of landscape and feeling and politics; it records the intimations of an integration of self in the South African context.

Perhaps one of the major influences on this form is oral, that is, I think I hear the fluid forms of daily speech, perhaps also the pulse of oral poetry in this poetry that is nonetheless destined for the blank page. And then there are sometimes implicit and explicit references to urban music, mbaqanga and jazz. There must also be the influence of church singing and of freedom songs. This is a poetry which demands to be heard.

Heard on the page, as it were.

It must also work on the page if it's going to stand up to the battering of time: the test is to craft the words which will carry the music. I'm thinking, for example, of a poem like Wally Serote's "Alexandra" which I was incapable of hearing in the 1970s. But hearing him reading this poem since then, I find it has a particular music, a particular thick-edged, broad-lined desperate moving music tracing an axis between life and death under circumstances of extreme difficulty which, I have to say, I have trained myself to hear.

And here I'd like to open a bracket and refer to, not a poem, but a story – I would say one of the most significant short stories to have been written in South Africa in the last half century, called "I take back my country" by Bartho Smit – a story that was retranslated for the Heinemann book. This story tells of a confrontation between a white art critic and a black painter, and describes in the most telling way how difficult it is for the art critic to appreciate the black painter's perception of the land. This confrontation, which begins with aesthetics but goes much further, is to my mind of radical significance. It is the kind of confrontation that I feel I myself am involved in, inside myself, when working on this poetry anthology.

Why did you decide to embark on a new anthology of South African poetry?

Well, in a way this anthology has two beginnings. The first was when I was at Wits University in the late 60s and early 70s. For us as white students, it was difficult to assess exactly what being in Africa might mean. Those were suffocating years, years in which I felt that Johannesburg, white Johannesburg, was under a belljar, and the blacks under that belljar were whites' servants. The masters and servants were together under this belljar, and Africa was somewhere beyond the glass, God knows where it was.

I was aware that this explained to some extent the fundamental unreality of our student poetry. Our poetry had a lot to do with emotion, a lot to do with self, but absolutely nothing to do with the continent we were living in. At that time I edited an anthology of Wits student poetry, with Kelwyn Sole and Robit Hairman: we were asking that question, but I think the content of the poetry itself was quite paltry. I feel I am now editing an anthology with the same question in mind but with a rich haul of poems to offer.

In the early 70s some poets were already exploring what it meant to be in Africa. But in the thin air of the belljar we were hardly able to hear them.

Yes, and I would name here in particular Wally Serote, Breyten Breytenbach and Wopko Jensma, all in different ways and all exploring from different perspectives. As I have said, I don't believe that I was able to hear Wally's voice clearly at all. Breytenbach – I remember that you and I had a project to translate Breytenbach into English. I remember walking into the library at Wits, picking up a book of Breyten's, closing it and forgetting the whole project because the Afrikaans was so inaccessible to me. Wopko's voice I did hear, but it was too broken, too violent, too eclectic for me to fully comprehend at a time when I needed the organic beauty of, say, Neruda, or the soundscape of Dylan Thomas or Gerard Manley Hopkins.

Then you left South Africa.

My father had been a political prisoner for nine years and our family left South Africa at the end of 1973. I went a long way away from Africa, much further away than I had been in Johannesburg: I had to make a space inside myself for Europe, at some point turn my back entirely on South Africa to get into the theatre work I was doing here in Paris, to get fully involved in a new European culture.

And then in 1990 – this brings me to the second inspiration behind this anthology – Mandela's release had a powerful, unforeseeable effect on me. I remember sitting in front of the television from the moment he was released, in the afternoon of 11 February, until late into the night, just watching the moment of release, flicking through the channels to see that moment again. Just watching it over and over and crying, and crying uncontrollably, not fully understanding what was happening to me. Later, trying to assess that moment, I saw how there was a connection between it and the release of my father from prison; allowing myself some 20 years later to actually experience the full release of emotion which I couldn't express in 1973.

But more widely than that, trying afterwards to come to terms with the fact that in South Africa I, and many, if not almost all white people around me had been living half a reality, a reality that was cut off from the possibility of relating in any meaningful way to almost all black people. And asking myself ultimately, in the months following February 1990, what kind of response I could find, sitting here in Paris, to what was happening in South Africa, to what was shifting inside me.

A connection made finally between your European self and your South African self?

Well, it had always been there. In all those years I'd remained involved in South Africa in one way or another, I'd translated a book of Breytenbach's poetry, and I'd written my own mosaic of memory *The House Next Door to Africa*. I found that the only response I could have to Mandela's release was in terms of text, because in many ways South Africa had become a text, or rather, a series of texts for me. So, I started putting together what became *The Heinemann Book of South African Short Stories*. And then my next question – one that has absorbed me far more intensely – concerned South African poetry.

Why more intensely than short stories?

Well, partly because of the nature of South African poetry, beginning in the late

1980s and going through into the beginning of the 1990s, particularly as revealed in *New Coin*. The kind of synthesis that interested me somewhat abstractly in the 1970s suddenly seemed to become possible on the page. Of course this was related to the malleability of South Africa under the pressure of intense change. Poets seemed, in the face of a reality which was cracking open under their feet, to be finding a more lyrical and yet socially conscious voice; now this seems to me like a rediscovery – a connection back to a voice which affirmed itself strongly in South African poetry in the 60s and early 70s.

In other words, it seemed to me that there was a surfacing of a particular form of poetic energy which could be explored in its own right, but which would also allow one to see what was happening in the 70s in a new light; and this in turn suggested that what was happening in the 80s and 90s had a lineage.

What do you mean by lineage?

Well I *don't* mean a certain form of white English poetry in South Africa that goes back to a European tradition, to Thomas Pringle, and further back to English romanticism. I'm thinking more about an autochthonous South African lineage which doesn't have a direct European root.

It seems to me that it is now possible to see the emergence of such a lineage. I would make a direct connection between poets such as Tatamkhulu Afrika, Antjie Krog, Karen Press, Kelwyn Sole, Seitlhamo Motsapi, and those writing 20 years earlier. We are witnessing the rooting of a new tradition in South African poetry which is African in nature though it obviously remains open to a multitude of influences — European, American or African. After all, poets are like magpies, they're always bringing back bits of this and that to their nests.

What else characterises this poetry?

One characteristic which becomes particularly clear from a Paris perspective, is a certain raw music, and at the same time an awareness, often a desperate awareness, of what is happening amongst people in the environment where this music is being sung. There is none of the formal distance which abounds in European society; there is a directness, an awkwardness and an immediacy which comes out in what I think is the best poetry. There is a sense of malleability. For example in a poem like Karen Press's "Heart's Hunger" there is a sense that the poor are not necessarily doomed to despair, that poverty can inform and sharpen a voice.

You mean a relationship between economy of language and personal economic circumstances?

I go back to something that Njabulo Ndebele said in an interview somewhere, that he

76

would be happy to listen to whites when they stopped speaking of guilt and started speaking of loss. The great divide in South Africa is an economic divide. The true dialogue will happen when there is no longer a swimming pool between rich and poor. You can't have a true dialogue when there's a swimming pool between you. So, yes, the economy of the poem also might actually be reflected in the economy of the person, the economy of a lifestyle, the 'lean' line. It's interesting to note the number of poems in South Africa which are written with short lines. I'm not suggesting that it's a defining characteristic. It's just interesting, statistically.

Turning back to the 60s and 70s, you mentioned Breytenbach, Jensma and Serote as precursors to a South African tradition.

Not precursors: I would rather situate them as initiators whose work could not be fully heard by someone like myself at the time it was being written. They themselves had precursors and here I would mention Ingrid Jonker, some of the poems of Sydney Clouts, Adam Small and the remarkable poems by Jolobe and others in that collection called *The Making of a Servant* which was published by Ophir/Ravan in 1971, in the excellent translations by Rob McLaren and Z S Qangule. I don't think this is a full list and I am sure that in many poems one would find the inklings of what is being more fully developed today.

And of course one would have to take into account all the oral poetries of South Africa. Stephen Watson's book *Return of the Moon* deserves mention in this context because I think that this book, like no other in South Africa to date, has sought a link between the oral statement and a contemporary form; and I don't know whether Watson should be considered as the author or the translator – probably a bit of both – a mediator across time, revealing the beauty of the 19th century/Xam statements to a contemporary culture. This startlingly original work should be seen as one of the attempts to visualise, to recover the precursors to the lineage I'm talking about.

What else do these three 60s/70s poets have in common?

The rawness, the political statement, the power of metaphor, the sense of music . . . and there is also something essential, and it concerns language – which language one writes in and which languages one is conscious of. Here in France a man by the name of Berman, who is involved in the theory of translation, says that all texts in all languages have at the boundaries of their consciousness the existence of other languages.

Now I would say that it's this consciousness of other languages that was precisely excluded in the 60s and 70s and is even today excluded from so much poetry – and I mean particularly English poetry in South Africa. Just as a white person walking in the streets of the city might entirely exclude black languages from consciousness, so this can be reflected in poetry.

The three poets I've mentioned were already moving across language walls. This is essential to the creation of a new poetic territory in South Africa. Breytenbach was obviously clearly conscious of any number of other languages in his writing. He came to Paris in 1961, and there is an increasing consciousness of both French and English in his poetry at that time, along with Zen, surrealism and other influences. He also speaks of Afrikaans as 'a bastard language', a phrase which suggests political reasons for introducing hybridity into one's writing in South Africa. Serote is influenced by African languages and township English, which transforms his use of English sometimes brutally, sometimes subtly. Jensma actually seeks to integrate bits of different languages and different syntax into the rhythm of his poetry, and writes in English, Afrikaans, the *tsotsitaal* and *goemataal* of the 60s, as well as playing with bits of blues songs and jazz forms.

In the 90s, English is becoming Africanised and this Africanised English is being used with a lot more confidence than in the 70s – we're now seeing wordplay, multilingual punning, and so on. In the 70s there was none of this unforced integration of language, because social reality was so compartmentalised.

Poets are often loners who cross borders between communities. I would take Jensma as an emblematic figure; I would associate his madness with the fact that he crossed into forbidden compartments, he took on the madness of South Africa. There's a sort of conglomerate effect of language in his poetry, coming from his heterogeneous experience . . .

Cronin talks about this quite consciously in *Inside*. Gwala also uses the rhythms of different languages even when he is writing in English, and he should be associated in that respect with the trio of Breytenbach, Jensma and Serote.

I think that today, as you suggest, there is a more integrated form of poetry which takes into account these diverse languages. If one is to talk about a poetry, rather than 'poetries' of South Africa, the poetry I'm talking about does I think stand more consciously at the frontier between languages.

However there is still as much of a wall as ever around African-language poetry. This is reinforced by the limited publishing possibilities in African-language writing, still overshadowed by the old language boards and tied up with the prescribing of books in the education system.

We must come to a point where there is more attention paid to the act of translation; and I hope we witness in South African poetry more and more poets giving themselves over for a time to the translation of poetry that has already been written in South Africa.

Look, for example, at what I think is possibly the most significant anthology of South

African poetry to date, *The Penguin Book of South African Verse* edited by Uys Krige and Jack Cope, which tried to put together poems of different languages, even though it kept them in their different compartments.

This compartmentalisation, kept in place by violence, is really what apartheid did to people's psychology. What do you see happening as the compartments become more permeable?

An extreme fragility. English poetry of the 60s and before was designed to keep the outer world in general, and Africa in particular, at bay; and it maintained a semblance, or an illusion of solidity by constructing an apparently coherent window-frame of words through which to look. When one takes that window down, when one takes the wall down, one is simply standing naked in the wind with nerves exposed.

Not exactly emotion recollected in tranquillity.

Well, I'm not saying that a poet shouldn't have some distance, nor am I trying to make any absolute statement against more formally crafted poetry. But it is obvious that the poetry I'm talking about is qualitatively different from the protected (and in the South African context, I would add the adjective *defensive*) poetry of before.

This is made more apparent when one thinks of the position of poets in South Africa. There isn't a well-defined margin from which poets can write as in Europe. The poet doesn't have a clear place in South African society that I know of today. The exceptions are perhaps when the worker poets in the 80s stood up and performed their poems, and perhaps there are black poets, particularly in rural areas where traditions are still alive, who have a defined role. Poetry in any case, in any part of the world, expresses a very fragile position existentially, and even more so in a country like South Africa where there is not a large place given to literature, and a place no wider than a hair's breadth given to poetry.

Could you pick out some poems from your anthology which could be called essential?

Well, going through the contents list alphabetically . . .

Tatamkhulu Afrika's poem "The Mugging" for many of the reasons I've mentioned: for its ability to express fragility; for its strange ambiguity; for his almost 'enjoyment' of what is a near-rape situation; for his ability to use poverty as a way of 'seeing' the land; for his statement "the lava of the land"; for the music of it; for the compassion of it, for his ability to conquer his own romanticism.

Breytenbach's "Your Letter" because he manages to talk about the death cells at the same time, in the same breath, as he talks about love, as he talks about memory; for his ability in the face of pain to use memory as a resource, lyrically.

Cronin's "Walking on Air" because of its jauntiness, because he is able to reach a form of orality in the political tradition through this poem, but lightly, even though the context is so heavy; to find a new form of lightness, walking on air; the economy of it.

Ingrid de Kok's "To drink its water": so dry and sparse, such a thirst for return; and here she finds a music as taut and economical as one of those one-stringed instruments that have to be pressed against the body to resonate.

Jensma's "Spanner in the What(?) Works" : one of the most remarkable poems I think to have been written in South Africa, for the way in which it cramps together so many different possible existences and against that places his own intense need to make a statement in the oppressive, suffocating atmosphere of the 1970s. And its humour.

Motsapi's "River Robert" because it is able to look straight at disillusionment and not go sour at it, bends the language to it without breaking; he finds a music of disillusionment and humility and neither sinks into despair nor attempts in any way to rise above it in hope. Motsapi's music is a challenge for me, I have to reach for it, but I love it also for the challenge. I think this is easily his most successful poem.

Mthimkulu's "Like a Wheel" because of the sheer simplicity of it; one of the loveliest poems to come out of the *Staffrider* period.

Mtshali's poem "Amagoduka at Glencoe Station": it's a film, such a clearly stated vision of these people at the station without self-pity, without romanticism, just looking and seeing and listening to the music that's being played.

Andries Oliphant's "The Hunger Striker": what a strange poem, because in the face of pain the hunger-striker is able to evoke memory and then take these wild metaphorical tangents out of despair and still maintain a music; what thick painterly imagery Oliphant can bring to a lean emotion.

Karen Press, the poem called "My Thirty-seventh Year" but for very personal reasons, because of the last line of the poem, "I've no rope, my father left no rope" and because of my own preoccupation with my father. Karen Press has such a wide canvas, but in this particular poem, she's writing without a safety net about her own emotions and I love something about that quality.

Wally Serote's "Alexandra": that particular thick line which I have to ask myself about just like the critic in the story "I take back my country"; the music. I can't forget the way I've heard him read this poem.

Kelwyn Sole's "Poem from Botswana" which has been with me for a long time: which is such a good hard look at dogs. When Sole looks, he looks hard . . . and there's a lot of compassion also, in that poem. Poverty and compassion.

Chris van Wyk's "The Road": memory – and that ability to graft an adult perception on to the perception of a child without betraying the child in any way. A beautiful poem about loss of innocence.

Stephen Watson's translations in *Return of the Moon*, in particular "Song of the Broken String"; that one, for me, is the one that can bring me to tears: extreme vulnerability, and yet the song of it, the song of vulnerability.

Listening to you listing these poems, what runs through all of this is that South Africans carry on singing through everything, through despair, poverty, violence; even the violence is woven into the song but the song continually carries it beyond itself. If one begins to talk of a South African aesthetic, that quality of a transcendent song must be a key part of it.

Yes, yes. And this is true of so much of Antjie Krog's poetry. The poem of hers which is not in this anthology because I think it is untranslatable, but which keeps ringing through my mind, is the alphabet poem in which she sings the South African alphabet. That's a great anthem.

Interviewed by Alan Finlay

MIROSLAV HOLUB (1923-1998) from the Czech Republic, worked most of his life as a researcher and immunologist in Prague. His poetry is well-known internationally, and has been published in many languages. He wrote essays and also published over 150 scientific papers. He was interviewed during the *Fault Lines* readings in Cape Town in July 1996.

Books of poems published (a selection):
Selected Poems (Penguin, 1967)
Although (Jonathan Cape, 1971)
Notes of a Clay Pigeon (Secker & Warburg, 1977)
Interferon, or On Theater (Oberlin College Press, 1982)
Vanishing Lung Syndrome (Faber, 1990)
Poems: Before and After (Bloodaxe, 1990)
Intenstive Care: Selected and New Poems (Oberlin College Press, 1996)
Supposed to Fly (Bloodaxe,1996)
The Rampage (Faber,1997)

What is the common root of art and science?

The common root of both is something which is nobly called 'creativity,' which I would call the art of getting proper ideas or, more exactly, the proper questions which are very specific for this artistic discipline or for that scientific discipline. Otherwise they have very little in common. Maybe there are some human capacities, faculties which can be used in both; like imagination, like the ability to think analytically.

How does science influence your writing?

Just in my own relation to reality. I am worried about what can be labelled a 'soft centred' approach. I think every fact, every norm, needs some scrutiny, analysis and critique. This I have from science. Because reality, the human, the natural reality, is so complicated I think that in poetry clarity of expression is essential. I don't like poetry which is a jungle of words, of feelings. I need clarity. Seamus Heaney called my poetry the 'fully exposed poem': my poems are fully exposed and consequently they are comparatively easy to translate.

In your book Vanishing Lung Syndrome *the title poem ends in a landscape where only surgeons write poems.*

The poem is about a rare disease which looks like losing one lung. The lung would be completely replaced by a cavity, and it's some sort of comment on the human soul. In another poem I say the action of a successful surgeon is the first poetry – following Aristotle's division of philosophy into the first philosophy and the second philosophy. The first philosophy is the solution of the practical questions of life. Mozart died of kidney failure. There would be a solution to the kidney failure if he lived now. He would have gotten a kidney transplant and would have written a couple more symphonies.

What kinds of questions can poetry ask that science cannot ask, or answer?

Well, poetry is a series of questions. In a poem you get something which is the basic metaphor. The question is, can this idea (it's not a philosophical idea, it's a poetic idea) be made into a poem? The second question depends on the education of the poet: how many people have already had the same idea? If we had a computer memory, we would discover that somewhere somebody has written almost the same poem. In science, questions are a consequence of the present trend, the present paradigm of science. They are derived from the ruling theory and must respect the given technical possibilities of the laboratory. So this is just another set of questions. Basically, as Peter Medawar, the British biologist, has said, "Science is the art of the soluble". Maybe, to paraphrase, poetry is the art of the imaginable.

Why are you so strongly against mysticisms, which are surely just human wisdoms that have existed from the beginning of time, so to speak?

Yes. I don't like superstitions including long-standing superstitions. Reality is changing, everything is changing on this planet and this universe, so why should human attitudes not change? But you know, I am speaking for myself. It's not a prescription for all. If everybody would be of the same opinion it would be a wasteland. I respect people with quite a different approach. For me one of the greatest Czech poets was Vladimir Holan, who was some sort of an introvert, a mystic of words, a deeply schizoid and isolated human soul who believed only in his own capacities. For me it is essential that truth is dependent on information, on available informations. For others, truth may be a result of an isolated personal mediation, intuition, insight and so on. To speak philosophically I would say that this may turn into a grave mistake. But speaking about poetry it may turn into an interesting poetic voice.

So for you creativity is about finding a new way, because we're always in an entirely new situation?

I don't like these sublime words like 'creativity,' but yes, I would say that creativity is something like deep and radical innovation. Is there something like a human nature, a human essence which would be unchanging? I doubt it. I think the human essence is changing as well as the essence of every creature or every phenomenon in the world is permanently slowly changing. Of course it's invisible. The human essence doesn't change in a hundred years. We know very little about the deep psychology of medieval man or of ancient man or of a hunter and gatherer.

In the introduction to the Penguin edition of your Selected Poems, *Alvarez writes that you are interested more in the question in the poem than how it is said. Yet a lot of poets would say that what's important for them is the music of the poem, exactly how it's said. For some poets song is the essence of poetry.*

Poetry may be chanting, it may be close to a song. Chanting is the way of Russian poetry or of some Latin American poetry. Typically Czech lyricism is the lyricism of a song. Seifert, the Czech Nobel prize winner, called many of his poems songs. I was educated on hexameters, my first education in literature was Greek, classical Greek. Strict metres bring some limitations to the formation of images and of ideas. I reject those *a priori* limitations, I want to be free in finding out the contrasting situations which form the ruling metaphor of the poem. On the other hand a poem is definitely not just prose chopped into shorter lines. Even free verse has rules and these rules must not be upset, otherwise you get lost in some sort of inaccessible or less accessible prose.

How do you see your poetry in the context of Czech society, which has had so many upheavals over the past 50 years?

When one is living under oppression in more or less difficult sociological or political situations one is usually inclined to write more vigorous and even, which is funny, more optimistic kind of poetry. When you are left alone, when you are free, you relax. You may even become sort of sour, depressed and nihilistic. I have the feeling that poets in the real happy situation lose a part of their essence. They are not sure what to speak about. They don't have anything to complain about. What I noticed in the Communist regime which was in a way a chaotic regime, was disorganisation at every level. The oppression was one thing, but the generalised and legalised mess, moral mess, administrative mess was another. In a condition of general chaos, poetry is the last resource of order. In a completely orderly open democratic society poetry just gets the opposite role, to create some sort of turbulence, some sort of personal chaos which may be interesting.

Having just emerged from many years of socialism, Eastern Europe style, how do you feel about the global capitalism of the 90s?

That's not easy of course. Who likes capitalism? Even for us having lived forty years under the so-called socialism, Russian Socialism. Even now capitalism is a slightly dirty word. We have been born in that Central European situation with plebeian leftist ideas. The commercialisation of life, commercialisation of culture, it's a menace. On the other hand, if the alternative would be poverty and famine and tribal wars, then capitalism is the better eventuality. An affluent and technically progressive society

84

without a free market might be impossible. Our poetry feels neglected in the new free market conditions. In spite of that, the mainstream of poetry doesn't try to approach people. The more we feel isolated, the more we isolate ourselves by esoteric and complex introvert, post-surrealist artefacts.

We have a similar situation in South Africa, where most poetry is not read, it's not listened to . . .

Well, when was poetry really read by many people? It was just that in some cultures poetry was an attribute of a knight or a warrior. Otherwise poetry was just an issue for a very limited number of people.

In your talk the other night you made a distinction between artistic poetry and poetry which comes from necessity, spontaneously from people who might not even think of themselves as poets.

I think that the key question is: is it about some sort of esoteric problem or is it about the problems which everybody confronts in everyday life? I was struck yesterday, watching the sitting of the Truth and Reconciliation Commission, by what the poor tortured black victims were telling. In a way it was a cruel poetry and artistic poetry can't match it. And I would say exactly the same about a volume of Second World War poetry I read recently. There the most powerful poems are by plain people, a captain of a warplane, a victim in the Warsaw ghetto. It shows that poetry can happen everywhere. I once wrote "Poetry is everywhere, that's the greatest argument against poetry." I meant against poetry as literature, I meant against artificial poetry. Because I think poetry is embedded in everybody's life and it surfaces in the drastic experiences and during the more dramatic periods of human history.

Interviewed by Robert Berold

NATAN ZACH, born in Berlin in 1930, has lived in Israel since the age of five, and
writes in Hebrew. He is the author of nine volumes of poetry, a play, two collections of
essays, some children's verse, art criticism, and several translations into Hebrew. He
has worked as a theatre director, journalist, and university professor. His poetry has
been translated into many languages. He was interviewed during the *Fault Lines*
readings in Cape Town, July 1996.

Books of poems published:
Against Parting (Northern House, 1967)
The Static Element (Atheneum, 1982)

*This is the first international gathering of poets that I've been to. I'm struck by how
much people listen to each other. It brings out the best in the readings.*

International meetings have been one of the greatest experiences of my life, and I've
been to quite a few of them. This is probably my thirtieth. All over the world. You find
people who you don't know, who you don't know anything about, and you discover
that you have a common language. You find that apart from belonging to your own
country, you belong to some kind of international community. I assume the same
would happen with physicists who meet internationally, except that they would be
mainly worried about their physics and their theories, and would not develop
interpersonal relationships as with poets. Because poets are much more socially
involved, not only with the 'politics of the language', as one Israeli poet put it, but with
a great many other issues outside the field of their so-called specialisation. They may
also be more open and candid, especially when they are not afraid, when they are not
in their own country, when they don't have to worry about their rivals getting a better
place on the reading order or things like this. In an international conference you don't
mind, your voice will come through – or not, if you have nothing to say. Many of us
know each other from previous encounters. There's a core of people who already
belong to the jet age of poetry.

*Almost all these poets come from countries which had experienced war or
dictatorship or some other political violence at some time in their lives. In such times
poetry has a vital function, a spark which is shared by ordinary people. The poets
gave a sense of knowing how easily things could become dark again. It is this shared
feeling of vulnerability that creates bonds . . .*

Sometimes within half an hour. I listened to the East German poet Jürgen Fuchs, and the minute he had finished reading I knew he was my friend. The minute he had finished reading I said I want to translate his work. And he put under my door – the Germans are very polite – he pushed under the door before leaving two of his books with a letter and a poem which reacts to a poem I read. Before that we almost had nothing in common! Alright, we both speak German. But he belongs to an entirely different generation.

Your generation of Israeli poets is credited with breaking with the compulsory nationalism which was prevalent in the 1950s. How did this come about?

Our predecessors had this slogan: "Always we." We didn't want to be 'we', we wanted to be individual voices. One of the ideas of the change we introduced in the 50s was we are responsible only for each one of us, we are not responsible even as a group to the group. We were attacked at the beginning, we were outcasts, but we enjoyed it just as young people in their twenties enjoy being revolutionaries. At the time we didn't realise what we were doing and what an impact this is going to have on Israeli poetry. It has actually changed Israeli poetry unrecognisably. As a result Israeli poetry of the 50s, 60s and 70s are entirely different bodies of poetry. We didn't want to introduce a new common conception of poetry, we wanted to enable every poet to express himself individually – but with the knowledge that I am not responsible for you, you are not responsible for me, for what I write . . .

And that's not just in the realm of poetry . . .

Of course not! That's why I belong to Meretz, the civil rights party. A rainbow nation like Israel really is made up of immigrants from 70 countries of the Diaspora. You have highly cultured people from Germany and Holland and America alongside people who 50 years ago emerged from the caves of Tunisia. You have Russian communists who have become fascists under their oppressive regime. And now, all of a sudden, 200 000 black Ethiopian Jews. How are we going to handle this problem, unless we have the idea of an open society with no consensus? Unfortunately Israel is not yet mature enough to accept this kind of pluralistic society, and there is always the problem of a religious, ultra-orthodox reaction.

You say you were individuals, but you were also poets in a country under extreme pressure, where there have been six or seven wars in the last 50 years. Did that not unite poets?

The '82 invasion of Lebanon changed everything. People who have written lyrical poems for years find themselves faced with a national trauma which they cannot ignore, and they start writing political poetry or rather a poetry of protest, some of it like the poetry of our predecessors. But with one big difference: whereas they represented the Israeli consensus, we came out against it. I personally would never have written a poem like "The desire for precision" which is very different in its spirit from anything I'd written before. But this was within my experience. A poet shouldn't go beyond the limits of his personal experience. That's why many of us didn't write about the holocaust for instance: the holocaust is over, it cannot be changed. We have special tasks relating to the future of Israel.

Nevertheless the holocaust still overshadows much of the collective memory of people in Israel. Nearly everyone had relatives who were killed.

It was Adorno, the German-Jewish philosopher, who said that lyrical poems cannot be written after Auschwitz, a statement that was in a minute disproved by Paul Celan. On the whole, my generation has avoided the subject of the holocaust. It's only now in recent years, with the emergence of the so-called second generation of survivors, meaning the children of people who have actually been there, that we have a literature written mainly by Israeli-born writers that deals with the holocaust, after their parents didn't want to talk about it, suppressed their terrible memories. It was the Eichmann trial which made the difference. Because it was televised nationally, there was no way of getting away from it, you heard the evidence of hundreds of witnesses.

I myself wrote very little about the holocaust – I did not consider I had the authority to write about something which I had not experienced personally. Israeli politics, to this day, cynically exploits the holocaust in order to make other people feel guilty so they either contribute money to Israel or at least avoid attacking and criticising the state.

Your family, German Jews – how did they escape the Nazis?

In my last book there are two poems about childhood memories that came back to me when for the first time, five years ago, I went to Germany and a friend took me to the archives in Berlin. There I found out things about my father which I never knew, because he never told me, he never spoke about Germany. I found out when he left, the exact date, why he left – because a German captain of police came and warned him, a *Nazi* police officer came and warned him: "Look, there is a death sentence against you". This was in 1933, a short time after Hitler's coming to power. There was not yet a death sentence for all Jews. So he was warned and we had to leave overnight. This was one of the memories which I had previously suppressed all my life, it came out when I read these archives.

Overnight he had to leave the country where he spent all his life. He had served in the German army as an officer in the 1st World War. The first thing which he does when he comes to Paris, he goes to the German – Nazi! – Consulate and he reports his new address. Good heavens, what kind of culture bred people like this? Had he stayed in Germany another week he probably would have been shot on the street without trial. Here he is in France in relative security and safety (he could not know that the Germans in a couple of years would occupy Paris as well) and he goes to the consulate as a good law-abiding German citizen – here's my new address, the papers of my wife, and please register also my only son – who was me, you see. I read these documents and all of a sudden a new aspect about my father, my family, my background was revealed to me. This caused a kind of bitterness which I never felt before. It opened up something which was very suppressed and very hidden, concealed even from my consciousness, and so for the first time in this summing up book which came out six months ago, there is a German section.

The holocaust must have affected Israeli poets, even those who had not experienced it directly.

As I said, younger poets are now releasing experiences, terrible experiences – in Israel – as children of parents who were in concentration camps. Like a friend of mine whom I've known now for 15 years and all that time he never spoke about this. He told me now that for 7 years his mother prevented him from going to school in Israel and locked him up in the flat. She didn't want him to go out because she was worried, concerned that he might not come back. For 7 years the boy was locked up in a room here in Haifa, he can't go out and meet anybody. Of course he is very neurotic but we never knew the circumstances. All of a sudden this bursts out, comes out in confessional form, that for 7 years he was a prisoner in his own home in Israel.

How would you compare the slow genocide of black people in South Africa, through forced removals to barren rural areas and other forms of attrition, to the Jewish genocide?

However atrocious, I wouldn't compare it to the Nazis. We always make the distinction: the Nazis set out and actually burnt in the gas chambers 7 million people, that's why we always react very strongly when Israeli politicians are comparing the Arabs, the Palestinians to Nazis. The Palestinians have not gassed 7 million Jews. They are fighting what they consider a war of liberation. What chance of a war of liberation was there for European Jews? From time to time the Palestinians have perpetrated terror atrocities against women and children, unjustified and evil, because there is this evil spirit of fundamentalism amongst them, but it's a different issue altogether and should never be compared with Nazism. And, mind you, I am a member of the Israeli-Palestinian Writers Committee who believe and campaign for the establishment of an independent Palestinian state and protest against the occupation of their lands and the atrocities committed against them. As Ka. Zettnik (a pen-name derived from Kazett, German for concentration camp) wrote, Auschwitz is a different planet. In Cambodia something very similar happened, they also had their Auschwitz, but Cambodia's also a different planet — to massacre a million of your people.

I take it you're not really sympathetic to any kind of nationalism.

Not really sympathetic? – that's an understatement. Look what happened in Israel, with the best intentions of building up a safe homeland for the Jews rejected by most countries. It took only a relatively short while and we've become as nationalistic as any other, we became as oppressive a military power as some of the regimes we denounced. There is not much difference between our treatment of the Palestinians and the South African treatment during apartheid of the blacks.

But how does one dismantle nationalism?

There is a good chance that nationalism will dismantle us before we dismantle it! Maybe economic pressures could work, as in Russia, economic bankruptcy and the pressures of the great powers as well as the pressures of enlightened public opinion. But I don't know. We couldn't get the entire enlightened world to force Iran to cancel this Fatwah, this death sentence on Salman Rushdie – the entire civilized world came out against Iran on this issue and has achieved very little. This goes to show that when you're faced with a fanatic or religious nationalism which is willing to make the greatest sacrifices in order to prevail, there is very little you can do.

You spoke of fundamentalism as an evil spirit . . .

Islamic fundamentalism is a horrible one; Jewish fundamentalism is not far behind. Culturally, there exists also the danger of being flooded by this American trash sub-culture, just as dangerous to the human spirit as fundamentalism. The twin dangers strangely enough hate each other and appear to exclude each other. In the fundamentalism of Khomeni, anything to do with American culture and television is tantamount to Satan's voice. But in a way they work together in destroying this kind of liberal and enlightened nineteenth century spirit which has managed to survive, albeit partially, into the middle of the twentieth century. They work together, fundamentalism and American machoist capitalism, to cripple culture and render it impotent.

Do you feel that it's a mixed blessing to be Israeli at this point?

Yes, it's a very mixed blessing. I fear that now, with the right-wing Likud and its orthodox partners getting stronger and stronger, we might be on the road back to the Middle Ages. They've got the money to run the country, they've got the army. The Israeli ambassador to South Africa told me the other day that he's resigning. Some of the Likud people are criminals, with corruption and other charges against them. Life in Israel — this is something that can't be explained, you have to experience it, to be there, there is always hatred, even amongst ourselves, even amongst Jews, old folks against the young, Jews who go to the army and serve three and a half years while those who sit in the yeshivas are exempt from army service, there's a lot of resentment and hatred. We have a country with the highest taxation rate in the world. And if I were to tell you what a professor in Israel makes – we never tell anybody, not to look ridiculous.

How important is poetry in Israel?

Without poetry, without the writings of the Founding Fathers, men such as Herzl, the State of Israel would not be, because all the ideologues of the State of Israel, all of the people who dreamt the Zionist dream, were writers. Achad Ha-am was a philosopher. The Hebrew literary tradition goes two thousand years back and at the same time people like Bialik and Brenner rebelled against Jewish Diaspora Orthodoxy and turned to Zionism, furthering the creation of the State of Israel. But once the State of Israel was normalised, many of these writers were kicked overboard, there was no further need for them.

You grew up in Germany, you studied modernist English poetics in England, you write in Hebrew. Are these all influences in your work?

Until I was 20 I hardly read anything in English, I read Hebrew and German. In German I read Hölderlin, I read Heine and the German Romantics and Expressionists, everything I could lay my hands on. For 40 years I've been working on a translation of the poet Else Lasker Schueler, she was my favourite – she, Georg Trakl and Rilke were my favourites. Then came the discovery and formative influence of Anglo-American modernism: Yeats, Eliot, Auden, e.e. cummings, Wallace Stevens, William Carlos Williams, Ezra Pound. In comparison, I find contemporary English and French poetry very disappointing, it's become very closed, esoteric and domestic. They write like some club of minor dispirited intellectuals who have no longer any hope that poetry might really change culture. In my short stay in South Africa I've found much more vigorous and impressive English-writing poets here. In Germany occasionally you find some interesting poetry though it's not internationally known, and nothing to compare with Brecht. Celan is really the only great post-war master.

What is your involvement with other Israeli poets?

Very intensive, despite the lack of time for more personal contact. I teach at the Haifa University, I publish a series of poetry pamphlets, each pamphlet dedicated to one poet, many of them unknown. It's an attempt to help people who find it difficult to find a publisher. I translate a lot, I participate in poetry workshops. There's an enormous thirst in Israel for publication, everybody seems to be writing poetry.

All these people who are writing, what are they reading?

The other day I was in a town about one hour's drive from Tel Aviv, this was at some kind of festive occasion. After the readings a girl in her twenties came up, she had read three poems which I quite liked. So I said "What do you read?" She said "Read?" She was amazed, as if to say "If I write it's enough – I have to read?"

In the poem "'Delicate" you speak in the persona of a somewhat tired but tolerant man.

Well, I am . . . I am too old to be impatient with the young . . .

The language is conversational but the subject matter is not like that, the subject matter is serious.

Well, this was the general intention. You might say the most serious poetry conveys your accessibility as a private human being. In my most recent book, for the first time in my life, I wrote a few autobiographical poems where I speak directly and without any attempt at concealing my childhood experiences in Israel, a thing I would never have dreamt of doing in the 50s. Let's say I felt it was a summing up, because of age and other reasons. I haven't published a book for 12 years. This one book really contained three different books written over these 12 years. I didn't arrange them in any chronological order, so as to increase the disharmony and dissonances. I didn't want a smooth book where each poem glides into the other. I didn't want continuity. I wanted the clashes, fractures and incoherence of a daily life.

How do you respond to the current move to the right in Israel?

As a poet?

Yes.

When you are 66 as I am now, and you start reacting in poetry to let's say the Likud government rise to power, there is the danger of becoming a mere propagandist. I wanted to maintain, at all cost, my personal voice, to even retrieve some of that which I've lost during my 'political period'. How then do I respond? I have a weekly column in a newspaper where I don't publish poetry. I appear on radio and television. I participate in organising demonstrations. But I keep my poetry to myself and my books. I'm afraid my muse does not easily respond to things that are forced on it from the outside. During the war in Lebanon and the Intifada I wrote spontaneous political poems. Even "The desire for precision" happened like that. I heard these kinds of things on the radio and instantaneously I responded in a poem. The poem has to come from the very depth of me, I have to feel this *must* be written.

92

Interviewed by Alan Finlay

PHILLIP ZHUWAO was born near Harare, Zimbabwe, in 1971, and spent his childhood moving with his family, who were evicted from several farms, finally settling in Kuwadzana, Harare. His collection of poems, *Sunrise Poison*, and his two novellas, *See the Barbarous Lands* and *Iron Fleece*, are to be published in 2003. He died in Harare in 1997.

Book of poems published:
The Red Laughter of Guns in Green Summer Rain
(chainpoems written with Alan Finlay)(Dye Hard Press, 2002)

This interview, the only published interview with Zhuwao, did not appear in New Coin, *but in issue No 6 of* Bleksem, *a small journal of writing edited and published by Alan Finlay in the 1990s. This version has been re-edited from the original recording.*

Where do you come from?

I was born on a commercial farm in Zimbabwe in 1971. Along the Mabunt road, near the white Rhodesian barracks. It was a commercial farm belonging to an Afrikaans man – a tobacco farm. All along the Lamakonda road up to Banket they grow tobacco. I was born there, in a little mud hut with a thatched roof. My mother came from Mozambique and my father from Barotseland, Zambia, from the Lozi tribe. His family all migrated to Zimbabwe in the late 1950s, to look for greener pastures. After he was educated in Zimbabwe, he came to South Africa to work on the mines. He came back to Zimbabwe in the late 1960s and married my mother. My family lives in Harare now. I have three brothers and three sisters.

When did you first start writing poetry?

I started seriously writing in 1990. Before that I'd written bits and pieces, but I didn't think of it as poetry. It was something like copying. I copied Japanese haikus, James Joyce, Gabriel Okara, but mostly Dambudzo Marechera.

What do you like about Dambudzo?

He says the truth about everything – the way we see life, those near us, our society – the truth that comes from the heart. But now I know much more about life than to copy from Dambudzo. Where I write from, it's my own experience, personal experience. What I've seen. What I've felt. My relationships with people. My loves.

Do you always write from the self outwards?

Firstly the self. I'm much more interested in the self. I'm not interested in the ordinary man in the street. No. The ordinary man doesn't interest me. Some people say my writing is selfish. But I have to take care about this personal thing before anything broader.

You write with very strong images . . .

I imagine a lot. I've got a lot of fantasies. I think this came because of my short-sightedness. I mean I couldn't see what was happening. I couldn't see the real thing. I couldn't see the flowers, everything, the knives. So I'd imagine a lot of things in my head. I only got glasses recently, most of my life I could see almost nothing. In class I could see nothing on the blackboard, so I failed my exams. I had to live in my mind. I'd see things in my head instead of seeing the real things.

And your nightmares?

They started where I was born, on the commercial tobacco farm. We had migrant workers from Malawi, Zambia, Mozambique, and there was a lot of talking about witchcraft, hyenas, people dying, graves, cannibalism. I grew up being afraid of the night and the darkness, closing the doors fast at night, being fearful of sleeping alone. Then my grandfather started punishing me whenever I got naughty by throwing me into a cattle kraal. This affected me subconsciously so that whenever I dream, I dream I'm being chased by bulls. I had the same dream last night, being chased by bulls. Then at the end it was lions. It's quite frightening. It came from my early childhood, my grandfather trying to frighten me with bulls. Now it is affecting my whole life, I can't spend a week without dreaming about black bulls running after me, snorting after me. The other thing about my nightmares is pits. I always dream of somebody throwing me in a deep black pit, an endless pit.

Have you ever written about this?

Sometimes I write about it, but not much. I'm scared of writing about it. I wouldn't like people's judgement when they read about me, about this. So I don't write much about it. But when I do people get scared. People start asking me questions about death. They start asking me why I'm so fascinated by death, bulls, pits, graves and all. But it's something that began in my childhood, when I was young. It's still something that's within me, something that's still torturing me in a way. I'm thinking of writing about it but I'm scared of how people will take it.

You don't have to publish it . . .

Ja. Maybe by writing it, I will get exorcised. It will be like breaking something. But then the whole thing is so scary. I think sometimes by writing it it's like keeping the whole thing within me. So I try to keep away from it sometimes, and at night it comes back, scaring me.

You're in the process of finishing a novella?

Ja, I'm about to finish my book *See the Barbarous Lands*. I guess in a month's time it will be ready. This book is everything about my life. It's everything. Once I finish writing it I guess I hope to be free. I've got no hopes about it but I think I will be free after I finish writing it. I'm telling something that had been captured within me, imprisoned in me. Writing it out is a big exercise in myself, in my soul. Although I think some people are going to get angry when the book's out. I don't mind. A lot of people are going to feel betrayed – friends, members of the family.

You've read very widely. Which writers attract you the most?

What they call anarchist literature. Fascist literature. Rider Haggard. Céline. Ezra Pound. Nietzsche. A few people wonder why I'm so interested in these writers whilst I'm black. They wonder why I like reading Rider Haggard when I'm black. They don't know. I can't explain to them. It's really difficult to explain. It's like when I read these writers I feel there is something between us, something we both understood. Something the people have never got to understand. I feel a sort of brotherhood with them. Writers like Céline and Dambudzo.

You'd call Dambudzo a fascist writer?

Some people would call him a fascist writer. Really I don't know what a fascist writer is, but I've seen him being put in that category, as a fascist writer, as an anarchist. I don't really know what an anarchist writer is. But I associate myself with those kind of writers. Those who, by telling the truth about their perceptions, get betrayed, ostracised, removed from society.

Why do you think Dambudzo was ostracised?

Because he didn't live up to the society's dreams, society's hopes, the family's hope. According to the black family, once one has finished school, once one has finished university education, one should get a job, marry, buy a beautiful car, a beautiful house. But he didn't do that and society and his family felt betrayed. Suddenly they threw him out of society. But we can't live up to all these aspirations of society. We can't all marry the beautiful girl. We can't all own a beautiful BMW. We've got different destinations, we've got different karmas. I think that's the problem with my career as a writer also. My family hope a lot. They thought that by educating me and my being clever and all that, I ought to do something for them. A sort of repayment for their troubles. But then I discover I can't. I've got to live up to my own fantasies, my own poetry world. They say I'm not responsible, I'm selfish. This I don't understand. They say my poetry comes first, before my family, before my friends, before my career. So at the end I'm damned.

In black African society they are suspicious of a man who writes poetry. They don't trust a man who writes poetry. They think a man who writes poetry is a queer. So it's very difficult to go around parading yourself as a poet among the black people. It's like they start staring at you, trying to find out how you are queer. Everybody starts raising eyebrows, asking how much you earn through writing poetry.

The same for a poet in white society . . .

I think white society understands the poetry world, the art world, much better than the black. Although poetry has been in the black society for a long, long time. Oral poetry has been a mediating instrument for the black shamans. I don't know why today they don't respect black poets, are suspicious of black poets. I think it has something to do with having a regular job. Being a clerk, a lawyer, a doctor, an accountant. They can't understand why one could aspire to be a poet.

Once you're a poet you're on your own. And you're alienated even from other poets.

That's true. That's everywhere.

Still, a lot of people take Dambudzo to heart. A lot of young poets.

Because there's never been a poet like Dambudzo in the literary history of Africa. He was much more powerful than Ngũgĩ wa Thiong'o, than Chinua Achebe –

What about Okigbo? Okigbo's got lots of power . . .

Ja . . . but not as radical as Dambudzo. Okigbo has got a lot of American power and all that. But not as Dambudzo. Although Dambudzo's power was a bit British. Okigbo sort of wrote for the people, whilst Dambudzo wrote for himself. Most African poets write for the people. For ideologies. For the government. For tribes. Like what you have here – Zulu oral praise poetry. That's what most black African poets do. Few write for themselves.

So in a sense your poetry is actually a betrayal of the oral tradition?

Ja, I would say so. My poetry's something to do with me. Not with the ordinary man in the street. Not with my friends. I sometimes think I'm like Céline. I'm much more interested in myself, in my pain, in my sufferings. I always think that my pain and my sufferings have been much more greater than the man in the street. So I'm no longer interested in other people's pain. Like once, one person asked me what I would say if

I was ordered to go to war. And I answered "bullshit!" I mean I can't go to war and fight for anyone. I don't think I'm even patriotic. I don't think I could call that a selfish perspective. It's something that has been between me, where I grew up. One had to fend for oneself.

Interviewed by Sam Raditlhalo

TABAN LO LIYONG was born in Sudan in 1939 and lived until 1962 in Uganda. He has taught African literature in Uganda, Kenya, Australia, Papua New Guinea, USA and Japan, and has published collections of poems, and essays on literature and culture. Since 1995 he has been professor of African Literature at the University of Venda.

Books of poems published:
Frantz Fanon's Uneven Ribs (Heinemann, 1971)
Another Nigger Dead (Heinemann, 1972)
Ballads of Underdevelopment (East African Literature Bureau, 1975)
Cows of Shambat (Zimbabwe Publishing House, 1992)
Words That Melt a Mountain (East African Educational Books, 1996)
Homage to Onyame (Malthouse, 1997)
Carrying Knowledge up a Palm Tree (Africa World Press, 1998)
The Defence of Lawino (translation of Okot p'Bitek's Wei pa Lawino)
(Fountain Publishers, 2001)

What were the first influences on your writing?

It would be difficult to say who influenced me. I'd prefer to say so and so lit the fire, gave me the courage or gave me the urge to write. What started me on writing was not other writing, it was hearing stories told by the fireside. When I went to school, in 1945, we had a period for telling folktales in the vernacular. This came every Friday morning. During that period each student was to tell a story, and it went in turns. There was no way you could escape it. If you had no story, you would sit down in shame in front of the students, facing them. So, I heard a lot of stories, including stories which were told so well that I envied the tellers – my fellow primary students. Sometimes I write my stories as a tribute to them because they told far better stories than I could ever tell.

Some of my teachers were writers themselves and so the mystery of the world being translated from the spoken to written word had been broken a long time ago. I was taught by people who had written. I just said OK, this is the sort of thing that you do when you have the time. So when it came to my own writing, it was the coming together of all those things, plus other books that I had read.

Like Nietzsche . . .

Nietzsche was one. Nietzsche read the work of the Roman general Marcus Aurelius, who had been in Britain and Germany. He had written that Germans are a hardy group, a strong group who will go to all lengths in order to achieve something. So then Nietzsche decided that the Germans were the chosen people and they could outdo the Jews. So he said: if the Germans had those qualities which Marcus Aurelius said they had, they could raise themselves up to be higher than the Jews. Translated in an African context, OK, then the Kaffir can also raise himself to the level of the Mulungu.

Then of course another one was Karl Marx, overturning the tables against the lords. He overturns the tables against the rulers, the traditional rulers, so that he can release the creative forces from the majority of the people on the ground. That also, I think, is a good idea.

Of all the people who gave us new insights into what can be done, revolutionary insights, I think these two stand out. And then of course let us not forget the translators. Kwame Nkrumah translated those ideas into the African context. Before Nkrumah, no African country had got independence. Yes, not by himself, he worked with the Black Americans in the States including William Du Bois and George Padmore in London.

Looking back to the 60s, when you first started writing, do you feel you adequately served the needs of creative provocation on one hand, what Chris Wanjala once termed the Tabanic genre? Given the chance to do it all over again what would you do differently?

East Africa was the centre of turmoil, literary and cultural turmoil. Nairobi, Dar es Salaam, with Makerere hosting the Commonwealth Writers Conference in 1960. It was all part and parcel of that political movement. Politics went first and then cultural and literary activities followed closely behind. It was cosmopolitan. Whether you were Kenyan, Ugandan or Tanzanian, if you were in Nairobi you were accepted, if you were in Makerere you were accepted. You did not think of yourself as being a foreigner, you just participated. So we did a lot of things then which cannot be done now because of the intensification of nationalism.

You wrote a denouncement of what you termed eunuch scholars. That to me is the essence of the Tabanic genre, the dislike of writers and scholars sold into bourgeois power groups. Could you elaborate on that?

I don't like a scholar who just reads and accepts; or merely reads to gather facts, datas. I prefer to have scholars who put themselves and their positions into their reading. In Africa, you don't just go to a funeral to cry for the person who has just died. You go there so as to mourn your own dead. The same with reading – when you are reading Shakespeare or Ngugi or Achebe you should think about yourself, your own predicaments. When you are reading *The Beautyful Ones Are Not Yet Born*, you don't laugh at it and say "this is what the Ghanians do to their people." That thing that happened in Ghana can also happen somewhere else, including South Africa.

"Search for knowledge everywhere" – that is a Muslim injunction – "even if it takes you to China." The question is why should anybody limit himself? If they are going to be in the English department then for goodness sake let them know everything about English, know everything: Chaucer, Spenser, Shakespeare. Search everywhere. It is only when we have blinkered scholars who hold that Karl Marx is only for the political economists, Darwin only for the biologists, that I quarrel. The type of scholar I prefer is the one, who after he has understood what is going on, would like to do something about it. Yes, practice must be part of it. Every reading must be in the context of the reader's personal and communal position: as a call to a debate, an invitation to action.

In keeping with your early expectations and optimism, the piece "Student's Lament" first published in the East Africa Journal in 1966, still stands out as a central piece, at least to my mind, of doubt about the pace of the change.

Let me tell you how it came about. As students abroad we used to burn up a lot of those midnight candles: study, study, study, study. Here I am trying my level best to master difficult concepts, later to go back with these things to fertilise the home. But at home people are saying "Oh, he is difficult." But isn't it the measure of the material that I am handling which is difficult, rather than me trying to be difficult? What was I sent abroad for if I'm not supposed to master those difficult things and transmit them home? Was I supposed to concentrate on the soft, easy matters only? So I sat down to write that thing. I wrote it, wrote it, wrote it for 36 hours without sleep. After I finished it I took a big breakfast and went to the library, where I worked, to shelve books. Fifteen minutes later I was caught by the librarian, sleeping on my feet, holding the books up. He took me to his office and sat me down. I said "I was working . . ." He said "Then you should not work here also." And fired me. Nobody till today has ever referred to it.

How do you respond to the charge by certain critics that your poetry is more cerebral than emotive? I think of lines such as these from Another Nigger Dead:
> *"to give up and curse God*
> *to despair too soon*
> *even the blind struggle to see*
> *have courage everybody."*

Some time ago I decided I will write essays in which I will explain things; I will write poems in which to hide things; and I will write stories just to laugh or to have fun. So in my poems I follow up some trends of thought. It is like someone making an etching, a picture, a mural picture. You don't do it in one sweep. You do this and that and that and that. So go through the etchings and you finally will arrive at some answers. Follow the line(s) of thought and you will get its meaning, or some meaning, at any rate. "To give up and curse God" – that comes from Job. Job did not despair, so why should we be the ones to give up too soon?

Ngũgĩ wa Thiong'o decided to go local, to live traditional. Somehow or other I don't like it very much. He is a man who should be challenging, to reach for higher ideas, higher ideals: but to curtail himself and say "I turn my back against using English" – that is the same as despair. Maybe even Ngũgĩ has despaired on the intellectual side of things and so he is going back to the people, his people. So this despair is there. It affects us all. Whether it is Okot p'Bitek, Ngũgĩ, Ayi Kwei Armah. Our generation has gone through a lot and we have seen the rise of nationalism and also the failure of African national leaders. We have seen it all and hated most of it.

How do you analyse the failure of African nationalism?

There were two parties in Kenya, Kenya African National Union and Kenya African Democratic Union. The Americans and British said they, the parties, should become one party and they agreed. Then Oginga Odinga wanted to start another party, Kenya People's Union, the Americans came and had him banned. Later on the Americans came again and said there should be multi-party politics in Kenya and Oginga Odinga should start another party. So the question becomes: if you as a nation do not keep in mind what exactly you are going to do then the nation will be pushed left and right by foreigners, especially those with money. Today they say this, tomorrow they say that, then they say another thing. So you end up losing your way.

Initially writers were needed to boost nationalism. But it seems that as soon as they weren't promoting the parties in power, they were kicked out or persecuted.

That literary conference of 1960 was held because Makerere University literature staff, English department realised they needed to light the fire from West Africa. So they brought across from West Africa Gabriel Okara, Chinua Achebe, Christopher Okigbo, John Pepper Clark and others to come to Makerere. And when they came there Ngugi gave Chinua Achebe his *A River Between* to read, and Achebe read it and gave him some comments about it. So the fire had been lit, passed from West Africa to East Africa.

Things were going fine – except at the political level things were not going fine. Obote wanted to eliminate the Kabaka of Buganda and other native rulers. At one time Kwame Nkrumah had eliminated the native rulers in Ghana. That is why Obote kicked out the Kabaka too, because Nkrumah had done it. When Nkrumah introduced the idea of African High Command, Julius Nyerere opposed it. Only later on to shoulder the liberation wars in Southern Africa.

In Kenya the Kikuyu, a majority tribe, were in control and the Americans and British at that time liked it. Their logic was that a bigger tribe should be supported because it already has a lot of people who can man the state. And they never even thought that at a future time, a ruler could come up, like Daniel Arap Moi, who is not a Kikuyu. They never thought that could happen. So they gave all the help they could give to the Kikuyu and Kenyatta including the muscling of all the opposition. They said we have pinned all our hopes on Kenyatta and Kanu, and any other position is going to mess up the categories we have brought in here.

We saw this happening. Some of us tried to say something against it. But rural politics is different from any other. So I wanted to say in my writings what was hurting us. If this is how things are, what is the use of staying here? Why witness future murders? The seeds are now being sown and there is no way we can do anything about it. But a writer has to be the trumpet blower. Or the whistle blower. If there is an off-side or hand ball, or foul, you blow the whistle. That is what I was thinking about.

What are your views about literature in African languages?

In East Africa we do not have African languages and literature studies. In 1945, when I went to school, we were taught in the vernacular for the first three years and then after that we started learning English leading progressively to learning in English only. Only the bigger languages were taught as school subjects: Luganda, Swahili, Kikuyu, perhaps. But otherwise African languages were left behind.

South Africa is a bit different, thanks, left-handedly, to apartheid. Apartheid preserved African languages and some parts of African culture. So you had and have departments of African languages and African literature in an African country. These were never seen elsewhere before. In the South African context people have been writing in the vernaculars all along. So for you to say a Zulu wants to write in Zulu is old hat. You have done it all along. But in the East African context, Ngũgĩ's novels will be the first major novels written in Kikuyu.

Did you know Dambudzo Marechera? His work reminds me of yours in certain ways.

Marechera was my godson intellectually and culturally. We came together for the first time in 1979 in West Berlin but by that time he had already got in touch with my writings. We studied without boundaries, delved in intellectual enquiries without limits. Ayi Kwei Armah is the third member of our trio.

Marechera did well for his short life. He accepted the challenge of Oxford, but it blew his mind. He found himself singing alone and out of tune because there was no other African at Oxford of like mind. That is what the problem is. You get students who go to the aged and reputed universities like Oxford. In the context of their behaviour and the behaviour of the white youths in Oxford, he was just a normal student. But in the African context everyone would have said: "You are going to Oxford, that is where the English are studying. You are supposed to come back a better scholar, a better gentleman," and so on. But when you actually go to Oxford you find out that the Oxford undergraduates are scoundrels, scandallers, fun-making aristocrats. Few go there to study hard. They play games. They socialise. They are sons and daughters of kings and lords. You meet them and find out more hollowness in their inner circles. But if one of our boys goes there and comes back and behaves in the same way, people will say what is wrong?

Isn't it difficult for an African studying in Europe to accept that the intellectual contribution of Africa is never acknowledged?

Terence, a dramatist, one of the humorous comic writers of Rome, was a negro. Aesop was a black fellow from Ethiopia. Plato, Pythagoras and others, the pre-Socratics, had been to Egypt before returning to Greece. Some of the ideas of the Greeks are of African origin but the Greeks never acknowledged their theft. That's how it is. If there is something that is African in Egyptian languages, it should have its correlative in the present African languages. The French-speaking West Africans have Egyptologists: Theophilus Obenga from the Congo and Sheikh Anta Diop from Senegal. So the question is – and I am struggling with it – why shouldn't we also learn Greek and Ancient Egyptian to learn about ourselves in ancient times?

What evidence is there that Africa had its intellectual excellence?

The library of Alexandria contained a lot of ideas, not only African ideas but also Asian and European ideas. Egypt was an intellectual centre, an intellectual thoroughfare. Plato came there after the death of Socrates and studied for ten years before going back to Greece to write and teach. Timbuktoo was not a hundred percent black university. It had everybody including Asians, including Europeans. Where a place is a magnet for intellect then everybody brings their intellect there and comes and participates. We have had times when we were already interacting at a high intellectual level with the outside world. That is also why something or other in the black man in America makes him take his African past very very seriously.

Why, in your view, did Europeans divide Africa into north of the Sahara and south of the Sahara, with only the south inhabited by Africans? Hegel, for instance, in his Philosophy of History, *says that Africans occupy the territory south of the Sahara, and that Egypt was Africa connected to Asia.*

They went by race and by colour, in evidence of the Mediterranean littoral, around the Mediterranean sea. The African coast had been inhabited for some time by Arabs, 'coloured people' in quotes, who were already a mixture of races like what you would call coloured people in the Cape – people who have black blood in them as well as foreign ingredients. So when European racists wanted to talk about Africa, they would leave out their cousins: the coloured people of Northern Africa were excluded. They said these are not the real Africans – for the real Africans, go to Africa south of the Sahara. But strangely enough they got their information about the Africans from the Arab historians. People like Ibn Khaldun had done a lot of travelling in Africa.

If you are a white racist and you are faced with a human being who is black, how do you tackle him? How do you confront him intellectually? The answer is simple – find some way of categorising him. Look at the stories that were told about us, even in Shakespeare's *Othello*. Othello is wooing Desdemona by talking about some people whose heads were beneath their shoulders and so on. In the white man's mind, the black has always been a problem because the metaphysics of Europe are told in either/or, white/black. Black is the colour of darkness, the colour of the devil. In the white man's mind there lurks a big black god or a big black devil and he doesn't know how to come into contact with it so he fears it and therefore he has to find some ways of numbering it amongst those things which have to be destroyed. And so racism developed out of that, that which lurks at the back of your mind, which frightens you at night.

European thought and political power has dominated the world for over 500 years. How do you envisage the end of its hegemony?

European hegemony is not going to end that quickly. Until Europe becomes poor, Europe is not going to leave its own prejudices. It is only when people are poor that they begin to realise that their categories were wrong. When they realise that they have failed then they say, look, maybe the way we have been looking at the world is wrong. Maybe other people have some other valued approaches, outlooks towards life, and we might as well learn from them. This has been going on already. Europe, and its extension into America, they are becoming aware of this. Anthropologists like Margaret Mead were interested in saying, how does a child in a poor third world area survive under conditions which would have killed a white child? How do blacks, how do Bushmen, the Australian aborigines, how do they or how did they survive without the benefit of modern medicine, science and so forth? How do they survive? If poverty comes to America or Britain, will the white child be able to survive? Because they are more concerned with their survival as the white race and custodians of the values of the white world.

But it has started to change. During the Korean war all the American GIs who were arrested and detained, when they were tortured, they spoke out very, very quickly. Whereas no Korean would confess or inform. And the poor Koreans defeated the Americans, right? Then the Vietnamese defeated the French and defeated the Americans too. So it is only when things change that people start to change their attitudes. Like here, in this South African context, till this change of 1994 came, few whites had believed that there would ever come a time where the tables would be turned. So now white people are talking about affirmative action. And now some of the things that blacks have been doing are also being tried by the whites. Some whites are appreciating African ways, becoming humans.

The Europeans, when they came here, found us with our pants down and they defeated us. So we went to Europe or America, we went in order to study the secrets of the conqueror. Why did he come and conquer us? And if we are still activists, we should still continue studying in order to look to future confrontation with that system so that we can recover ours. And then we can build a better one, between our recovered culture and the one that the Europeans have. So we are to study the European ways in order to overcome them, in order to challenge them, in order to find out how they operate. In order to master them. And to transform them to take in African ingredients.

If you leave the world to be led by the categories of the white man, these categories always ask for confrontation: either/or, good/bad, black/white. One of these categories is going to overthrow the other, right? That's the danger of following the white man and his either/or philosophy. What we should be doing is say, this is the African way, this is the Chinese way, this is the Indian way, and so on – non-binary opposition, but polygamous co-existence; acceptance of horizontally lined multiple choices. All these categories, all of these ways, are ways of rescuing man from going headlong into oblivion. It is our task, Africans, Asians, to bring to the table of nations all the heritage that belongs to us and do it very forcefully.

And it is also up to Europeans to see where theirs have failed in order also to integrate ours within their categories. But when they are still very rich and powerful, they are not going to do that in a hurry.

You trace the modern African identity to the 13th century . . .

Yes, when the nations of Islam were powerful, pushing towards Africa, towards Asia, towards Europe. They crossed to Spain. They took over Spain and were only defeated in France. In Africa, we ran. We ran southwards because we couldn't be Muslim. Or we ran because our kings, who had total power over us, could not hold us any more. People at the peripheries could run, so they did. And continued looking for safety, taking with them whatever gods, and ideas of their gods and of their cultures as they could. And also tactics for defeating the next group. This, according to me, is the single most important cause why Africans ran, why Africans migrated southwards. Now fortunately or unfortunately it is because we ran that black Africa is not Muslim. Because those who remained in Northern Africa are mostly Muslim now. Most of Nigeria is all Muslim. Northern Nigeria, Northern Ghana, Northern Sudan, Northern this or that – Senegal is mostly Muslim.

What is Ali Mazrui's position regarding Islam?

Mazrui was an African when he was in Makerere. When Mazrui went to America he recovered his Muslim standing since his people directly came from Oman and there was no more reason to identify fully with Kenya, Africa. His great-grandfathers had come from Oman and they used to be rulers on the East African coast. So Mazrui has recovered his standing in the Muslim world. He is their best scholar, he is their best informer on us and against us. Underline that one, *against us*. There is now even a Kenyan Muslim Political Party and he is a founding member of it. Last year he was in Zambia promoting the advent of a Muslim Party there. Like most Muslims, when they become older they become devout believers because they want to square matters with their maker. And he is gloating at the fact that Islam has a foothold in Africa. He used to go to Nigeria a part of the year to do research there – his scholarship grant gave him the chance to do that. Every quarter of the year he would come to an African country to do some studies. I mean that programme he did for the BBC, 'The Africans', it glorifies Islam rather than anything else, he even runs down the traditional African culture.

How would you characterise African philosophy?

The African family system is unique. In all our traditional languages we have a word for all members of our extended family. Knowing who you are related to, therefore knowing how wide the tree is. Knowing that you are not alone, you are with others and they are also with you. When it is a funeral or marriage or so forth, the whole tree comes together. Nobody grudges the other anything. Everything is shared. The idea of sharing, and knowing that no human being is a human being by himself or herself. This is the African way which unfortunately both Christianity and Islam are wrecking. It is something which is really unique.

In the 13th century, let us say between 700 and 1000 years ago, we were running. We had to rely on one another in order to survive. I think we should always think in terms of survival. How did the Bushmen survive? We must ask ourselves that. That small and wily fellow must have more life that the rest of us. So instead of looking down on him we should actually raise him up and say: "Look, tell us, how do you do it? How do you make this scanty nature give you something so that it can keep you going and has kept you going, despite what everybody is saying about it and you?" We have that in our knowledge of agriculture, our knowledge of healing.

Then of course, there's another one also, our outlook towards life, towards fate. Rather than think foolishly, we actually are great optimists, we are very, very optimistic. And Mazrui also said somewhere that Africans are forgiving. We make sacrifices and we forgive. Why? Because we are very optimistic. We actually don't think the darkness will last. We don't think any darkness will last and if Mulungu is strutting like a god we sometimes laugh at him because we know he is not what he pretends to be. So we can easily forgive him because we know he is far from reality, he is putting on a show and at the end of the day the show will come to an end.

That attitude towards life has kept us going through thick and thin and since we have reached the 1990s without crumbling there's no way anybody is going to make us disappear any more. There are some areas where our survival tactics are better than what other people think.

106

You've said that the clues of what Africa is or will be can be deduced from what Africa was or has been. History, in its wider sense, more than any other discipline, holds the key to the self-knowledge of a people without written records.

We should never forget about history, either of our past high performances or the history of our subjugation, of our being down-trodden. And also the history of others who were downtrodden and arose from there and climbed up. This is where the Jews are different from everybody else. They say "Don't forget – never forget." You can forgive but never forget, because if you forget the same thing can be repeated. The same thing that hurt you before can come back in another guise and you'll never even notice it. If you had been burnt before, you know how fire burns. So please remember that we have been burnt and we should not allow ourselves to sleep otherwise we will be burnt again.

If somebody makes you think that we are now equal whereas the naked reality is that there are differences between where we live and where others live, then you are a fool. History is something we should worry about. You should read and envy. Jealousy is destructive, but envy can make you challenge, make you accept challenges. You envy somebody his cows and sheep and say, why are they fat? why shouldn't mine be fat? If you're jealous you're going to kill them. Better take up the challenge to say, I should also breed cows that are bigger and sleeker than his. That is the path of envy: accepting a challenge. Wrestling with a challenge.

What is your view on the direction of contemporary African writing, given that your generation had written so prolifically about the demise of nationalism and the future of nationalism?

I think it would be better for today's writers to follow the fates of individuals. Not write about Africa this, Africa that. A priest, who is head of a breakaway church, what are his hang-ups? The head of the army, what are his plans? So we need to go for individual types. It is better to delve in-depth on individuals and find out what their problems really are and reveal them from within. Because otherwise it is generalisation. Otherwise it is simplification, over-simplification. Glossing over nasty facts about our people. Being protective of African characters. Partial revelations are half-lies. He or she is no writer if she lies. You have to go into depth. It would be better, really, to choose a theme and explore it in depth.

Obviously you think it's important for writers to study . . .

Yes, they should know their craft. You can't write if you don't read. Just as you can't be a good dancer if you don't go to see how other people dance. If you can't sing, how can you write songs? So it calls for professionalism, really. New writers should be aware of all that has been written. Even about writing. So when you are writing you should write that which is in your blood, in your backbone, in your back yard: you should already know what has been written by other South Africans.

If you can read Afrikaans, read their novels, poems, plays. And also find out what they have said about you, about other characters. For somebody who knows Afrikaans, it is foolish of him to read only novels in English about the South African situation. As the Arabs would say, seek for knowledge everywhere. Don't blinker yourself. Political prejudices should not prejudice you against using another language. Until you've read them, how do you know what they said?

Never forget this: the story being told is one thing, the moral being displayed is another thing. A story is never a story but it also has a central idea, a central thesis. Writers also think, have ideas. And embed their ideas in their works.

Your dislike of Negritude was as fierce and as direct as Mphahlele's and Soyinka's, if not more. There are lines that move some of us like "strange news called negritude." What would you make of what I perceive as essentially a return of Negritude in another guise?

Yes, Negritude cheated us. Senghor should have created Senegal as a Negritude state. Nkrumah should have created Ghana as an African personality state. Then we would have seen Negritude in action, African personality in action. But they philosophised and left it at that. Since they were not only philosophers but politicians, they should have put into practice what they were believing. That is what the fundamentalist Muslims do. They do not only advocate an idea but they also put it into practice. That is what the Boers here did. When they believed in apartheid they put apartheid into action. At least Nyerere with his Ujaama villages, and moving people from one place to another, tried to put into practice what he believed.

For me knowledge is very powerful. Any knowledge has claws and teeth. If you don't see the teeth and the claws of an ideology then it is useless, then somebody has emasculated it. When ideas are conceived by people in the realm of action but those people don't put them into action, that's where the problem is. These ideas then become dreams. To be realised by who? nobody can tell. So if we are going to have a Renaissance, well and good but let us have it fully orchestrated, fully ramified throughout all walks of life.

How would you propose we build an African literary culture?

Please let us shy away from 'Africa.' 'Africa' is too big. Your area is South Africa and Southern Africa really. Leave the Eastern Africans to do their own thing, and the Central Africans, the Western Africans, the Northern Africans. It is when we want to be continental in our conception that we end up just making a dot here and a dot there and so on and call them African.

In this SADC region, you need to translate books not only into English but from one African language to another including books written in Mozambique, in Botswana, in

Zambia and Zimbabwe. We need to have access to the books that have been written. It should not just be a Vendan writer or teacher recommending Vendan books: it should be someone else who is not a Vendan, who knows the relative importance of Vendan books, or Tsonga books, or Sotho books who does the identifying and recommending.

You need translation centres for translating these books. Then you also need exchange of scholars and exchange of writers so that they move around as our children, not as foreigners. You need literary and other competitions within the SADC areas, including even a version of the NOMA awards for SADC countries. Maybe it will be sponsored by Castle Beer, I don't know. In Europe they used to have aristocratic or rich patrons. Here we need also cultural ambassadors, not the radicals who cannot wear suits but do their hair like yours. We need ambassadors who can go to a De Beers board meeting and say "Ladies and Gentlemen, do support art – do support this idea, it is a good idea." You need those. It requires a lot of doing, and a lot of planning and if you plan it the wrong way, if you do it precipitously, it can be knocked down.

Doesn't this contradict something you said in your inaugural address here in Venda, that the problem with most African social scientists and writers is that they limit themselves to specific tribes and specific religions.

I was talking about tribalists. Because even amongst the Sothos there are Bapedi and that is not the end of it. How can anyone just specialise in the Bapedi and not know how the Bapedi are joined to middle and southern Sotho? You have to do it like the kite. The kite has two types of eyes, one for seeing the world below and another one for seeing a rat, right? You are out there and you are 50 yards up, you can't see a rat but the kite can. Even some of the doves, they can see a small grain on the ground, they adjust their lenses. They can see panoramically and they can also zero in. So that is what I am talking about. It doesn't matter if we have those who zero in, so long as we have the people who can put things into context. The ones who are going to talk about continental Africa, they should be able to see a variety of things. That would be it.

Critics have not been very kind to you. They say that your writing echoes bourgeois or even racist criticism, propaganda. "His thoughts are permeated with Indo-Western decadence." How have you reacted to this?

The lucky thing about it is that the only literary criticism that I've read about myself is this one by Christine Pagnoulle. Otherwise I have just continued doing my own thing. I have never read whatever other writers and critics have said. For one simple reason – knowing them and knowing their limitations, their intellectual limitations – I am likely to be infuriated. And then, secondly, I think I explore a wider field than most of them, not just of Africans but of other people, so I feel few of them can do me justice. So I am ready to go through life like Cassandra. Cassandra in one of the Greek myths is a prophetess, but she's doomed not to be respected, not to be believed. When she tells the truth nobody takes action. So I've accepted it. It is my fate because I am still active. I mean it is easy to pontificate when somebody is dead and the work he has produced is over. But if he is still producing, whatever report you make it is an interim report. I'm not interested in reading interim reports about me because I'm also an activist in the field and in that way I rub other people up the wrong way. So if I am supposed to listen to what they say, they will tell me to go the wrong way, to go their way. So I think they better do their own thing and I do my own. Maybe by the end of this century, when I have stated most of my major theses and have had them published, then will I have the luxury to sit in the gallery and follow the debates on the floor.

Interviewed by Susan Rich

INGRID DE KOK was born in 1951 in Johannesburg, and grew up in the mining town of Stilfontein. She studied in Canada and South Africa. She works at the Centre for Extra-Mural Studies at the University of Cape Town. She was co-editor of *Spring is Rebellious: Arguments about Cultural Freedom* (1990) and advisory editor of *World Literature Today: South African Literature in Transition* (1996).

Books of poems published:
Familiar Ground (Ravan, 1988)
Transfer (Snailpress, 1997)
Terrestrial Things (Kwela/Snailpress, 2002)

You lived in South Africa until 1976, and then in Canada, then returned to South Africa in 1983. How have these changes in geography affected your work?

I think geography is a powerful influence generally. A primary input. Its effects are difficult to identify, but they seem to be there, unavoidably. Growing up in a hard, flat, dry place, a demanding physical environment has probably influenced the way I see a great number of things as well as the way I respond to landscape. I'm interested in geography and space insofar as it relates to the notion of home: to issues of migrancy, loss and return; of home and home-coming, home-leaving and home-defining. I'm sure that crosses with other concerns, especially those which are gender-related.

What was your experience of Canada after growing up in South Africa?

It was liberating to spend time in a country like Canada where one could actually confess to being confused about something, to have two views and the time to find a considered way to have an opinion. Like most of my contemporaries, my political experience was obviously powerfully anti-apartheid. Therefore, perhaps of necessity, also powerfully judgmental. It was bracing to go to a place where even the people who were on one's side, on what one assumed was the 'correct' side, had a variety of views. And where the atmosphere was not punitive, but exploratory.

Why did you choose to come back?

It was partly personal, partly having been on a trip back to South Africa and finding that I couldn't be anywhere else; and partly because my writing was making it clear to me that my writing base should be South Africa. But Canada remains in my consciousness as an important 'other' home. It was kind to me.

111

What are your views about the ongoing debate in South African poetry on the responsibility of the writer? How do you see the relationship between poetry and social activism? Do you think the poet or the writer has any specific responsibility to his or her community?

Seamus Heaney engages with this creatively, I think. So do many of the significant poets of the century, in one way or another. My own view is unexceptional. I think the poet's responsibility is to write a good poem. It's a social responsibility as well as an individual responsibility (if indeed it is possible to distinguish between the two). I think that's how you respect your readership, engage with your community, make a 'contribution' – by doing your best piece of work. And it's a big thing to do, it's not a small thing. It's easier to do the other stuff, it's easier to be on the writing boards and arts councils, run workshops, mount readings, easier to 'have a profile', easier to do and be hundreds of other things than to actually take the piece of work that you're working on and work on it again. But this is probably the minority view. And of course writers engage in other activities as citizens, members of parties, activists.

Which poets do you find yourself drawn to, that you return to and read again?

At the moment I am reading Eavan Boland, Jeremy Cronin, and mainly Irish novels. And next year I intend to reread John Clare, and Robert Lowell. But which poets do I go back to? Over how long a period? Robert Frost, Emily Dickinson, Elizabeth Bishop, Thomas Hardy, John Donne, and Akhmatova, Neruda and Rilke in translation. And occasional, possibly unexpected poets that don't seem to fit: like Tennyson, oddly. I'm interested in what he does in "In Memoriam", as an extended, though probably failed, formal exercise – in the "In Memoriam" stanza and how it registers grief. I'm compelled by elegy, basically, in traditional forms but also slightly odd forms of contemporary elegy.

You are obviously very interested in form. What about the forms of these poets attracts you?

One of the current aspects which attracts me to Frost (and the commentaries on him by Brodsky, Walcott and Heaney in "Homage to Robert Frost" are exemplary) and also to Hardy and Bishop is how violences are contained in their poems. I'm interested in the formal representations of the furies, of grief, violence and anger and how they play themselves out, are reordered, in the delicacies and constraints of quite formal work.

The poems in Transfer *seem to have more concern with form than your poems in* Familiar Ground. *The recent work seems to be tonally quite different. Is there a way that you see that your work has travelled from the time of* Familiar Ground *to now? Certain trends and obsessions that are apparent to you?*

112

I don't know if it's different. Some of the poems in *Familiar Ground* are also quite formal, and I still write some sort of free narrative verse. There probably is a shift, after all it's a ten year period. But I'm not sure what the shift is or what it means except that I'm attracted to tight expression and always have been, even before *Familiar Ground*. I know the contemporary arguments in favour of looser, experimental, exploratory forms, and I respond to numerous examples of that work. But I think one can be as experimental within inherited forms.

Can you talk about a particular poem, a poem that you could use as an example of how your writing process happens?

There are a variety of processes. Different poems produce and are produced by different processes in me. The "Small Passing" poem from my first book developed from hearing two or three comments – one was a comment about the white woman having no right to make her grief central, another was hearing Zinzi Mandela talk on Canadian radio about not being able to touch her father in prison, only being able to see him through the glass. And, in retrospect, of course, the process was about putting together those disparate hearings into a poem. I think that's my practice in some poems such as "Transfer" – where the first sentence, "All the family dogs are dead" is a disputed sentence. My brother thinks he said it and my ex-husband thinks he said it! Anyway, somebody said "all the family dogs are dead."

But this pattern is only one point of entry. I don't think I have something called 'a writing process', or, if I do, I don't recognise it.

One of your poems that I keep coming back to and reading again and again and again is "Mending". I wonder if you can talk a bit about where that poem evolves from.

MENDING

In and out, behind, across.
The formal gesture binds the cloth.
The stitchery's a surgeon's rhyme,
a Chinese stamp, a pantomime

of print. Then spoor. Then trail of red,
Scabs rise, stigmata from the thread.
A cotton chronicle congealed,
A histogram of welts and weals.

The woman plies her ancient art,
Her needle sutures as it darts,
scoring, scripting, scarring, stitching,
the invisible mending of the heart.

It took a long time to write – maybe a year, and its first form was very different, originating as a response to someone's broken marriage, only later developing the stitching metaphor. The language itself, the working of the poem, is what generated the poem, not something as definable as a prior 'idea'. But it is intended to carry a sense of the wounding of, and healing by women, and perhaps their ambiguous role in the healing of nations, or this particular nation. Having to stitch itself together. Wounds and ruptures. Mending is one of our most domestic metaphors. And it's a complex act. It is done alone but it references women's work over the ages, as well as torn things, repaired things. And needlework suggests precision, obsession, cross-overs, coverings up and undersurfaces. Not to mention fine motor control! Perhaps the poem is also about the act of writing a poem. Anyway, it's a sort of a six-month poem.

A six-month poem?

I usually put finished poems away for a while. I don't pull them out or submit them for publication for at least six months. When I look at them again I often turf them. Once or twice I haven't let them rest fallow, but exposed them to light prematurely, and I've been sorry.

The subtle way that you weave political subjects into your poems is characteristic of your work. Are you actively concerned with doing this?

It's not an intentional act or an active project. If it were, given how I work, something would go wrong. I am not as conscious as your question assumes.

In your forthcoming chapter "Memory on Exhibition" in Carli Coetzee's and Sarah Nuttall's book Negotiating the Past, *you quote Derek Walcott's Nobel Prize speech where he says "Break a vase, and the love that reassembles the fragments is stronger than that love which took its symmetry for granted when it was whole. The glue that fits the pieces is the sealing of the original shape. It is such a love that reassembles our African and Asiatic fragments, the cracked heirlooms whose restoration shows its white scars."*

I wonder if I'm following you correctly to connect this metaphor to the formation of collective memory that South Africa is undergoing at this moment, the process of being able to see all the cracks, making them explicit in the reassemblage. I'm thinking in terms of the Truth and Reconciliation Commission, of public exhibitions such as Faultlines *and* Miscast *and* Streets. *Do you believe in this reconstruction process?*

I do, but it's a conditional "I do". I can't imaginatively conceive of another route, but there is no safety in this one. There's something heroic about the reconstructive attempt, though everything depends on the quality of the deconstruction. Walcott's image is very apposite, though he is talking about the fracture of Antillean society. And very moving. It's about keeping the scars present, but in a reconstituted form. That seems psychically to be right.

In your poem "At the Commission" I noticed the absence of a first person narrator. Instead there's an omniscient observer. I wonder about that choice? whether that was intentional?

> AT THE COMMISSION
>
> *In the retelling*
> *no one remembers*
> *whether he was carrying a grenade*
> *or if his pent up body*
> *exploded on contact with*
> *horrors to come.*
>
> *Would it matter to know*
> *the detail called truth*
> *since, fast forwarded,*
> *the ending is the same,*
> *over and over?*
>
> *The questions, however intended,*
> *all lead away from him*
> *alone there, running for his life.*

It wasn't intentional in that I didn't think "Now I will write a poem in which there is an omniscient narrator". 'Positioning' oneself in relation to the testimonies of the commission is of course fraught with danger, not just for poets, but for reporters, anthropologists, scriptwriters, and mainly ordinary citizens – all those who are attending the hearings or reading, watching or hearing the reports. I think problems arise no matter how you write about the Truth Commission. The appropriating voice that 'shares' unbearable pain and loss is problematic. The omniscient narrator is problematic. The engaged analyst is problematic. The only way through it, perhaps, is for lots and lots of different things to be written about the Commission's burden. It seems an unavoidable dilemma: I don't know how you can write in South Africa and not reference this major revelatory complex mixture of truth and lying in some way. Yet it also seems impossible, invasive, to do so. The only way I can is to acknowledge the moral torment involved, and then set it aside, or inside. This is not of course a unique set of moral or aesthetic questions. Terence de Pres and others have written with intensity about the responsibilities but also the dangers of writing about the Holocaust, and of course, there are other examples.

That does raise the question of artistic appropriation of others' experience generally. How do you negotiate that potential mine field?

I don't share the view that certain topics are the province of certain people whether by gender, by race, suffering or by origin. In South Africa this argument is intense, and in all likelihood will get more acute. I don't believe in it, I don't think it should be given credence. I think it's dangerous for art, I think it's dangerous for morality. Of course people, black or white, do appropriate experience. I can see historically why and where the strong feelings about artistic appropriation originate, and I do think those of us who are white, who were beneficiaries of apartheid, should negotiate with an appropriate sensitivity to the past, with what a friend calls 'historical decorum'. Black people have gone through massive suffering and humiliation and appropriation. It behoves white people to be a little restrained, respectful, suspicious of themselves as knowers of reality. But I'm against literary ghettoes, homelands, apartheid reproduced in ideas and expression.

This kind of mindset has affected South African poetry. In the Canadian journal West Coast Line *you wrote "In my view whilst some experimentation occurred South African writers with rare exceptions and regardless of whether they were politically engaged or not, lost sense of a wider context of artistic engagement. In formal terms poetry stultified, xenophobia reigned, the self-congratulatory text became commonplace."*

Given this – in what ways has South African poetry improved since 1994 – or do you see any signs of hope for a poetry culture emerging in South Africa?

Not really to any significant degree. There are shifts around but I think it's too early to say what the consequences will be. There are a few more books published, there are more visiting writers, there seem to be more readings. More cultural buzz. And there's more variety and commentary in politics and ideas generally. This will certainly have an effect on what people read and how people write, particularly young, black, writers who were assumed to fit into certain writing patterns.

In 1995-6 you were poetry editor of New Contrast. *What was the quality of work like?*

Not as memorable as I had hoped, though there were notable exceptions. But I was not there very long. My sense is that maybe we need a more generative notion of poetic apprenticeship, of the hard taskmaster – or mistress – that poetry is. Many younger poets seem eager for exchange, and there are few opportunities available to them. Acceptance or rejection by a poetry journal is a poor substitute.

What are the signs of change?

Well, the rap stuff which took over from worker poetry has helped because it has loosened form, and re-introduced linguistic and performance playfulness. When writers feel they can play, developments are possible. And the use of all the different SA languages start setting off things against each other. I especially like Lesego Rampolokeng's scathing multilingual jive attacks. But fundamentally I'm interested in

116

lyrical poetry. I go to a range of events; read a variety of poets. I listen, I hope, relatively intelligently, but my interest is in lyrical poetry. And maybe it's in fiction that developments in writing first show. Novelists seem to be working backwards rather than forwards. The trajectory used to be forwards from suffering to a future utopia. Now I think there's a reflection on history, the past, whether personal and national, and then individual and national compromise. It seems more realistic, and sober. Also more depressing. Surely the nation – whatever it really is – can't function adequately, never mind celebrate, until it's gone into deep mourning and depression. One can't possibly expect this culture to just transcend the violences in its current memory. There's got to be some psychic reckoning, and that's a slow and arduous process.

Given the tiny audience for poetry in South Africa, what motivates you to keep writing over the long term?

Well, it's what I do! So the tiny audience only impacts as a kind of hazy, secondary consideration. I think the audience that will read me is primarily South African. It does, however, matter also to be occasionally published in journals and anthologies elsewhere. It's about testing yourself within a broader international writing community. In South Africa it's a relatively small, sometimes generous, sometimes mean-spirited family affair. If one is selected for a foreign journal, or for translation, it's largely without much knowledge of who you are, what your profile is, more about the work itself. So you get some inkling of your relation to other writers internationally. The selection of a poem ("Transfer") in *The Best American Poetry 1996*, guest-edited by Adrienne Rich, was important for me. It felt like a gift, it came from nowhere. But I have no mission to make South Africans read lyric poetry! Writing and reading this sort of poetry is solitary and demanding. So be it!

117

Interviewed by Robert Berold

The Botsotso Jesters are a performance poetry collective. They also publish a literary magazine, *Botsotso*, and publish books of poetry and fiction under the imprint of Botsotso Publishing. At the time of this interview, the members of the group were Anna Varney, Siphiwe ka Ngwenya, Ike Mboneni Muila, Isabella Motadinyane, and Allan Kolski Horwitz.   In 2003 the group consisted of Muila, Horwitz, Ngwenya, Zachariah Rapola, and Napo Masheane.

ISABELLA MOTADINYANE was born in 1963 in Soweto and at the time of her death in February 2003, she was living in Orange Farm. She worked as an actor and performance poet.

IKE MBONENI MUILA was born in Soweto in 1957, and grew up in Venda, Limpopo Province, returning to live in Soweto in the 1980s. He studied acting at the Soyikwa Institute. He is an actor and performance poet.

SIPHIWE KA NGWENYA was born in Soweto in 1964.   He is a writer, theatre director and performance poet. He organises poetry readings in Soweto under the auspices of Timbila Poetry Project and the Jozi Book Club. A selection of his poetry was published in the 1992 anthology, *Essential Things*.

ANNA VARNEY was born in Johannesburg in 1959. She is an artist, graphic designer, mother, and poet. She co-organises an annual exhibition of manuscripts and handmade books.

ALLAN KOLSKI HORWITZ was born in Vryburg in 1952. He works for a social housing association and member-controlled provident fund. His fiction has been included in two collections by Botsotso Publishing. His first book of poems *Call from the Free State*, was published by Outposts in 1979. His poetry was included in *Essential Things* (COSAW, 1992) and *Throbbing Ink* (Timbila, 2003).

Books of poems by The Botsotso Jesters (collective and individual poems):
We Jive Like This (Botsotso Publishing, 1996)
Dirty Washing (Botsotso Publishing, 2000)
Purple Light Mirror in the Mud (CD with music, 2001)

How did Botsotso Jesters start?

Isabella: It was 1995. Allan brought us together, we met in Pretoria at Lisa Combrinck's place: me and Ike and Allan and Lisa and Roy Blumenthal and Phedi Thlobolo. We discussed poetry and we said we're going to come up with something collective.

Allan: . . . then Siphiwe joined. We started looking at common work that we had. Lisa dropped out, Phedi and Roy dropped out.

Anna: I was still very shy, I joined later. I made some contributions to the first collective poems.

Ike: We had our first performance at Wits, at an Open Day.

Siphiwe: We also performed at Sandton Library and during the Arts Alive Festival here in Joburg. And then Soweto, Chiawelo Community Centre and in Eldorado Park at the library.

Allan: To prepare our first programme we rehearsed for about three months, so it was very intensive. Every Sunday we used to meet. It took a while to develop the programme, because our concern was that it shouldn't be something slapdash, it should be really sharp, professional, something that held together. We wanted to perform group work as well as individual work.

Was group performance work something new for you?

Siphiwe: I was inspired by poets of the 1976 uprising, Ingoapele Madingoane and Matsimela Manaka, they used to perform as a team. So performing as a team was a good idea to me.

Allan: We were mixing individual work, group work, song – it was varied. So it held people's attention, which was obviously one of our concerns. If it was too dry people would get bored.

Siphiwe: Yes, people were surprised. After the Sandton Library performance people kept asking: how did you come together? They thought we were students from a college or university.

Isabella: Another one came to me after a performance and said, "Can I ask you something?" I said yes. – "Did this white guy teach you this whole thing? at college?" [she laughs] How can you teach somebody to write a poem and to perform?

Political poetry is not very popular these days, yet you have been very critical of current politics in poems like "Land of Plenty" and "Freedom Chanter." How have people responded to these poems?

Allan: People have been quite open. A lot of people have told me these poems were powerful and that they had something to say.

Siphiwe: What we write about is the way we live. Maybe it's a problem to them who still follow their parties.

Anna: . . . party animals . . .

Isabella: Performing political poetry, people associate you with Mzwakhe. If it sounds something like him they say: well, this one is a poet.

Ike: Not everyone is a politician. There is also the everyday life struggle of an individual. If you only do the political stuff, you are denying those who are fed up with day-in-day-out life experience and difficulty. It's not wise concentrating on one line.

Allan: I believe even our more political poems go deeper than just rhetoric. The metaphors and images are taken from daily life, but they are connected to broader political concepts.

Anna: It's just that it's not narrow party politics or the recognised traditions of politics. Politics in the sense of how we live our lives.

Allan: The political question became: has the transfer of power really made a difference to the basic needs of millions of people involved in the struggle? Our collective poem "Freedom Chanter" examines that and concludes that no, it hasn't happened. But we weren't just poets in some abstract sense, we were also people caught up in a much broader political movement. We tried to connect the two in a non-dogmatic way. We were working towards a general consciousness of what human beings need and what people are struggling for; with all the contradictions and weaknesses, all the betrayals and problems.

Are there other poets you feel are trying to deal with these issues?

Allan: Yes, Lesego Rampolokeng – his work is not narrowly political. And Kelwyn Sole – his work is connected to larger issues. Not many others. COSAW was supposed to be an organisation that brought together arts and political struggle, but COSAW has collapsed. So there is a vacuum and there aren't any clear signs at the moment of that vacuum being filled.

Anna: I don't put politics over there and give it attention and then give the rest separate attention. It's all one vision.

Siphiwe: Yes, poetry is about everything. A lot of people ask me, what kind of poetry do you write? And I say, I write poetry. Poetry is poetry.

Isabella: It depends on what the poet is inspired by, you know. Like I was inspired by those tight trousers, Botsotsos, so I just wrote about it.

Anna: Have you ever looked at a toothbrush politically?

Allan: Well the political aspect is the price.

Rhythm, movement, plays a strong part in your work. You break the line into non-logical forms, jumping around, impressionistically. How did this style develop, did you influence each other, are there other influences from other poets?

Ike: We do somehow influence each other. Like for example, Sipihwe did put some influence in me while I was in the dark, when I didn't understand what I was writing. His work really challenged me to rework and look at what I was writing. Also Lesego — in one way or the other he does influence me, although I do not imitate him. I like the influences that people gave me, they have brought out the poet inside me.

Allan: I'd say Ike and Isabella have probably influenced each other the most.

Anna: Influences can be very subtle and not always easy to discern. There are times I've written something and later realised I probably wouldn't have written it if I hadn't heard Ike's work, for example.

Siphiwe: With the rhythm part I have been influenced by our oral traditional poetry and also rap or dub poetry.

And another feature of your work is the mixing up of languages.

Ike: In that I was inspired by poets outside South Africa, books I read in the library. That's where I found mother tongue mixing with other different languages in one poem. That's how I got into writing in tsotsitaal, the so-called isicamtho, mixing it wittily. Tsotsitaal is a very alive language. It's not stagnant, it differs from one place to another. People who are staying in Hillbrow talk a different tsotsitaal from people who stay in Cape Town or in Soweto or in Giyani.

Anna: It's probably the most representative of all the languages in South Africa, and also the most creative and witty.

Isabella: People ask me: are you still busy writing in this pidgin language? They think that when you are a poet you've got to write in English only.

Siphiwe: Tsotsitaal is an easy language to communicate in and a lot of people use it. Of course kwaito musicians use it in a way that is derogatory or obscene. It's being used now in community radio stations, the Voice of Soweto, Soweto Community Radio, YFM. But with our poetry we use it to communicate, not offend people.

Allan: It's a pity that kwaito got stuck on sex, the level is pretty low, it's cheap thrills, sensationalism. It hasn't been broadened to deal with other issues. Maybe its something for us to consider, to start writing lyrics for kwaito bands so that they have something more substantial to put across.

Isabella: Some years ago Brenda Fassie was singing in tsotsitaal. You know, that stuck in my mind. Oh Brenda – Brenda is forever a pantsula. You are what you write.

Allan: How a poet uses language is taking responsibility, saying – yes, this is my experience of the world. So many different languages, each one expressing often another understanding of the world; but also the commonalities, the links between languages. I always thought that was a very strong element of our work, that we did have different languages.

Ike: English was never a pure language, it's a mixture of all different languages coming together, the so-called Anglo-Saxon English. In the same way, so many other African languages, when they're brought together, they form the so-called tsotsitaal or isicamtho. In my work I mix Venda and Tsonga and Zulu to show that from this kind of mix I come to the pure tsotsitaal. This guides my readers, to show them that I didn't jump into tsotsitaal, I'm from somewhere to tsotsitaal.

How does tsotsitaal work as a written language, if it's constantly changing from place to place, time to time?

Siphiwe: The tsotsitaal spoken today differs from the past. And they differ from the one Ike is using because Ike uses the old tsotsitaal mixed up with the new.

Allan: It's important to always have a translation, because in ten years time who will understand the version, the brand of tsotsitaal that's spoken today? It's constantly moving.

Anna: . . . because the language changes and thought patterns change too.

Your publications are well designed and full of interesting graphics. How do you see poetry and graphic art meeting?

Siphiwe: If you look at *Staffrider*, as it was published by Ravan Press in the 1970s, poetry and visual art, they went together. With us too, even in performance, Anna does some art works as backdrops.

Anna: We bring together different languages. It's collage work in a way. Visuals take the whole thing further.

Ike: If you're aware of your surroundings, whatever you are looking at brings so many ideas to you.

Anna: Written words on the page become visual in themselves. Words contain images and if you are also looking at images, then you can bring the two together. Obviously

122

with performance it's different but there you can do backdrops and create a visual environment.

Allan: There's a long history of feedback between visual arts and poetry because they both deal with essences, they are both crystallisations of experience. A poem or a painting or drawing is immediate, quite sharp, so there's a place there for fusion. I don't think anyone could look at *We Jive Like This* or *Botsotso* and not see that there is not this marriage.

Anna: In my own work, being both an artist and a poet, I don't prioritise one or the other and there's always a tension between the two. I'd like to see the visual side being picked up even more in our publishing.

You published a number of issues of Botsotso *in newspaper tabloid format. You've also published* We Jive Like This, *a book of your individual and collective work. What's next?*

Allan: There is a new *Botsotso* coming out in the next month. It will be the ninth issue. And there's a book-length collection of poetry by Donald Parenzee, Vonani Bila and Alan Finlay. And there are some other possibilities for another book of our own work.

Obviously you think carefully about distribution because you've always gone for large-scale distribution. At one time Botsotso *was a supplement to the weekend paper* New Nation, *and after* New Nation *closed down,* The Sowetan.

Siphiwe: I've heard that some people who bought *New Nation* bought it because of *Botsotso.*

Allan: That might be overstating the case, but it did have a lot of impact. It really was a disappointment that *The Sowetan* wouldn't continue with *Botsotso* as a supplement. But that I suppose reflects on South African business. They pay lip service to supporting the arts but they don't really want to. The fact that *The Sowetan* wasn't prepared to take it up says something about the priorities of the newspaper industry. It would have been interesting to test the readership of *The Sowetan* about *Botsotso.* I believe there would be a very strong response in favour, if readers were given the chance to give their input.

You're carrying on with mass distribution through Win *magazine. Can you tell us about that?*

Allan: *Win* is a free magazine – 60 000 copies are distributed all over South Africa through spaza shops. It deals with a lot of socio-economic issues like health and education. They've asked Botsotso to contribute two pages of writing, mainly poetry, so the autumn edition of the *Win* magazine does carry a small *Botsotso.* This will get to a really massive audience. People who wouldn't generally be exposed to poetry are going to see some South African writing.

A wider readership will mean a wider range of contributors. What's your editorial policy concerning the selection of work for Botsotso?

Ike: *Botsotso* is selective. People need to read something which is substantial and challenging. We can't be expected to publish anything just like that, because we want the magazine to reach the masses.

Siphiwe: We want to publish work that will last . . .

Ike: . . . exactly, work that is substantial.

Isabella: We don't want to end up with people drafting things, and sending them over to us because they think *Botsotso* can take anything.

Allan: We're looking for something that's original, that's lively, that touches on how we live now. Something that to some extent does reflect where we are, today.

Where is South African poetry today, in your view?

Siphiwe: Some people thought poetry would die when what it fought for was achieved. But I see that poetry is still going. The present poetry is more critical than in the past I think, most people who write feel free to write their feelings and their thoughts.

Allan: Most literary magazines have a very limited circulation, they don't reach a very big readership or audience. Bookshops, book chains don't carry poetry and make no effort to promote it. Poetry won't ever die but at the moment we don't live in a time when there's clarity, when there is a clear direction. It's a time of individualism, a time when people are out for themselves. Our backs are up against the wall. It's a corporate world now. If you don't have something that people are going to buy, who's going to support it? In South African poetry, there's always been a number of streams. In apartheid society, English poetry was dominated by old colonial modes, old standards. There wasn't a sense of South Africanness. On the other hand, poetry in African languages was marginalised, in the same way that all black culture was marginalised. We are in that crisis still.

Anna: There aren't patrons any more. We're living in an age now where people have to know how to market themselves and they've got to be more business orientated to make sure their life in public continues. Artists are sitting back and feeling sorry for themselves because they don't have a profile. It's time for us to get up and do something about it. Business people ask poets to perform for free at their meetings and we agree. We talked earlier on about tsotsitaal coming on in advertising and so on. I think there's a lot of art in advertising these days and maybe that's today's form of patronage. Perhaps we need look more at that, putting the arts in advertising.

124

Siphiwe: Some companies have wanted me to compose poetry for conferences, or when someone is coming to South Africa from abroad.

Anna: We shouldn't sit around with begging bowls. We've got to get up and be proactive.

We have the slogan of the rainbow society, different cultures coming together. But there isn't really much content to that.

Allan: In the absence of broader political direction it is left to advertising literally to create the new culture. Knowing the American model and having lived in America, I can see it's going to be a disaster because it's superficial. YFM for instance – they were going to have a poetry programme. Every time I've spoken to them they're not quite ready to do it. The same thing with KFM, Khaya as well, also supposed to have a poetry station.

Anna: Look, we decided there should be a journal and we made a journal. Let's start our own radio station!

Isabella: Botsotso always breaks boundaries, you know.

Ike: I really find it interesting that in the New South Africa, with such a big office of Arts and Culture, we experience a dying culture of learning. One cannot really understand how it comes about.

Is censorship coming – or is it with us already?

Allan: Yes, there is censorship. But it's not comparable to the Nationalist government. For instance *New Nation* which is an ANC/SACP paper ran an issue of *Botsotso* which had two poems about Slovo, one which was like a praise poem and the other was very critical. They published it and that I thought was a very good sign, they never came to us and questioned it. The John Pilger programme on TV created a storm but the fact is it wasn't banned and that is still a healthy sign. Unfortunately a lot of the critique of what's going on comes from the political right wing rather than from the left. The right wing talk about democratic values and so forth, which is pretty ironic. But I suppose in the end the key thing is that there are enough people who are ready to fight for freedom of expression. Clearly *Botsotso* is part of that struggle.

Anna: You don't get a sense of censorship like you used to. I don't feel censorship has come, in fact the media is more open than it's ever been. Mandela is getting called to court – when have we ever had a president having to go to court over a rugby issue?

Ike: But censorship is there in other ways – at times one can really feel it. There are certain places where you can't just talk in any language you like. When you start mixing languages they start looking at you, saying you can't use this street language here. You don't read an African language in *The Sowetan* for example.

Allan: The fact is that the crudest, most destructive forms of apartheid have been smashed and we've got a chance to rebuild. South Africa is a far better place to live in, in 101 different ways. I don't think anyone would say let's bring back the past.

What is your sense of our political culture today?

Allan: For me the thing that is most distressing is that the sense of solidarity has broken down completely. There always were opportunists, but now it's very open and it's unashamed, people don't apologise for it or see it as negative. Opportunism has now been legitimised across the spectrum, and that's a very dangerous thing. No doubt our arts will reflect that in the same way that art in Europe and America is quite decadent now. Clearly there's an international crisis, it's not just South Africa. Corruption is everywhere.

Anna: That's where the voice of the artist comes in. We are meant to be leading society with a shout about things that are wrong.

Ike: Like when I ask a politician where is my tax money going, he will open a bible telling me stories, unfinished stories . . .

Interviewed by Robert Berold

JEREMY CRONIN was born in Durban in 1949 and grew up in Simonstown. In 1976, while lecturing in the Philosophy Department at the University of Cape Town, he was arrested under the Terrorism Act, and jailed for seven years. He is the deputy general secretary of the SA Communist Party, and a member of parliament for the African National Congress.

Books of poems published:
Inside (Ravan Press, 1984)
Even the Dead (David Philip/Mayibuye, 1997)
Inside and Out (David Philip, 1999)

I think of you primarily as a lyric poet, exemplified in your new collection by the poem-cycle "Moorage." But then you have another voice, a more public one, the one of "Even the Dead."

I think there are many contradictory pulls upon all of us, and I am not an exception. For me poetry, in a variety of registers, is one way of exploring these different pulls, of seeking through it all some kind of anchorage, moorage, integrity. Lyrical poetry is what I feel most affinity with. I have said in other interviews that my earlier lyrical attempts were problematic. It was only when I was in prison, between 1976 and 1983, that I found a lyrical voice with which I was relatively happy. I found I was able to speak, from prison, of love, of the death of my first wife, of personal things like that, with some integrity, unabashedly. I felt that lyricism emerging from an apartheid prison cell had a social rootedness that I had not been able to achieve before. I'm not suggesting, of course, that you have to go to prison in order to be able to write lyrically! It was, however, an existential reality for me – no doubt connected with a sense of the irrelevance of a young white South African's emotions in the middle of the granite apartheid years. Prison connected the emotions to an historical reality. I should add that in the prison collection, in many of the poems, I found in poetry the space, rhythms, disciplines for working through a bereavement. I was not allowed to attend my wife's funeral, or participate in the usual social rituals that enable one to cope, more or less, with the death of a loved one.

Do you feel that on release from seven years of prison you lost that impulse or found it difficult to find a voice for that impulse? In prison the sense of time and introspective space must have been very different.

Yes, it was difficult, (although I wasn't complaining about being out of prison!) It was not just the reality of being outside, but also of being rushed off my feet by the heroic, exciting, complicated, frustrating political events into which I was released in 1983. Through the 1980s I continued to write a great deal – but it was largely notes, observations, many of which eventually found their way into the *Even the Dead* collection. A lot of that material was jotted down through the 80s; but then it never really became poetry to my satisfaction. Maybe it was just that I didn't have the time that I had so abundantly in Pretoria prison. In the new collection I have quite deliberately set out to recover another lyrical place from which to speak. You are right to suggest that the most intensely lyrical section of *Even the Dead* is the poem cycle called "Moorage." As in my earlier collection I am trying to explore the intersection of the personal, the emotional and the broader political realities of our time. My relationship with my second wife becomes a point of moorage, a kind of lyrical anchorage for the events covered in the collection – roughly through the 1980s into the present.

The poems in Inside *were about the impossibility of love because of bars, prison regulations, space between yourself and the loved one, and then death. In their different ways these are the great romantic themes.*

You have put your finger on something I was trying to work through in the new collection. I was deliberately trying to quarrel with the fatalistic assumptions of much lyrical writing. I wanted to write poems that were about the possibility of love rather than its impossibility; about the erotic in the quotidian and not in a forbidden zone outside of it, about love and marriage, love and rearing kids, love and shopping, love and jointly sharing the task of trying to outwit the security police. I was trying to connect a lyrical voice with the project of normalising our society and lives, of making the too-good-to-be-true be true.

But that attempt surely is threatened now by a new elite, people occupying new positions of power, transforming the nature of power a little but not that much, and basically declaring the struggle over . . .

. . . saying we're in charge now, we will deliver change to you, your job is to be obedient and silent citizens?

Yes.

That kind of closure is not going to succeed. For better or worse, the contradictions in our society remain very powerful realities. The culture of mass participation developed in the 80s has been fragmented and dissipated but it hasn't disappeared, nor will it easily disappear. But certainly there is a real struggle now to validate millions of ordinary people's hopes, aspirations, experiences and energies. How often these days do we hear the word 'culture' only when it is connected to the disqualifying words 'of non-payment,' or 'of unrealistic expectations'?

128

So how do you find an aesthetics which will satisfy the lyric poet in you, while you are working in a political milieu, with things coming at you full blast?

I suppose aesthetically I want the poems that I write to emerge from that full blast, from the conversation that is going on around all of us, in many registers, whether it be other poems, political debates, literacy classes, soap operas, the Truth and Reconciliation Commission evidence, or the monologic voice of CNN. Poetry has got to take its chances in the midst of all of that, it must emerge from public conversation and return to it. I would like poetry to be a fully-fledged citizen in the midst of our complicated reality.

Some of my poems emerge directly from political interventions I have made, at other times the reverse happens. Recently, for instance, I was doing a political education input for the ANC Women's League, and I said that the clenched fist of solidarity was in danger of being displaced by the pointed elbow of individual competition among former comrades. The image, which just spilled out in the course of the input, seemed to strike a chord, and I thought I should try it in a poem, which I have done. This weekend I did the reverse. I have been working on a poem about freeways and on-ramps, imagery referring to neo-liberal ideology and its assumptions. At this weekend's ANC-SACP-COSATU Tripartite Summit I was asked to do a paper on the present global economic crisis and I played around with the same imagery – I didn't dare recite the poem as such! That's part of aesthetics for me – for these things to be feeding each other, to be trying out different audiences, trying to connect different discursive practices.

Would you say the function of being a poet, politically, is to be anarchistic?

Maybe. One hesitates to generalise about these things, and different poets are legitimately different. But for me, the anarchism inherent in poetry is located in the stance it adopts towards language. Poetry tends to be disruptive of received meanings, it bites the heels of discourse, it makes visible hidden assumptions and assumed hierarchies embodied in our ways of speaking.

Can you give an example of that?

Well, one of the intellectual challenges of our times is to take on the deadening dogma of market totalitarianism, neo-liberalism and its zealous belief that there's some kind of one-size-fits-all economic policy model for the whole of the universe. It is hard to speak and think in English without uttering the Washington Consensus. It is the seemingly transparent self-evidence of this whole contemporary dogma that, I think, poetry, amongst other discourses, should seek to challenge. This is why I have been playing around with images of freeways and on-ramps. In our post-1994 South Africa we have been given the impression that we are about to catch a great global freeway, some kind of planet earth N1 (N1 North, of course). An endless horizon of non-stop growth awaits us if only we take the correct on-ramp (privatisation, deregulation, liberalisation and a budget deficit of 3 percent). What most of the Third World is discovering, of course, is that you just keep going around on the same on-ramp, as they tell you to tighten your seat-belts, more and more. There is no freeway north. Most of the world is heading south. Poetry can disturb the assumptions of this prevailing dogma. Poetry can use the resources of language, like imagery (of freewaysperhaps), like narrative (comparing the neo-liberal grand narrative with Nongqawuse's cattle-killing narrative, as I do in *Even The Dead*) to disrupt the seemingly obvious.

How do you explain that the past few years have shown a distinct dwindling of cultural activity in South Africa?

I would be cautious about asserting that too assuredly. Obviously there's been a certain loss of energy, if you compare the mid-90s to the 80s. For understandable reasons there has been a certain hesitation in finding new voices, new themes, and new places for poetry and culture. We cannot simply go on repeating. But I don't want to exaggerate, I think it is important not to be unduly pessimistic.

There are many new possibilities, new spaces now. Back in the 1980s, and much to my initial surprise then, I was able to read poetry to mass rallies. There are not that many mass rallies around at the moment. But what I couldn't do in the 80s, that I have been able to do now in the 90s, is to read poetry quite a lot on radio and even on TV (I have sometimes squeezed in some poetry into what was meant to be a more political interview). So there's that space, the broadcasting space which didn't really exist for anything other than an apartheid-aligned culture. And I am not just referring to the national broadcasters, there is now a whole network of local community radio stations. South African poets need to engage with these new possibilities. South African poetry must also claim other spaces, the school classroom, the university lecture theatre, the prison yard, a range of civic places like these. There is, of course, also a reciprocal influence – poetry can be performed into new spaces, but new spaces are also likely to influence the shape and themes of that poetry.

Recently I was lucky enough to be invited by Poetry International, along with some fellow South African poets, to read and discuss in Rotterdam. Apart from reading poetry, I was asked to present a short paper on "Oral poetry and printed poetry, the poetry of the street, and the poetry of the study". I found myself wanting to refuse the temptation of playing too easily with those dichotomies, which perhaps characterised the last decade of South African poetry. Poetry should, as I said earlier, become a full citizen of the new South Africa, it should not have to choose always between either the street or the study (both forms of exclusion and marginalisation in their different ways). Poetry should also occupy the town hall.

In your poem "Five thoughts concerning the question: what happens after Mandela goes?" you explore how Mandela embodies a telescoping of time that is the South African reality. Can you say more about this?

130

I first became sharply aware of this telescoping reality when I was doing some writing on the veteran Western Cape political activist, Dora Tamana. Mama Dora, as we knew her in the United Democratic Front in the early 1980s, had been active in the 1940s and 50s, on the Cape Flats. She had pioneered, in those decades, what we would nowadays call 'Masakhane', setting up food co-ops, children's creches, and other voluntary community organisations. She died in her eighties, in 1983, the year the UDF was launched, but she had played an inspiring role in the formation of many of the community organisations that affiliated to the UDF.

Tamana's life story embodies the telescoping of time – her grandfather, as she remembered, carried British army lead in his body, from the time of the frontier wars of the last century. She was personally at Bulhoek when her uncle was killed by Smuts's army. The Bulhoek massacre was directed at a syncretic Christian movement that had occupied the ground – illegally – declaring it sacred to their sect. Tamana's son was an MK guerrilla who was wounded and captured by Smith's Rhodesian forces in the late 1960s. Her grandson was shot with police buckshot in the 1980s, during the youth uprisings in the Cape Town townships. What an incredible continuity, and an incredible telescoping, within one life, of different times – from iron age resistance to the first wave of globalisation last century, through third world liberation movements of the 1960s, to the urban youth intifada of the 1980s. That, in its way, is the immediate history of South Africa.

Mandela also embodies this compacting of time. In his autobiography he remembers how political sentiments were first awakened by the vivid tales of elders about primary resistance to colonial dispossession. His personality was shaped by his experience in his uncle's Tembuland royal court. This was not Versailles, but the modest kraal of an aristocracy that was just emerging from early communalism. Leadership, in these conditions, had to be earned, daily, and it was based on more or less direct, personal contact with subjects. Colonial occupation was at once hastening and suppressing the formation of this emergent stratum. In my poem, "Five thoughts . . ." I was trying to reflect on some of this. Mandela is an anachronistic yet entirely inspiring and relevant world leader, at the cynical end of the 20th century. When politics is equated with all that is corrupt and sordid, Mandela strides across the global scene bearing his paradoxical blend of aristocratic born-to-rule dignity, African pride, and homely directness. When any other late 20th century politician hugs children you can bet it is election time, Mandela is different. Much to the consternation of his bodyguards he plunges constantly into the midst of crowds. Daily direct contact is, for him, what leadership is all about.

It is not just time, of course, that is telescoped in the South African reality, but also space. Apartheid, if we step back just a little, was not as anomalous as we sometimes have claimed. In many ways the spatial project of apartheid, the division of territory into a colonial metropole and subject colony, was what happened to the world, from the last quarter of the 19th century. The anomaly of South Africa is that metropole and colony, first and third worlds were not some thousands of kilometres apart, but the two kilometres between Alexandra and Sandton, Mamelodi and Waterkloof.

Does this telescoping of time, in particular, provide resources to South African poetry that might not be so readily available in other cultures? We aren't that far away from the positive aspects of the primitive. The poet as shaman, as healer, as keeper of songs and stories, interpreter of dreams and trance states – these are things that are known mainly by anthropologists in other cultures, but we have the opportunity to observe them, if not first hand, at least in some postmodern forms.

I think you are absolutely right. But let me come at your question from a slightly different angle. The modern project, whether in its early liberal or in its Marxist variations, privileged production. This was not all wrong, as we might now realise after being bombarded in the last 25 years by the privileging of finance and daily stock-market psychoanalysis – the market is nervous, the market is reassured, the market will not permit this or that. However, the privileging of production in the paradigms that dominated most of this past century drastically ignored the re-production of life – rearing of kids, shopping, gendered power, and a sustainable relationship with nature. (These are the central themes of the poem-cycle "Moorage"). In 1956 the Soviet Union was able to send up a sputnik, but down on the ground people (usually women) still stood in queues for a loaf of bread. Modernity treated nature as something to be conquered in the name of production. A different perspective on nature is to be found in earlier cultures, and, as you correctly say, these are to be found in resources that remain dynamic within our country.

Among the cultural resources there are strong oral traditions in our country – how do you relate to these?

When I was a participant in the CODESA negotiations in the first half of the 1990s I became aware, in a new way, of African orality as a significant political reality. The negotiations were not, of course, exclusively oral, there were printed documents of all kinds, but much of the work was indeed talking – talks about talks, and then, well, more talks. The negotiations were our national talking cure. Now, the original position of the ANC-alliance was that the negotiating process should involve a two-sided table – the apartheid regime on the one side, the liberation movement on the other. But FW De Klerk dug in his heels, and insisted that the talks should be multi-party. This is how we ended up with some twenty parties in the talks. The strategy from the side of De Klerk was, of course, to load the dice with a dozen or so compliant bantustan and other ethnic parties. But things did not work out like that. The apartheid regime was singularly inept at keeping its allies in line, it relied on rigid positions, heavy-handed hierarchies and on printed negotiating mandates.

My African comrades in the ANC, by contrast, were able to talk the process through,

132

to influence in discussion, to engage fluidly in bilateral and multilateral situations. I do not want to exaggerate this aspect too much, it was not the only factor, after all the political positions of the ANC were democratic and massively supported. But I am quite convinced that part of the ANC's negotiating success had to do with this kind of oral capacity. I don't know, perhaps it goes back to the traditions of the communal village lekgotla.

Do you have any general perspectives on contemporary South African poetry, since the negotiations and the elections of April 1994?

I am reluctant to advance general perspectives. In the first place, I am not sure that I have my finger on the pulse of a broad range of current South African poetry-writing. But, secondly, general perspectives are often normative manifestoes for one's own poetics, in contrast to everyone else's way of doing things. But, at the risk of falling into the latter trap, it seems to me that at least some current South African poetry, particularly poetry that is trying to be relatively political in its themes, is grappling with the shortfall between post-apartheid aspirations and actual realities on the ground. This is not, in poetry, just a question of political theory, but of poetically constructing speaking places, subjective positioning in language that does justice to the complexity of our reality.

I recently had a brief debate with Breyten Breytenbach in the *Sunday Independent* around this. Breyten is, probably, our most accomplished lyricist, he is able to invest landscape and sexuality with a great anarchic surge of libidinal energy. But his 'poes-modernism', as he jokingly refers to it in his latest collection *Papierblom*, is not, in my judgment, able to sustain an effective political positioning in regard to South Africa (whether you are talking about political politics, or gender politics, or environmental politics). The challenge in our new situation is to continue the momentum, to sustain an ongoing struggle to transform and increasingly democratise power. We need sustained engagement. Libidinal subversion is hit-and-run. Breytenbach ends up by declaring the whole post-1994 situation a sell-out. He can wash his hands, we have let him down.

Kelwyn Sole, another fine poet, with sensibilities different to Breytenbach's, also, I believe, ends up with a moral and poetic closure, declaring the revolution 'betrayed'. I am not saying that poets, or anybody else, should not criticise the many political errors and confusions of the post-1994 reality. But reducing it all to 'sell-out' or 'betrayal' leads, I think, into an aesthetic, imaginative and intellectual cul de sac.

At the other extreme, are some of the recent lyrical-epic poems of Mongane Wally Serote. Faced with the shortfall between reality and aspiration, Serote incants the aspirational, over and over: "ah / where / where are those moments which can be magic / and dazzling / and can bind us together / us / the human race / . . . Where / where is that moment / which can startle us to life." Aspiration is here in force – reality, the specific, actual struggle fades away. (Colin Gardner has noted this tendency in Serote's writings sensitively, but pertinently, in the latest *English Academy Review*, number 14). I am sure most of us who are writing poetry in South Africa at this time can recognise both of these kinds of tendencies in our writings. They are, however, problematic. It is critical, I think, to avoid intellectually lazy and often self-righteous expressions of betrayal on the one hand, just as it is important to avoid the endless reiteration of ungrounded aspiration. I think that a relevant South African poetry should force the actual and the desirable into continuous dialogue. Let them discuss, let them quarrel, but compel them into the same aesthetic, linguistic and subjective space.

LESEGO RAMPOLOKENG
& IKE MBONENI MUILA   June 1999

Interviewed by Robert Berold

LESEGO RAMPOLOKENG was born in Orlando West, Soweto, in 1965. He is a full-time writer and performance poet who has performed in many countries, both solo and with musicians such as Julian Bahula, Soulemane Toure, Louis Mhlanga, and Gunther Sommer. He has written a play, *Fanon's Children*, and collaborated on plays and filmscripts.

Books of poems published:
Horns for Hondo (COSAW, 1990)
End Beginnings (Shifty CD with Kalahari Surfers, 1993)
Talking Rain (COSAW, 1993)
End Beginnings (German translations) (Marino, 1998)
Blue V's (German translations with CD) (Edition Solitude, 1998)
The Bavino Sermons (Gecko Poetry, 1999)
The h.a.l.f. ranthology (CD with various musicians, 2002)

IKE MBONENI MUILA was born in Soweto in 1957, and grew up in Venda, Limpopo Province, returning to live in Soweto in the 1980s. He studied acting at the Soyikwa Institute. He is an actor and performance poet, a member of the Botsotso Jesters performance group and on the editorial committee of Botsotso Publishing. He writes in English, Venda, and isicamtho.

Books of poems published:
We Jive Like This (with other Botsotso Jesters)(Botsotso Publishing, 1996)
Dirty Washing (with other Botsotso Jesters)(Botsotso Publishing, 2000)
Purple Light Mirror in the Mud (CD with other Botsotso Jesters, 2002)

When did you first encounter oral poetry? What effect did it have on you?

LR: Oral poetry doesn't necessarily see itself as such. I came across it in the streets and in my home as well. For instance my grandmother, when she was in some kind of excited state, moved to anger or joy or whatever, would rattle out some lines that would put quite a number of people today going as poets to shame. That's why I've always gone out of my way to say, for me, my grandmother was the original rapper. She would rattle them out on the spot, what in the US they refer to as free-styling, meaning when you go out on stage without having written anything, creating extemporaneously as it were. But as I say, I did not recognise it as poetry itself. It was just the way in which my grandmother would express herself at certain times. This country's best poets will never be known, will never be recognised, because they do not even see themselves as poets, just as people putting words out there, in the street, mouth to ear, that kind of communication.

And then as a kid I used to listen to Radio Freedom. They would have a slot where they had poetry, I suppose just a means of mobilisation. And they introduced it by having these sounds of AKs going off to add some power to it. This rattling of guns and the static that's coming from your receiver, all these noises, this person reading poetry – it was electric, you know, that's what I think ignited that first spark.

And then again I had the good fortune of being dragged by my cousin Vincent to these not necessarily 'cultural' gatherings, people like Ingoapele Madingoane, Maishe Maponya and all the rest of them. I could recite "africa my beginning" without batting an eyelid, you know, at the slightest provocation, because I thought it was one way of getting some attention. And I *did* get some attention, and that I suppose got me rolling. Unfortunately for me the first few times I tried to read my lines at these places they chased me away. It was just sad, these were people I idolised and I wanted to show them what I had picked up from them. I was only about 14 or so. It was '79, around there.

Were you listening to any recorded oral poetry then?

LR: I subsequently came across the work of people in the Diaspora who were doing pretty much the same thing as these guys were doing, putting the word to the sound of the drum, maybe with someone playing horns. I saw a definite connection between what they were doing and what people like Linton Kwesi Johnson was doing. The difference was that the dub poets tried to infuse drum and bass rhythms into the word itself, whereas these other people were not doing that. Dub poetry is a specific genre, a specific form of poetry. It comes out of reggae music, the instrumental side of reggae music, where the drum and bass get pulled out and brought back in. You take that and build it into the poetry itself. Only then does it become dub poetry. I read somewhere that Ike is the king of dub poetry although I doubt that Ike has ever written a dub poem in his life, let alone being king of one. He might be the king of whatever he is doing, but it's definitely not dub poetry.

Then there was the underground British scene as they called it, Mutabaruka, Jean Binta Breeze, Oku Onuora and Michael Smith in Jamaica, and in the Americas The Last Poets and Gil Scott-Heron. And then there were those Africans in exile in England who came together and called themselves African Dawn, that was Ahmed Sheik and Merle Collins who was from Grenada I think. There was a definite link between what all those people were doing and what people in the Black Consciousness movement were trying to do, and I suppose that's what set me off.

I'm one of those people who are tied by the word. But we are not necessarily doing the same thing. What I am doing is as different from what Ike is doing as it's different from Lemn Sissay, and it's worlds apart from what Benjamin Zephaniah is doing. You can put us all under the spoken word form, it's all the word in motion, the word moving from mouth to ear, the word lifted off the page.

136

What about you, Ike, how did you meet oral poetry?

IM: Long before understanding written poetry, I was used to poetry being chanted. It was like a way of life in our family. My mother used to say, maybe at times when she was happy, my son, can you sing the praise names of the Muila family? And then I'd start chanting my praise names. . . then maybe somebody would sing something, maybe someone takes a izgubo or a drum and starts playing, and then they'll be chanting. When I started coming to understanding what is praise poetry and how it's written and how it becomes formalised, it was then that I realised that, hey, people come from rich cultural backgrounds. It doesn't matter whether you're Mosotho or Muvenda because there is that thing in a family unit that one has got.

Before my father passed away he was like a Zionist and he would get possessed sometimes and speak in tongues, things that he himself didn't understand. He was communicating with the gods and the gods were saying this and this and this.

I got into drama and studying, it was around 1987, under the Soyikwa Institute of African Theatre. They didn't want us to do scripted plays only – we had to workshop and write our own thing, we had to create characters, create our own music. That is how the interest got into me. When really something is happening to a person, you find yourself expressing yourself in your first mother language. I started by reading Venda poems and then mixing with the students of music. We performed in the library.

Staying with your roots kept you going . . .

IM: When you go back to your roots and feel the real stuff, it's then that the real artist in you develops. The artist which is not from a certain convention. It might be something like an avant-garde which doesn't have a head or a tail, it doesn't matter. It allows you to progress instead of retrogressing. But if you start distancing yourself from where you come from, it is then that the writing just becomes banal. This is what happens if I start distancing myself and displaying this kind of pride which is like shit across the street, which is never nice.

Coming back to the 70s, it was clear that Madingoane took poetry to a place it hadn't quite been before.

LR: "africa my beginning" was IT for me. I celebrated that piece, and I celebrate Ingoapele Madingoane today. I think that guy held spirit and injected spirit into the stagnation that had taken over. And also gave some direction, of course, to a whole lot of other people and influenced other people and inspired other people to do that. There was a real difference between the poetry of the 80s and that of the 70s. One wing of the poetry of the 80s was one wing of the liberation movement, created by people who specifically went out of their way to put into their poetry a line that sought to bring people in line with the UDF. As opposed to the 'zimzims' as they were called – the kids who were in AZASM, the Azanian Students' Movement, when I was a student. People who had embraced BC at the time.

Ingoapele Madingoane's poems went across lines, they just sought to sound a wake-up call, to conscientise people across the board and get people to realise that they were not the slaves that they were made out to be. That was definitely it, in political lines, for me. If you go into that whole *Staffrider* era, you come across the work of people like the Allah Poets, Dashiki, Lefifi Tladi who were writing and reading pieces. Even Jaki Seroke, PAC now, he was putting some really good stuff down, I believe. I might have problems with them on other levels, but they were putting some lines through that had quite a lot going for them.

What stopped the impetus of the late 70s poetry?

LR: I suppose all the States of Emergency and people jumping and running and stuff. You had to go deep within yourself to be able to project whatever it is to grab the attention of people. What killed that flow we're talking about, for me especially, was that there came this new aesthetic that if you recite your lines in *this* tone of voice, that is poetry. It became a standard, it became the rule by which people had to recite their lines, you know, that's why hundreds of people started coming out and going blah, blah, blah, blah, blah, blah. And that's why we stood a very sorry chance of becoming a nation of poets. Because anybody who could actually project their voice in a certain style could be classified as a poet.

The 80s situation had to be. It was essential. The bring-on-the-poet-to-lick-the-stage-clean-for-the-politicians thing. And then the conmen who talk 'possession by the spirits of the ancestors' hustle. Imagine having to negotiate with your forefathers to take possession of your tongue at exactly a quarter past eight, when you're due on stage. Those guys didn't have any watches, man! And judging time by sun and moon is not reliable! The 80s. Mzwakhe. It doesn't matter whether you liked his work or thought his stuff was 'work', he opened a crack in the literary structure and occupied it. And for that he gets my respect. The old goats that gloat at him today are the ones who lifted him high yesterday. Bad roll of the dice. The mass democratic movement propped him up once, and then what? He dropped. So everyone runs around cackling away in their little farticles. I say biggup to him, and flash my lighter in the direction of the dynamite up the wrinkled butts in Parliament.

What were the aesthetic pressures in the 70s?

LR: I did not like being beaten into form. Achmat Dangor and company gave us all those workshops, and tried to tell us what constitutes poetry, and this and that and the other thing, that you can use western forms, or whatever, as long as you threw this amount of politics into the poetry, then that was it. That also killed it off for me.

138

This country has killed off, across the political spectrum, a whole lot of talent, to use that phrase. People killed off their art because they were busy fighting a cause, which was the thing to do. They were fighting a cause and it killed off whatever was within them, as the essence of their art, it did that.

How does that affect people trying to do something new, new forms?

LR: I don't think the history of this country has actually allowed for people to break from the norm. You either conform or you are out, that has been it from the beginning, and that's so sad.

There is a racist element about attitudes to form as well. Some people who go as oral poets are buying into this idea of the black person as being a person of body and heart and not so much mind, and whatever it is they recite is from somewhere other than the brain, you know, it comes from elsewhere, they're just a medium for it. This is the aesthetic cross that black artists always had to bear.

Ike, you write in tsotsitaal/isicamtho. How did you arrive at that?

IM: Isicamtho is a rich kind of language. It's all over – in Louis Trichardt, you find that they use a different tsotsitaal, which is different from the one we're using in Mofolo, which is different from the one being used in Hillbrow, or in Cape Flats, you see. And each poet has got his own way of commanding the language. It's not just throwing in phrases and then it's finished and klaar. It's a cultural exchange, maybe that one from Giyani will make us feel the way they communicate around Elim. If I go from here and go to Elim, once I blom, it will be taken as it is, they won't show me their own way of blomming.

Blomming?

LR: Hanging out, at the street corner, at the shops or whatever. What is a blom? it is a flower. Basically what you're doing is setting your roots on there, and you're just flowering.

Isicamtho came spreading out of influx control laws. People came from all sorts of different corners, not only South Africa, but beyond, and they had to somehow find a way of breaking through and across language barriers, which was different from what was happening on the mines, that was a baas to boy situation. People had to find a way of merging the Zulu and the Sotho and the Tswana with Afrikaans and English and all sorts of things – they tried to create and breed anew some kind of communication, and that's what it came out of. You've got to find a way of saying whatever it is you want to say, articulating your concerns.

IM: Maybe in the very same family unit, you find that we are talking in Venda, in

Sesotho, in Tsonga. Those languages, when they come together, something new crops up, like a new language will be born. These days adverts and radio stations pick up the very same language, the street language, and use it, and it does really have an impact to the masses.

LR: The way my mother and her husband speak in the house is, I suppose, how they used to in Sophiatown. It's got much more Afrikaans, or 'Kaffirkaans' rather, thrown into it than the other languages that we hear, and the way in which I communicate with my friends, with Ike for instance, is different from the way in which my sister, who is eight years younger than I am, communicates with her own friends.

For both of you now, 1999, you're not appreciated by your community. You're not really performing in Soweto. Lesego, you're better known overseas than in South Africa. How do you understand this?

LR: I have to go to the extent of whoring, of prostituting myself elsewhere. That's the best way to put it, in fact. I don't know if it has anything to do with history, but in South Africa we seem to be bogged down in this need to celebrate the empty. I don't want to sound high on this one, but we do definitely celebrate mediocrity here. If you listen to the stuff that's being celebrated in South Africa, quite a lot of it doesn't really do anything for me or for anybody except to open money bags – which is fine. I suppose I could have done a different kind of whoring and gone to Parliament, and sang the praises of the old goats. I could have done that, but I don't think my conscience allows me to do that.

There is also this moral point that's always being poked in our faces, that you have to write for the masses. But those masses are not defined, you just have to write for the masses, and there is this standard that's being placed on just how high the word should jump or not for it to be celebrated. I've always believed that if you say this is the level the masses are, and pitch the word at that level, what you're actually doing is contributing to keeping those masses at that level. I don't go with that at all. In my case, it's also to do with *what* I've got to say, not so much *how* I've got to say it. Form and content, you know.

How useful have literary critics been about oral poetry?

LR: No use at all. People who don't even understand a single word that Ike's saying are happy to say he's good or bad. I read somewhere that Seitlhamo Motsapi is so great blah blah a brilliant performer who uses music blah blah. Much as I love Seitlhamo's work, I doubt that he has ever dropped a word onstage, let alone with music. Most of what I've read is people yapping a lot on issues they know crap about. Critics who cut you down to small size – or worse, blow you up with too much praise. I'm part of no group no school no cult, I'm out here to shave the beards off these little gurus.

140

Do you still perform or try out your work in Soweto?

LR: There have been times where I've tried out my work in front of drunkards and children because I thought they were the most open-minded, the most intelligent, in the sense of being able to tell me right off that how I was presenting my work was crap. I would do that, and it didn't matter to me whether they didn't understand what I was saying, but whether they could go with the flow of whatever.

Actually, maybe, I should just take this opportunity to announce that this year I'm going into retirement, I'm through with this performance crap, honestly, I really am. It drains me and for what? There's no fulfilment to be gained there. In the beginning what I needed most was not so much people appreciating what I was doing, but that I was able to appreciate it myself and celebrate myself, but beyond that you reach saturation point and do what? Can't keep pumping yourself up until you burst. So, from today onwards I'm going to walk around in a jacket and tie, and grow a belly and write vast tomes of novels.

Haven't you made these resolutions before?

LR: I have. And it really hasn't got me anywhere. The word has to be constantly given birth to . . . .

So you are going to perform your work anyway, whether people listen or not?

IM: I do this thing, this isicamtho, for self-fulfilment. If I created this isicamtho with the audience in mind, to worry how they're going to follow my stuff, it will be like I'm killing myself. I do it to fulfil myself and I mix with them, and the way we communicate, it's never the same, even though we are talking tsotsitaal, it's never the same way. I've got to be fulfilled inside, whether I get bread or no bread it's all the same, my only bread is my fulfilment. It shouldn't be stagnant political comments always – zabalazo, struggle, struggle. We've got to be creative, we've got to go with the times. There are a lot of pressures that we get, some people who appreciate and others who don't actually have that positive approach.

You get the attention of publishers more when you die. But I want to say – here's my anthology – do something with it, and then you don't have to wait until I pass away. I want to show my kids that, hey, your father was great when he was alive. I want it now so that when I die I die a happy person. I shouldn't have to wait for my brother to pass away to create a poem for him. This is my brother's poem, I create it while he is still there, and then he appreciates it. Or he takes it and puts it at the backseat of the toilet, it's OK.

If I have been labelled a king of the tsotsitaal dub, it's because of my originality. I hate academics not because of my poor education background, which no one on earth owes to me, but maybe because they ponder a lot on labels. I am a proud multilingual tsotsitaal poet – hasale dosale isicamtho madala – I don't know the likes of a dub if there is one.

LR: The oral word preceded the printed page. Long before the Assyrians started scratching on the bark of trees, the word was alive, and flying. There were the great poets of the Crete marketplace, those blind poets who served as newspaper poets who'd rattle their lines out; *The Iliad* came down the spoken word line. Those volumes that we hold in our hands trickled down from the spoken word, the oral word. Now that being the case, then I believe that even if paper stops being recycled, and trees stop being chopped down, and all the books in the world are burnt, the word will still be alive and moving, it will always be alive.

Personally, on that audience thing, I've been fortunate in the sense that I have been able to go out and build a core audience. I do have a core audience, be it here or elsewhere. That does exist. But the problem has always been that I've never wanted to write for an audience, for a specific audience. I've never been able to say three fans can't be wrong, or three million, I've just never been that kind of person. It's never about audiences. The problem with being too concerned with audiences is that as soon as you come upon a formula that works the first time, the second time around you think this is a working formula because this audience appreciates it.

Like rock singers who the fans want to sound just like their hits . . .

LR: . . .then you start writing for that audience, and that audience starts determining your view of the world and how you present yourself. There's no chance for growth there.

Do you feel positive about the future of oral poetry?

IM: I do have some hope. Even if I can pass away now, I will die with the hope that in the coming generation in South Africa, a new language will be born. When one has a positive approach one can see that with isicamtho a new language *will* be born. Even though I can resign and say I want to resign, and no more writing and sit and start enjoying vetcakes, somebody will take my lines and appreciate that positively, and then that will help to bring together a new language.

LR: I don't know about this cliché of the sky being the limit to whatever, I don't want to see the sky as any limit, I want to go beyond that sky, that's it – the sky can be the limit for whoever wants to see the sky as the limit, I want to go beyond it, I don't think there are any limits. I've got my own sky that resides within myself and I want to punch a hole through it, and go beyond that, the better for me to get to know myself.

142

Interviewed by Robert Berold

DONALD PARENZEE was born in Cape Town in 1948. He has worked as a community development architect and lecturer in architecture. He has also been a cultural activist, organiser of theatre productions, and teacher of creative writing at COSAW. Currently he works as a curator at the District Six Museum in Cape Town.

Books of poems published:
Driven to Work (Ravan, 1985)
No Free Sleeping (with Alan Finlay and Vonani Bila)(Botsotso Publishing, 1998)

How did you get involved with poetry?

I trained as an architect and that training happened slowly, over a long period, it goes back decades, from the late 60s through to the 70s. I qualified only in 1984, and in the years between I digressed into all kinds of other things. In 1970 I was working in the South Peninsula Educational Fellowship (SPEF), a cultural organisation which was part of what is now known as the New Unity Movement. I was still a student at the time, working in an architect's office, sporadically, and going back to study and so on. That's where I got involved with poetry. I started reading a lot of poets and doing things such as working with high school students, devising poetry readings combined with music, on a regular basis. I was already beginning to play around with mixing sound, slides, texts. For example we did something on Vietnam – we took a book which was a series of letters, and then we did it as a reading. I read up on Vietnam and took slides out of books and put the whole thing together and presented that. In SPEF I was very fortunate because I got involved in all the poetry recitals – and that was good for me. I read mainly poetry translations – Eastern European, Russian, South American, Greek poetry. I didn't really get into English poetry very much at that stage.

Where did you hear about these poets?

Dawood Parker was a mentor. He was very supportive. He had bookshelves covering the walls of his flat. He knew his music, he accessed all the new publications and was building a library. He introduced us to all these things. I could visit and use this library at any time, into the early hours of the morning, take home stacks of books and just bore through them. I got interested in Neruda, Brecht, Ritsos, Hikmet . . . socialist poets. I was surrounded by socialist politics, so the politics and the poetry were aspects of the same thing in a way.

143

The poetics of these writers was different from what was going on in South African poetry at that time. The poets you mentioned wrote with a lot of imagistic detail and sensual texture.

I just intuitively went and read, I mean I had no contact with local poets or anything like that. I just wrote, and it just came out, I didn't think much about what I was doing. I didn't actually think of myself as a poet. If anything, I thought of myself as a performer of other poets' works. We were all performers. It was about making a space, a space for that cultural activity to happen. We would work in a group, around a tape recorder. I would make my selection out of a stack of books, type the poems out, then we would just read around. Then people would say "OK, I'll take this one, that one." Then we'd read. And then we'd critique each other's reading. We'd do that for about two weeks, a kind of rehearsal, and then it would end up in a performance. We'd set up the stage and lighting, handle the advertising as well, design notices and flyers and so on . . .

It was about creating a space . . .

Remember that spaces for any kind of gathering – to say nothing of political gatherings – were completely closed down in the early 70s. You couldn't even speak over the phone without disguising your language. The security branch was all-powerful. They were looming in the background all the time. They used to visit Dawood's flat regularly, so we had to be very careful about how we moved because it could all be wiped out. I had to be very careful about the words, the poems, the images, on posters or flyers, things sent in the post.

Were there any poems that you felt were too dangerous to be circulated?

Not poems, but some images. Round about '76, with the student rebellion, there was this photograph that had been taken of students with banners saying 'Release the Detainees' walking in the school grounds. We were going to use this picture in a poster advertising a poetry reading, but then we decided, for security reasons, to censor that poster ourselves and make that part of the art. We blocked out the words, so you didn't know what the banners were saying – you saw the picture of these students walking. The artist got angry, saying we had defaced his work, we had censored his work. So we took that contention, that difficulty, into the work itself. I'm still not sure whether that was the correct thing to do. Today I'd say no, you can't do that. But then it was as if we were in prison, it was a real state of siege. This was a period when rebellion was going on – the ice was breaking. There was a tendency for people to think "Well so what, let's say it", you know, especially younger people.

What was happening in your own poems at that time? Did any of them appear in Driven to Work?

144

Quite a few of them. A lot of them were written as a direct response to those particular days, like "Origins", "Now To Begin", "Then The Children Decided" – all written as immediate responses to particular events and moments. I think "Origins" was written when I was staying in Retreat in 1976. There was teargas around and this is why you get these things in the poem. You got stopped by guys with FN rifles in the street who make you open the boot and stuff like that, just around the corner from your home. It was also all tied up with what was happening to me in my personal life, in my inner life at that moment, the tensions and the stresses happening there and also my ideas, and readings. You sit down and you write this poem in which the imagery gets drawn from all these sources, a broader sphere which comes into the words as they come out onto the page.

So the words don't necessarily make sense to you as you write?

The words just come out, the title comes – "Origins" – now what the hell, what was that? – and then the next one, and then the next one, and the next one . . . but as it comes out, you start shaping it. I've always written like that. Generally the way I work is kind of semi-conscious. I wouldn't say it's not done with intention – but all these poems, they're words that come out and place themselves on the paper. And then they take shape and meaning within different contexts. When I read the poem to people it adds – it gives the poem other levels, more layers of meaning. The poem grows and I receive these meanings back. Maybe a particular poem looks quite sharp and knife-like, in the way it turns down and twists in. But my sense at the time of writing it was that of a spontaneous kind of blur, a sense of putting out things. The farthest back I can remember is writing a composition in Standard 2 – it was a similar way of writing, not writing with a lot of thinking about what I was doing.

So you weren't working within any conscious aesthetic?

I never worked in the aesthetic of poetry only, or of architecture only. I've always worked in parallel fields and bridged across them and hopped from one to the other. Poetry and architecture are two very demanding, jealous disciplines. I find I have to work in one and then I neglect the other one – then of course then I have to move to the other one and I leave that one. Later along the way I got involved in photography. In SPEF I had started working with slides, images and texts – using them in presentations. That's similar to what I'm working on now.

What are you doing now?

Well two years ago, I met an artist from Oxford and we decided to collaborate – sending work to each other – visual work, words, messages. The project is called *In Transit*. She has come to work with me in Cape Town, and I've been to work with her in her home city, Oxford. We also met up in Malta and worked together there, responding to the place and its people, its materials. Mostly we use found materials, a lot of the time we use waste materials. We've used the documents of our lives too – photographs, posters, poems. We've now decided to work separately for the next two years, communicating, but minimally. And then have an exhibition.

So you're poet, architect, photographer and artist?

Some people meet me and they say "Oh you're a poet" and then other people will meet me and they don't know anything about my poetry and they see me as a lecturer. Or they see me as an architect. They know nothing about the other sides of my creativity, my identity.

This feeling of not being a professional poet or architect, does it bother you?

Not any more. It used to. You know, if you're a professional, you read the magazines, you must keep up in your field. But now I see a movement, people are rising up above their fields – it's happening all over the world. People who've been trained as architects, geographers, psychologists, artists, theorists, historians, they're sort of lifting themselves out of that embedded discipline, and beginning to say "OK well, now we're going to do it like this, we're not going to be confined by notions of professionalism." And this is why creativity is so important.

What is the difference between production work and creative work?

A lot of the creative energies within us or around us are automatically suppressed as we go through the systems of family life and socialisation. And this seems the same all over the world. I think we are now at a point where one has got to look for ways of opening that up. Of allowing people to be creative. Its a kind of healing.

How does that articulate with your politics? Global capitalism, the extreme form of what Marx called monopoly capitalism, oppresses people because of the omnipresence of images. TV is the narcotic of this image overload, and South Africa imports the most mind-numbing of TV. How do you fight it?

We are living in an environment where every utterance, your every expression, your intuitive expression of your own imagination, can be immediately caught and channelled. And then it becomes a political act to engage with that. One way you can engage is by entering into those structures, those hierarchies, those frameworks, and using their language. You can't go and dream off and send people letters about your dreams. You've got to write them letters within the language that they understand. One has got to engage with organisational structures, that seems evident. At the same time one really has to find a way of working outside and around those structures.

How did you experience working in cultural organisations? You worked in COSAW for several years.

146

My image of COSAW was of pylons of organisational hierarchies planted in among organic forms. The economic energy and the political impulses came down from the top. My experience of our creative work in COSAW was like organic forms growing around the legs of the organisational pylons. They become almost unseen, sometimes invisible and sometimes not.

How do you deal with the pressures of bureaucracy in your architectural work?

With difficulty. My particular kind of work has been designing buildings for communities. Because the budgets are low, one is forced to concentrate on basic structures. So the aesthetics tend to be sidelined by all the variables – the budget, the structures inside of communities, the way money is channelled through, the culture of the very people that you're serving, what they want, how their briefs come across, all kinds of things. You might have the awareness, but the opportunity to implement it is very, very limited.

So what do you do?

You innovate as much as you can. You find ways of redefining the aesthetics. For instance when I first started at Community Projects Office (CPO – a unit within the Peninsula Technikon), I had to design a community centre at Ebenhaeser, a community about 400km up the west coast. I struggled for a long time to find the design. What I eventually came up with was something that was, in architectural terms, a structuralist approach, although my natural tendency is more organic, even expressionist. In the end I had to turn that impulse around. I had to design something that would be buildable by a community in training, that is, a community learning to build in the process of building. So it became a number of separate pieces that repeated themselves over and over again. I had to perceive the building as it came up out of the ground, bearing in mind that people were learning to work with the material as the construction proceeded. I couldn't just hand over the plans and say "OK, this is the form that a community centre should take." I had to think of the process and that affected the overall design.

Presumably you would need a good knowledge of the community and of the skills available.

Well, unless you live inside of it, you never know the community really. It's not about knowing, knowing is not always possible. Sometimes you only meet the leaders of the community. Often it's a few men sitting on top deciding that they've got this big dream and then it never happens. Eventually you evolve a kind of sixth sense where you have a feeling about something and you know which projects to go to and which projects not to go to. You get toughened up because you get hurt quite a lot. Your imaginative fervour and your dreams get sort of torn up, and you have to make a collage to put it together again.

Your poems seem to be inspired by a sense that life goes on. If the way is blocked, instead of getting yourself fixated, you start looking for other ways.

Well, if a river runs down a hill and there's a rock, the river will move around it and carve out bits of geography, physical geography. That's the way things work. There's no moral rightness or wrongness about it, it's just the way things happen. Human beings are destroying the planet, you know, because of this other way of doing things, this notion that you work from a fixed belief and implement that belief. You often find that that belief is shattered in the way things turn out. Or otherwise it destroys things. Especially in an area like Cape Town or the Cape Flats, you can't go into a place thinking that everything is just going to float into being. You've got to assert and to enforce sometimes and twist people's arms to get things done. But in writing poems, you're in a relatively free space. You're not working with bricks and mortar and concrete.

So in poetry, being a freer space than architecture, it is easier to express ideas?

Poetry is shaped as much by emotions as ideas. After I'd written *Driven to Work* I began to see what was happening in my writing. It was like a weaving, you know, the way these poems work. A weaving of ideas in emotion. Some of them go under and some go over. Poems like "Detention" are very tightly woven. In others the feeling is a little bit looser, and it goes through the sun in the sky and the sea. Some of them are quite dense and almost meaningless when you look at them, but when you pick up on one thread and follow it, it goes underground, under the meaning and it comes up elsewhere again. That's the sense I have of it.

Thinking back, how did you find working in COSAW?

Being inside COSAW was a very rich experience. There were these creativity workshops that we were doing. It also happened in Natal with the Culture for Working Life project. And then it sort of spread around. That kind of activity was very, very interesting. It was a free-flowing approach to work. COSAW was a writers' organisation, but in workshops we would work through and between the other arts as well. We worked with music, with colour, movement and so on. In the 80s there were lots of interesting cultural understandings and practices. It was a culture of people working with each other rather than this other notion of work as a competitive ethos. People treating each other in a particular way, with grace and with gentleness, and not competing for the idea or the outcome or that kind of thing.

Driven to Work was very much about being hemmed in by apartheid. How do you understand it now?

Apartheid was never really the whole thing for me, it wasn't what I was writing about really. It was more about imprisonment or enclosure. Apartheid was not an exceptional situation. That's why the poets we were reading in the 70s had such relevance for us. They were living under oppressive conditions in Greece, in Chile, in Eastern Europe. It was the norm, an oppressive norm.

How is it different now?

Well a certain layer of restrictions have been removed. There's more freedom of movement, we're in a more normal democracy. But ironically, it is totally different, a very sharp break – a closing down of that growing ethos of the 80s, quite horrible in that respect. There's a lot of pain about being creative. I find also that the moments of the most brilliance are the moments of the most terror. And the 90s in South Africa has been a period like that, where a lot of people have felt the pain and the terror. Because we all had to go through changes and transitions, in a very sharp kind of watershed.

The internal psychological effects of apartheid and capitalism are now more obvious?

Now that apartheid has been removed, there's a popular tendency to believe we're living in a free society, which we're not. Society is driven, basically, by the same economic structures as before. People have become much more aware of just how repressed their psyches have been, and it's been quite a shock. But there is hardly any redress for this through political structures. So the inner liberation of the individual becomes the responsibility of the individual. And that's a very difficult thing to do. This territory is very much the terrain of the artist or the creative person.

The 90s haven't felt like 10 years, have they?

For me it just went by like that – shoo! – because I was in a dark space. And my sense is that a lot of other people have been going through that. It's been a spiralling down, and then having to find a level somewhere and then get out of it again. And it's still happening. It's a psychological adjustment that I had to make, from the notion that one could take over the power of the state, that one could claim power, in that box over there – and then everything will be OK, you know. When you get to a point where you realise that you are actually powerless, you either go and kill yourself or otherwise you find a way of accepting that powerlessness. Without being a nonentity, still maintaining your dignity and respect. And still doing something of value somehow. That happens when you go down to the bottom and then you begin building up bit by bit. People look at you as if you're nothing, even if two years ago you were a national leader.

Most people are reluctant to go down to the bottom.

Well people go down to different levels – or people find their levels. The early 90s was about political restructuring. Some people didn't actually go down very far. They just repositioned themselves.

Turning now to No Free Sleeping, *how did it come together?*

I never thought that I had a book until Allan Horwitz came and spoke to me about Botsotso publishing it. Then I got into the process of working and then it came out like this. As with the first book, it's only when you're asked to read it here and there that you actually begin to see its value. A lot of these poems were written individually for particular occasions. And they had impact at some point – like that one "For Ralton" for instance. That's a strange poem actually, because it's a bit archaic in the way it's using language.

Well it's an elegy, and the elegiac mode is slower.

You know, he was a young 17 year old when I met him – he was in the Oaklands Band at Oaklands High School – around 1985, dancing on platforms, singing about all kinds of things – freeing Mandela and all that. And then he went into the ANC and he worked in the pre-election phase and then he became totally disillusioned after that, I think. I don't know, I can't say for certain because I lost touch with him – and then I met him here and there and I noticed this difference. The next thing you hear the guy hanged himself. The poem was a story of a young guy and it reverberated through a whole range of people here in Cape Town. Then they had a commemoration here in Salt River – Community House – and the place was packed with people. So in a way he touched a lot of people's lives. His death shook people up.

And the poem "One Day" – how did that come about?

I was with this guy. We went to Copenhagen together. He was quite a character, talkative. We were driving the car one day going from one point to another chatting and it just came up by the way, that he had been tortured. And I said "But you! I mean, who would've thought that you'd been tortured?" I'd experienced this before, in Ovamboland once, there was a guy there also. You find out the horrible stories of what happened with Koevoet and so on, but you don't see it on people's faces or in their manner. You don't see it. People have a kind of grace. Well, the stories come out. Later on this same guy kept on doing crazy things. Later I heard he just went off the track.

Despite the 15-year gap between your two books, they are both about liberation. What is your sense of liberation now?

We received a particular framework of liberation, a political framework, you know, in the sense of taking over the power of the state. It is a 19th century notion that influences us so profoundly. While I have never found it necessary to throw out a basic materialist framework, my understanding of liberation has grown to include the multiplicity and fluidity of things. In one's living experiences, you respond to the realities that are happening around you. Eventually what one comes to is that one is very physically, sensually involved with the world. And that includes one's thoughts, and one's ideas and one's skin – things that you breathe. The world consists of energies. And these energies transform and translate themselves. We work, we live, we are energy fields – we are within energy fields and the things we do are packages of energy that we put out.

Interviewed by Robert Berold

VONANI BILA, born 1972, is the founder and editor of the poetry journal *Timbila*, and directs the Timbila Poetry Project in Limpopo province. He works as coordinator of the Limpopo NGO Coalition and edits the newspaper Community Gazette. He has written eight story books in English and Xitsonga for newly literate adult readers.

Books of poems published:
No Free Sleeping (with Alan Finlay and Donald Parenzee)(Botsotso Publishing, 1998)

Who is Vonani Bila?

I'm a hard-working, sound and sober poet with a long heart, on the side of the poor masses of South Africa/Azania. I'm the fifth son in a family of eight children.

I live at Shirley Village at Elim in the Northern Province, a community of about 10 000 people. Most live below the bread line. Poverty has become a way of life. Shirley has all the features of a neglected rural village: electricity is here and there but it flies away when it is windy or raining. People don't have water. Water is priority number one, two and three. Unemployment is about 60%.

Shirley was a missionary village where men and women were forced to accept Christianity against their will, shedding away African traditional practices such as tsima (spirit of working together and communalism) ngoma (male circumcision ritual) and vukhomba (female circumcision ritual) and other socially-meaningful practices. The missionaries (vaneri) were nasty people who pretended to be good. They grabbed large pieces of the land, condemned chieftainship since it threatened their power, and employed local people, including children, to work on farms and paid them peanuts. They levied tax upon the people of my village.

When did you start reading poetry?

It was in the 1980s when I was schooling at Lemana High School, one of the so-called better schools in the Gazankulu homeland. Lemana had black and white teachers – each with separate staff rooms. I came into contact with poetry while I was doing Standard 7. Of course at primary school we memorised poems like "My skiete jag", "Amakeya", "Xisiwana", "Twinkle, twinkle little star", without understanding anything of those poems.

When did you start reading African poets?

152

Only later, when I read Ingoapele Madingoane. I just loved his poetry, it was so moving, full of energy. I was born before the vibrant poetry of the seventies – in 1976 I was four years old – but I was inspired that Madingoane was brave enough to go forthright with that kind of poetry in such turbulent times. I read Mongane Serote, Oswald Mtshali, Mafika Gwala, Rashaka Ratshitanga, Dennis Brutus and other committed poets of this land. But more than that, I later read Caribbean poets like Edward Kamau Brathwaite, and Jean Goulbourne, embracing powerful lines like "This is the place where the dog/ eat the garbage so clean/ the poor stomach in pain."

My passion for poetry grew. It inspired some teachers at Lemana High School to recognise my work and offer me a class to teach poetry. This is the time I shared some of my early poems with my classmates. My friend Justice Ndabani would always be available to type out my poems, before sending them to publishing companies.

How were your books received by the publishers?

Between 1987 and 1990 I wrote three collections of poems in Xitsonga (Shangaan) – *Ntumbuluko, A hi Maxuxu* and *Vutlhokovetseri bya Vutlhokovetseri*. After waiting for two to three years, I got letters spelling out that the poetry market is over-flooded, that there was lack of money to pay for the printing of these books. My spirit was somehow dampened. I also wrote a collection of Xitsonga short stories, *Vutomi bya Hlambanyisiwa* (Life is Retold) which was conditionally accepted for publication, but then turned down. So I stopped writing in Xitsonga for a while, and tried my luck in English. I didn't really dream that I'd one day write a poem in English, given that I never schooled at a Model C school. I have always doubted my English, I felt it was too embarrassing.

How did you feel about leaving Tsonga literature behind?

Of course I felt sad, it's my home language. The Xitsonga poetry that I enjoyed reading were books like *Mihloti* by J.M. Magayisa, the political poetry called *Mbita ya Vulombe* by Zinjiva Nkondo who was in exile at the time, *Khanikhojo* by the celebrated and prolific B. J. Masebenza, *Vumunhu bya Phatiwa* by M. M. Marhanele and anthologies such as *Madaladala* and *Switshongo*. But I must also mention the drought of good Xitsonga books. There are probably less than 500 books of Xitsonga fiction and poetry.

Xitsonga and Siswati are the most endangered of South African languages. Our languages are being forced to die slowly. For instance, right now I'm attending the stocktaking conference of the SABC. I just learned today that there's a move to privatise the radio, meaning that languages like Xitsonga, Siswati and Venda which are regarded as so small are just going to die because the radio's the most accessible communication medium in rural areas.

When you left school in 1990, police crackdowns, student uprisings and detentions were still happening everywhere . . . what were your politics?

I just couldn't find a political home. For me the question was – we need rural development. The politics we were discussing were not so relevant to the situation in our village. I felt very isolated even though I belonged to the Shirley Youth Congress, which was part of South African Youth Congress.

But you kept reading and writing . . .

I ended up going to Tivumbeni College of Education at Nkowankowa to do a Secondary Teachers Diploma. Most people knew me at Tivumbeni because of my poetry, which I would read whenever there was a mass meeting called by the SRC. I performed my poems like "Flames of Uhuru," "Reality an' Vision" and other works by poets such as Sandile Ngidi who wrote the poem "The Halitosis of Reform", Benjamin Zephaniah who wrote "Man Woman Come Together" and "Modern Slavery", and Sandile Dikeni's "Guava Juice". People started calling me De Dum Dum, De Gish Gish, De Bom Bom. Others called me Man Woman Come Together. Most called me Uhuru after the poetry performance group I formed after attending Theatre for Development workshop at the Africa Cultural Centre.

Were you getting published?

It was at Tivumbeni that I celebrated my 21st birthday with my first publication – *The Open Door Omnibus*, published from Cape Town, included my longest poem, "Reality an' Vision". I showed the poem to friends and everyone at home, including my mother who was unable to read or write. It was like a new baby for a new couple. I will always treasure that moment. I thank Karen Press, the Cape Town poet who was so patient with me, responding to each and every letter that I wrote to Buchu Books. Other poets who motivated me to write included Allan Kolski Horwitz of Botsotso Publishing, yourself as editor of *New Coin* and Maano Tuwani – a poet who runs a community book service, Guyo Books, in Northern Province. Maano exposed me to a range of critical literature like Ali Mazrui, Franz Fanon and the poetry of *Staffrider*, New Contrast and other journals. After the college was indefinitely closed, I participated in a six week long Organisational Development Workshop at Akanani. It was an interesting course that involved more than 60 people from all over the country. We built a hall and a garden during that time. Drama and poetry were used as instruments to communicate issues of leadership, management and organisational dynamics.

After this I spent the whole year working at Akanani as a gardener, wearing a brown overall and police boots given by my brother. This was the time for me to practise all that I had learnt during the six weeks. It was great to earn an income of R300 a month, to go to town every month and buy groceries. Of course it was too little, but I

154

had never earned such an income in my life. When my father died in 1989, he was only getting four hundred and something rand a month at the Elim Hospital after working for more than 30 years as a cleaner.

Akanani was a politically active NGO, did it not shape your political consciousness?

It did, but I never believed in the ANC political agenda. I was inspired more by learning that one of the boys I grew up with, Rhulani, had joined MK while he was in Soweto. I took a passport and told my mother that if she looked around and did not see me, I will be in Lusaka – doing combat work under MK, fighting for my country. I wanted to kill oppressors and apartheid demagogues. I wanted to fuel war against Boers who forced my father to die of a curable disease. But my dream to join MK was not realised.

You channelled your anger into poetry. "Comrades Don't We Delude Ourselves" is one of the most outspoken political poems of the 90s . . .

This is a poem about the masses whose struggle has been betrayed by loathsome loudmouth fat cat politicians who live in villas and drive bombastic estate cars with a wheel at the back. It is a poem that catalogues the poverty that grinds the people of Elim. It asks why is the left too weak? It is written in a province rife with racism, where farmers in Levubu let dogs to rip Mrs Sambo's stomach open; where a 17 year old boy is forced to eat his own excrement by brutish commandos at Potgietersrus.

In what way do you see Black Consciousness now?

I was always attracted to keeping BC and/or African Consciousness relevant and alive, BC as expounded by socialist visionaries like Steve Biko, Kambarage Nyerere of Tanzania, Sekou Toure, Leopold Senghor, Ben Bella, Gamal Abdel of Egypt, Samora Mashele of Mozambique, and poet Amiri Baraka. The major shortcoming of Black Consciousness in South Africa is that it is now being rejected by the very people it freed. These are people who are presently running big corporations and government. It is further clouded by this notion that we are all equal, when in reality the whites have material resources and the blacks, especially the rural folk, the disabled, women and youth are still locked up in poverty prison. But the political parties who were supposed to build a BC vanguard are more interested in power now. My critique of Black Consciousness was its assumptions that all white people are the same. And it also presented black people as a homogeneous community which is wrong, black people are very different.

Would you say the ANC government has adopted a hostile attitude towards Black Consciousness?

Yes, and this is an unforgivable crime. The ANC left poet Ingoapele Madingoane to die in poverty despite his being one of the foremost poets who inspired and fuelled revolution in the 70s. If we are serious about rewriting the history of this country, the ANC-led government must honour Mothopeng, Mahlathini, Sobukwe, Es'kia Mphahlele, Jackson Hlungwani and all who contributed to South Africa's liberation cause through art and gunpowder. Come 1999 – The People Have Spoken, said Thabo Mbeki. Where are the jobs for all, health care for all, land, clean water and decent education? The roads are unpassable, have become dongas. Even roads in Pietersburg where some of our leaders live, are so terrible – but the leaders talk of tourism. Is it the people who have spoken, or big business? The struggle was lost in CODESA, even before CODESA, in exile when people studied orthodox economics. We were sold out by people whom we profoundly trusted. We have lost the Freedom Charter, RDP and liberation values and now some dupes who regard themselves as our leaders worship the IMF, WTO and World Bank.

So who are your political role models?

My political heroes are people who have really worked hard, like the rural activist Tshepo Khumbane. I read so much about all the work she's done for the people in her community. She influenced me seriously. And ordinary women and men who stayed in my village all their lives. How can these people manage to make a living in such a dry situation? They inspired me to make a conscious decision to live in the village, do things for the people, live simply and achieve all the great things for the people. Of course I wouldn't say I'm a hundred percent in the village because I work in Pietersburg but I always make sure that I live in the villages and take the struggles of ordinary people forward. We've just formed the Movement for Delivery which is a peasant kind of movement to push for the right kind of development in these areas, make sure that there's water. The way for activists now is to strengthen civil society movements, to challenge government's failure to spend more resources for poverty eradication, its willingness to pay apartheid debt, hold it accountable, ensure transparency.

Sexual issues often come up in your work. In your poem "Dahl Street" this theme comes together with your economic/political critique, in the figure of the prostitute.

A feature of my work is the image of woman. I love an African woman with laden breasts – she is a queen. An elephant woman who walks tall. She must be honoured. She carries the burden of rural poverty. She also carries the hopes and aspirations of the nation. This is epitomised in a poem like "Give me love, Rwanda". I also use the image of a woman, especially the prostitute, to gauge the pace of socio-political change and transformation in our country. Often it's embarrassing to write about prostitutes, but perhaps the duty of the poet is to ask embarrassing questions, to express deepest analysis and feelings regarding the extent of development in our country.

156

In most places that I've been – be it Elim Bar Lounge, Loa Hotel at Acornhoek, some derelict shebeen at Dahl Street or Flying High Night Club in Pietersburg where girls drink and dance almost naked on the dance floor of smashed beer bottles and cigarette stumps; be it the Little Rose, Hotel International, Jabula ngo busuku, Diplomat, Maxim, Mark Hotel in Johannesburg where young and old women alike compete over clients, or inner city of Durban and its beach hotels, or Earlside in Harare – I have seen prostitutes locked up in drugs, beer and anguish. My heart bleeds when I see rich and famous men buy prostitutes – our sisters, wives, our children and mothers. Then I ask myself: do our leaders care? I dance on the dance floor with beautiful girls, be it Hillbrow or Pietersburg – and I feel like crying when I think of the suffering, agony and anguish these stripping women and girls are forced to go through because of failing neo-liberal economic policies which our right-wing government fully endorses.

How do you see sex in this age of AIDS?

The most precious, engaging, fulfilling and electric activity has become a millennium bug. It makes me scared when I think of all the pain humanity is going through. A close friend of mine is HIV-positive. She recounted her ordeal when we were about to make love. It's a polluted well. No more free and safe sex; no more free state, no more free drinkable water. Our freedom has been poisoned, drugged, bugged.

You have a strong tendency to go for the texture of things, to evoke the senses. Like in the Dahl Street poem one gets hit by a wave of urine, grease, food and booze.

I like descriptive poetry, I just feel it's so strong if people can smell it and touch it and feel it and it creates a real picture in their minds, that for me is good poetry when you can see the actual image. This is what I admire in the Caribbean poets. I listen to them performing their work because of the strength of their voice, for instance Mutabaruka, I just see all the images whether they are carried through by his voice or on paper I just see these images. Caribbean poetry has influenced me with its strong emphasis on rhythm and visual aspects.

Why did you start your poetry journal Timbila?

Timbila is a musical instrument that is often played by the Vacopi, a group of Vatsonga-Machangani people in Mozambique. This was the instrument my late father used to play. I appreciated African music through listening to my father strumming this finger harp. When my father died in 1989, I broke the chords of his timbila. Now I'm calling this publication *Timbila* as a tribute to a loving father who made me what I am with little financial resources. He instilled in me love for the arts and I know he is the happiest man wherever he is because he has fathered a poet.

The second edition of *Timbila* will be out in early 2001 and will feature more than 30 fertile poets. It will be dedicated to my friend who suffered from depression, Letsoba wa ga Mamadi, a poet who was stabbed to death by a street kid across Dahl Street in Pietersburg in March this year. I will include his poem "Filling the Hollow Feeling", which he submitted just two weeks before his death. At his funeral, which was attended by more than 4000 people, I was given time to speak about him since he was the person who gave me shelter when I came to Pietersburg in 1998.

How do you find the energy to write, edit a poetry journal, a newspaper, and do your NGO work ?

I work for the Northern Province NGO Coalition (Nongoco) as Co-ordinator and there are more than 150 member NGOs, bringing joy and pain. These organisations expect me to somehow be their voice and be the voice of reason. I have to balance my interests as a poet and those of the Coalition and it's not easy.

I write two lines, I go to a meeting, I write more lines, I go to another meeting. It's just not good for a young poet because I've not written a single poem in the past six months. Come Friday and Saturday I just go to nightclubs and dance the whole night to relieve stress. My eyes meet poems, my ears listen to thrilling stories in nightclubs but I can't write a single poem about all I experience through my travels, work and night life. It's not good for a poet, for his duty is to cough poems out of his chest or breasts. I feel like I'm betraying my own poetry. I feel that my bones are tired, my mind so numb, so exhausted. I'm burnt out already.

Why can't South African literature have 10 or 20 small magazines?

The National Arts Council must stop ridiculing journals with meagre grants of R10 000 to R20 000. You can't call that funding. Without adequate funding for the development and promotion of poetry, this country will remain without a soul. A shell. Existing magazines such as *Timbila, Kotaz, Fidelities, Botsotso, New Coin, HerStoria, Carapace, Tyume* and *TurfWrite* must substantially be funded, perhaps enter into agreement with these magazines for five years. We need to read more than fifty new poetry books published in a year and funded by the NAC, PANSALB and other bodies created to support the arts. Just one anthology, three poetry books and one poetry CD are not what this country needs. We need more! We need funding for weekly readings of poetry, in live venues and on the radio. We need poetry in all public toilets or shall I say poetry scribbled on the walls of our public grey toilets must be recorded? If government can spend billions to buy fighter planes, submarines, corvettes and helicopters – things that are not priorities – it can spend more on the infrastructure and resources needed to grow poetry and the arts. Funding must not only go to big names. All this is possible if there is political will, ardent and cultivated leadership.

Before you burn out, do you have any poetry plans?

My new project is *For the Ear*, a book of my poems, followed by a visual exhibition of illustrated poems as well as music with words. It will be a collection of all my works. I play an acoustic guitar so I've got a sense of the kind of music that will move my poetry but I also think of working with other musicians.

My big dream is to organise a network of poets. This network would be controlled by poets themselves, and its ultimate aim would be to support local talent. We need commitment to make this dream happen. The network would organise readings and study groups in communities where poets and readers and critics and other people can meet regularly and share poetry. It would organise intensive poetry writing workshops throughout the country to sharpen the skills of poets and create opportunities for publishing, and to host poetry readings throughout the country in restaurants, shopping malls, community halls, stations, pubs. Poetry everywhere and anytime!

Interviewed by Joan Metelerkamp

ROBERT BEROLD was born in Johannesburg in 1948. He worked for many years in rural development NGOs, and edited practical handbooks such as *People's Workbook* (1981) and *The Southern African Chicken Book* (1999). From 1989 to 1999 he edited the poetry journal *New Coin*, from which he compiled the anthology *It All Begins: poems from postliberation South Africa*. He now works as a writer, writing teacher, and editor of technical books. With Paul Wessels, he publishes Deep South Books.

Books of poems published:
The Door to the River (Bateleur, 1984)
The Fires of the Dead (Carrefour, 1989)
Rain Across a Paper Field (Gecko Poetry, 1999)

When did you start getting interested in poetry?

When I was at school I had a kind of epiphany. I was not particularly interested in poetry until I was studying for matric, when one poem – it was Milton's "Lycidas" – suddenly came alive for me. It was like the universe opening up – I could hear these symphonic sounds. I didn't know what the poem meant, and I didn't even care, I could feel its power and its beauty. I read it over and over again until I memorised it. There was nothing in my English classes which had prepared me for an experience like this.

So then you went to university with this . . .

I went to university, but, you know, emotionally I was very infantile, about two years old, though I had a reasonably convincing adolescent mask. I was studying engineering, but another part of me was very confused, whirling around in my unconscious, which I tried to anchor in poetry.

Did you talk about poetry to other people?

Yes and no. I wrote poems (poems I was reading, not my own, I hardly wrote anything then) on the white tiles of my bathroom. It was, as I said, an anchor in an unsafe world. I read poems to Denis Hirson, who was my next door neighbour, and to my girlfriend, who I was trying hard to turn into my muse. I was out of touch with the 'real world', but what was the real world? In the white suburbs where we grew up, the undercurrent of violence was never far away. The police would raid the backyards and my parents said nothing. We were living a lie and nobody was telling the truth. But poetry, like the Lorca I found in the Hirsons' vast bookshelves next door, was telling me a truth I wanted to know about. Just the ring of the authentic voice. I memorised poems and repeated them to myself, like mantras. Most of the time I didn't know what they meant, I just wanted them in my life.

Were you ashamed of your involvement? I mean, it feels as if this were some clandestine activity . . .

It was – a secret life where I could feel my feelings. I knew it was something linked to a deep need in me. At Wits University I wandered into some English poetry lectures and thought – this has little to do with my experience of poetry. Ezra Pound wrote that a book should be like a ball of light in the reader's hands. That made more sense to me. I spent hours in the Johannesburg Public Library going through the poetry section. That's where I discovered William Carlos Williams, George Seferis, and Arthur Rimbaud.

You were lucky to find what you were looking for.

Not really, I knew what I was looking for, which was the intoxicating experience of being transported by a poem. I knew very quickly if a poem gave me that experience. I read essays poets wrote about each other, that guided my reading. After a few years of this, I'd become immersed in modernism. Later, in psychotherapy, I traced these searches to my own story. Perhaps it was not such an unusual story. I came from a family where there wasn't much love, but I was nurtured by a black woman. She was there consistently, from when I was born right up to my student days and beyond. When I was a baby she carried me on her back, and gave me a lot of warmth. I shared her food as she chatted to her friends sitting on the street corner. She wasn't a complete mother, she couldn't be, because she couldn't stand up for me against my parents, but she saved my life. I have a vivid memory of being strapped to her back, with her and another woman ironing clothes and singing, Sotho hymns vibrating through me, the smell of the iron, the highveld winter sun streaming through the kitchen. It was safety and bliss, which I have always associated with song and sensual warmth because of her. That survived in me and I nourished it with poetry.

I spent a long time in my adult life searching for that warm place, in poetry, in music and in relationships with women. Modernism gave me music. I was very attracted to musical poems, like Eliot's *Four Quartets*, Pound's *Cantos*, and most of William Carlos Williams, even though I couldn't really follow the arguments of the poems.

You might have come to the poems through music, but by the time you'd memorised them, you'd got to the meaning, in your own way.

Yes, the meaning was registering somewhere, but I trusted the music. It helped me to get into Pound's *Cantos*. However obscure *The Cantos* were, their music was not obscure.

Why didn't you take up music yourself?

I had some traumatic experiences. One was my father smashing my guitar to pieces because I was playing it while he was talking on the phone. Poetry was safer, it was dismissed as harmless I suppose. It was silent. Its power was a secret. It was a lifeline for me which I didn't want anyone to tamper with.

And these days?

These days it's different. I'm not so split. I'm mostly free of my prison. The music and the meaning (whatever that means) happen together for me. I can live my poetry out in the open. And I've finally got over my music traumas, I'm learning to play accoustic bass.

I'm involved at the moment with discovering myself as a jew. My parents denied their judaism, so a whole rich heritage was denied me. But it's there, in my genes and my unconscious. Probably looking to books for the truth is where my judaism surfaces. We are, as Jabés said, people of the book.

Not just the bible . . .

Since I was a student I've been carrying around my own bible, made of poems. It's the gospel according to Vallejo, Jabés, Li Po, Amichai, Tsvetaeva, Sharon Olds and other poets, some of them South Africans. A shifting collection of sacred texts, which has become a mirror for me. Within this the *I Ching* is the central spiritual text – it too is made up of poems or poetic fragments.

You've read an enormous amount in translation.

I started to realise, even at Wits, that the twentieth century had given birth to a huge range of poetic forms. These came out of the shocks of history, the violence of the century. There was very little in English poetry to match the passion and risk-taking of poetry from Spain, Russia, France, Greece, Latin America and Africa. I felt differently about American poetry because Eliot, Pound, Williams were my route into modernist poetry. I find it difficult to read Eliot and Pound now, their conservatism depresses me.

What about Hughes? And Heaney?

Well they just didn't do it for me. Some years later I got into British poets who meant more to me – the Welsh poet David Jones and the Northumbrian poet Basil Bunting, and poets like Tom Pickard and Ken Smith – but again it was still through the music in their poems. Most of the British poetry I found – I don't know —

– too tight? Lacking the breadth of vision you were after?

Yes. There was wider and deeper emotional range in poets from other languages. The Penguin Modern European Poets series, edited by Alvarez, was appearing when I was a student. The volume *Four Greek Poets* — I remember reading it from cover to cover sitting on the lawn at the university. It had Cavafy, Seferis, Elytis and Gatsos in it. It was sensual, surreal and ecstatic, at the same time grounded in the land and in the political realities of Greece.

It's interesting for me that the poems in your first volume The Door to the River *contain elements of both narrative and concentrated image. The narrative isn't a distanced narrative, from an omniscient point of view. Every now and then the pure lyric will emerge – like the poem "angel", from your most recent volume. But even in this frugal, concise imagist poem there is a narrative element: as soon as you mention turning the corner to Claim Street, you're grounded . . .*

I think that Cavafy and Seferis helped me to see the historical and the lyrical together. After Wits I went to Cambridge University, in the early 70s, where I met two American poets, David Lehman and Lawrence Joseph. They were as passionate about poetry as I was. We read poetry furiously to each other. They introduced me to poets I didn't know. Joseph raved to me about St-John Perse and Camus' essays. Lehman had come from Columbia, the New York of Ashbery, Koch, O'Hara, poets who had turned to European rather than American poetry for inspiration. I think my out-of-touchness with reality scared them somewhat. I had a primitive sensual consciousness, even though I felt so deprived. Poetry provided a tenuous link to reality.

In two years there I got just enough distance from South Africa to realise that I had to move out of my trapped world. I started working in NGOs soon after I returned in 1973. That took me across the apartheid line, and once you do that, you can't come back. It was difficult, I didn't belong to white South Africa and I didn't belong to black South Africa either. I just knew somehow that white privilege wasn't worth the psychological distortions that it demanded.

In 1976 I was teaching in Soweto. I was there on 16 June in the hurricane of anger provoked by the police shootings. My life was saved by students from my school who locked me away in the bookroom. They said that if students from other schools saw me, a white person, they'd kill me. That compassion, in the midst of that anger, changed things for me permanently. I felt I would carry on working with black people no matter what. I joined EDA, a small rural development organisation on the margins of the left.

You didn't want to become a political activist?

I was too scared to. But underground politics wasn't for me. Politics is about power, there's no room for confusion. My experience with the white left in the 70s was not happy. They seemed to be so certain of everything. As Jabés wrote in *The Book of Questions* "Do not confuse justice and truth. Justice is done in the name of truth. And truth remains to be found."

I remember reading Rimbaud while in England. I came across this line "Men were gentle because they were strong". This one sentence gave me a lot. To understand that there was another kind of maleness, one that was stronger than the bullying egocentric kind. Of course, I still haven't got rid of the patriarchy in myself, even now.

How did you respond to South African poetry at that time?

To me the criterion was – and still is – is the line memorable? You cannot say that you like a poem and not remember a single line of it. In the 70s I found only Gwala did this for me, and Jensma, and Sole's early poems. I'm talking about poems on the page. *Staffrider* appeared on a wave of popular energy, and there were some remarkable poems in it. It came out of a context of township readings, a highly charged cultural activism where political expression was banned. In the 70s Gwala, Serote, Madingoane were forging the language into their own needs. I got to hear and appreciate that angry voice. It was poetry with a living urgency, with a real audience, a living oral tradition being turned into strong political poetry. I heard it because I'd begun to feel connected to the struggle too. But I couldn't really be part of it, it was the black experience. Only much later, in the early 90s, could I think of myself as part of 'we', both as a person and a writer.

When you became a father and a husband, how did it feed into your life and poetry? Your poem "A simple love" explores the problem of a split, it describes how you gave time to poetry by switching off to other people's reality.

I don't think one has to make a choice between poetry and other people, but then, in the mid-70s, I was close to psychosis. I was living between two worlds, and it didn't feel as if I could do much about it. I lived with words and images in my mind all the time in ways that weren't very functional to being a husband and father. I don't feel the same now. I don't see that poetry has to take me away from the world, rather it puts me more into the world – the world becomes more and more a text or an oracle. But then poetry was still a survival mechanism for me, it was unconscious, so I hurt people close to me. I knew I was in trouble, that's why I went into psychotherapy.

How old were you?

I was 30 years old by then, walking around completely involved in poetry but not writing. I'd written about five poems in ten years, yet my identity in my mind was as a poet. I'd met a therapist who I knew could take me on. She lived in Grahamstown. So I moved there. That's where I wrote my first book.

What made you finally sit down and do it?

My therapist asked me a very simple question: If you're a poet, where are the poems? She confronted me with the fact that it was easier going around being a potential poet than writing poems. So I took the risk and experienced the relief of writing, of bridging the distance between my soul and the world. It's very compelling. I worked at it, writing one or two poems a day for about a year. And in the course of that I discovered a lot about form. I was finding out the dimensions of certain experiences.

To make your own connection, on a different level, a level which brings you closer to your own reality: that is the antithesis of psychosis, it is integrating.

César Vallejo was very important to me during that time – I found in him a poet uncompromisingly meeting reality, distorting his own syntax where necessary, a poetic logic so clean that it carried right through his obscurity. I was more and more drawn to poets who were able to go into irrationality, the unconscious. That's where I wanted to go. I knew my truth was in there somewhere.

You didn't have to protect anyone against what was going on in your psyche, so you allowed yourself to be vulnerable.

Yes but I was projecting all kinds of anima and muse stuff. You can't fuck the muse. I've tried: it doesn't work. The muse is a goddess and she will abandon you if you don't respect her. It's an occupational hazard for poets, mesmerised as they can be by beauty. The same with the anima, the inner woman which Jung calls the bridge to the unconscious. The muse murmurs through language, the anima is within. I'll be trying to understand these things for a long time.

When did you know that you were a poet?

It was while I was writing "The Way Back", my first longish poem. The poem was a lyrical story of where I'd been, and at the end I found myself by a river, with the light falling over tall trees, and this heron fishing, bright in the sunlight. The poem ends:

> The heron becomes a storyteller fishing for his embroidered tale.
> The story is bright. He will tell it thread by thread.
> He goes home now. Not to a home, but a gathering.

Not to a home but a gathering – what did it mean? I didn't know, but the words insisted on being exactly those, they just wrote themselves down. It was scary and thrilling and satisfying. It was the first time I'd experienced in my own writing that kind of muse-energised flow.

You said earlier that you preferred Gwala's poetry to Serote's. Perhaps you can say more, it might say something about your poetics.

Well I have a certain attraction to the image and to associative poetry. I've always been less interested in conceptual poetry and in poems that circle round a fixed subject. I liked Serote's early poems because of their articulate anger, but I never found them as striking as Gwala's. For me Gwala got into the texture of things, his work was grounded.

I take a 'grounded image' to mean a reality which we recognise immediately, not a literary image. Also, perhaps, because it's rooted, it takes us somewhere new.

Well let's read a Gwala poem – "Night Party".

> Saturday evening
> Berea Road Station
> the 1044's long been gone.
> By the time
> I touch Mpumalanga
> at Zero-One-Thirty Hour
> got to zwakala
> into this wholenight gig;
> Winwood and Capaldi
> create Traffic on cellophane
> in a world
> already bored
> with riches and hobos:
> the same vile wealth
> that drugged Jimi Hendrix
> out of Life,
> the same nourished want
> that starved the sax bit
> of Charlie 'Bird' Parker
> to his grave.
> By break of Sunday's dawn
> with scanted
> crooked
> chimney smokes
> straightening me home
> the eagles have already
> flown in.

166

The images are clear and cinematic, the language moves, he commits himself to the specific. His anguish is that capitalism can and has destroyed black genius (his own included, no doubt). The poem changes gear right at the end to the powerful metaphor of the eagles.

You like to read poems aloud . . .

About the time *The Door to the River* was published, my friend Wally Gilbert and I started a business making wooden toys. He was a self-taught mechanical engineer. He was the first person I met with whom I could have an open-ended conversation on no fixed subject, and we spoke for hours on end. I read a lot of poetry to him, both my own and the poems I liked. My second book *The Fires of the Dead*, which came out in 1989, was dedicated to him. He had died the year before. The book looked both outwards and inwards. Things were dark in the late 80s, repression became cruder, PW Botha's thuggish government was getting desperate and killing people everywhere. In Grahamstown the police set up a searchlight at the 1820 Settlers Monument and beamed it across to the township so the casspirs patrolling there could see better.

In your 1999 volume Rain Across a Paper Field, *although there is a thread of narrative, the concentration is much more on pure lyric.*

Possibly the style in this book is too pared down. It came at the end of ten years as an editor. I don't think I can go any further in that direction. I need to go into new territory after this. When you are virtually a full time editor, reading other people's poems every day, you can become too flooded with words to hear your own lyrical impulse. That's why I've stopped editing poetry.

Yet a poem like "the return" has a lot of surreal images as well as narrative –

Well it's more grounded, to use that word again. The lyric impulse is there, but it gets further, to a kind of spiritual place, probably because the poem is grounded in political and psychological realities. That poem was a moment of real clarity, almost a revelation, that there is a future, a future after global capitalism, and that that future is beginning already.

Your poems are not only rooted in the immediate physical, but also in the immediate psychic, so they feed your own integration . . .

I usually write because I have to.

But a good deal of your creative energy went into editing New Coin *for ten years. How did you tackle it? What were your criteria for selection?*

When I took on *New Coin* I wanted to follow the example of Jerome Rothenberg, who'd put together some excellent anthologies in the 70s. One was *Technicians of the Sacred*, a collection of 'primitive' poetry transcribed mostly by anthropologists, with avant-garde twentieth century poetry alongside it showing similar themes and forms. Another was *America A Prophecy*, which he edited with George Quasha, in which some canonical American poetry was put together with more marginalised poetries, like sermons, blues, Shaker ecstatic religious poetry, homegrown surrealists, etc. I thought I could find similar marginalised poetries in South Africa, non-literary poetries if you like. So I was on the lookout, among poetry being sent to *New Coin*, for work that took emotional risks, or reflected the surrealism that surrounds us in South Africa. And I found it and printed it, even if the writing was sometimes clumsy.

I got into correspondence with everyone who sent in poems, trying to give helpful criticism, recommending poets for them to read. There was a certain inappropriateness about this at times, and some arrogance too on my part, but mostly people appreciated the feedback. The first few years were hard, there was little coming in that I really liked. You can't print only what you like, you have to fill up a quota of pages. The more important thing is that I didn't print anything I didn't like. This made me some enemies right away, but there was nothing I could do about that.

In a way you generated the poetry you believed to be there. Had you not had that vision to begin with, these voices would not have emerged.

It's true in a way. I can think of one poet, for example, who had given up writing for some years. I contacted him and asked him to clarify something in one of his old poems, and just because of that little encouragement, he started writing again, and hasn't ceased. *New Coin* got its own momentum, and the poetry started cooking. The juxtaposition of different styles and genres helped it cook further. Many of the linguistically innovative poets were black poets: Rampolokeng, Motsapi, Nyezwa, Zhuwao, Muila, Dladla, Bila and others. Why nobody in academe (with the exception of Kelwyn Sole) has registered the importance of these poets is beyond me. It really makes me wonder whether these professional literary people are able to read.

With poems written out of necessity, you can recognise them immediately. They usually have an idiosyncratic but coherent vocabulary, unique forms, a taking on reality at several levels at once. It doesn't matter how much or how little education the poet has had, the signs are unmistakeable. And always there is a hunger for reading. Phillip Zhuwao, with a primary school education, had by his early 20s, in the literary barrenness of Harare, read Akhmatova, Mandelstam, Rimbaud. The necessity to read and write takes over the poet's whole being.

It's frowned upon to look at it like that, especially in academe.

168

Because it's dangerous. To so inhabit imaginative reality and express through your mind and body things which almost overwhelm you, is not easy. And they are not nice things either, much of the time, they make demands on the reader and people reject them. Some of these poets have had no recognition at all. We're living in a society which denies ecstasy and denies pain, poems too are consumer commodities. Plus there's the decline in reading in general. It's not surprising that poets and other artists retreat into alcoholism, consumerism, academia, or some other suicide of the soul. To survive creatively you really have to believe in yourself.

You've said that you were prepared to publish some and not others – again, how did you make the choices?

If a poem did nothing for me then I couldn't print it. Of course I made some mistakes, rejecting some poems because I wasn't open enough to them. My sense of poetry broadened as time went on, but the criterion remained the same – the poem had to move me or engage me. I couldn't go by the writer's reputation, I had to take it poem by poem. It becomes like one big found poem, even though you find it in your postbox. And you've got to put each issue into an order dictated by its own logic, which is always different. Editing puts you in an impossible position, because you are custodian of a limited publishing space, so whatever you do is going to be unpopular.

And if you apply these criteria to yourself as a poet sending your own stuff to a magazine?

I try to live with a poem before I send it anywhere. Then I read it to people. They don't have to be literary people. By reading the same poem to different people I see if it retains its energy or if it runs out of steam after a few readings.

So you have to trust what you feel about it, there's nothing else really to go by?

What else is there to go by? In some ways it's worse when you've published a few books, when you're semi-wellknown. The South African literary world is tiny, and people are too polite about each other. Or they hate each other. That's why it's impossible to find reviewers. Nobody wants to say what they think or offend their friends. If they concentrated on the poems rather than the poet it would be better for everyone.

You've conducted lots of writing courses. Do you find them useful for your own writing?

I'm beginning to think that teaching people to read is more important than teaching them to write. Poets should know international literature and the literature of the past, at least know what resonates with them. If you teach writing you have the opportunity to introduce a writer to poets close to his or her own voice. Next year I want to work on a project with Mxolisi Nyezwa with rural writers in the Eastern Cape, which will establish libraries and small magazines. We will ask the writers to research what should go into those libraries, in both Xhosa and English.

You believe in the necessity of publishing: what do you think about marketing?

Your text goes out into the world looking for its reader. It comes from your heart and reaches someone else's heart. It's a mysterious and magical process which justifies a lot of the work of writing. I believe poems reach their readers no matter what. Marketing can help but the process happens more subtly than anything that marketing can bring to it.

So to return to your own work: what are you working on now?

I've just finished a biography of the Lesotho agriculturalist and novelist JJ Machobane. I've started writing my own story, partly poetry partly prose. Maybe this will allow me to integrate the past. It's hard to expose one's own shame and humiliation, but it's necessary. In capitalism we're all involved with shame.

How are you going to maintain your poetry?

I'll pursue trying to be honest with myself, I'll pray to God, the muse and my guardian spirits to engage deeper.

You mention God in South African poetry and people think you have ideas of grandeur.

But poetry, as Gary Snyder has pointed out, is a continuous line from the shamanistic, when healing, dance, chant, divination and poetry were all one thing. And poetry gives voice to both the human and the non-human, which has new importance as we are going into huge environmental crisis. All poetry that endures is a form of magic, an illuminated language.

Do you have any sense of the poet's task, the poet's obligation? Denise Levertov, for example, has a clear sense of the poet's duty towards poetry.

We all have a duty to use and practice our gifts, don't you think? No matter what they are.

In two of your major poems, "The Way Back" and "the return", you write of language being translated from silence or born from silence. Why is this important to you?

I don't know. To reach silence is like touching some absolute ground. I know that we

170

never escape from language but if I spend time in silence – I am speaking for myself – I can experience emotion more clearly. The spirit or muse of non-verbal poetry is real for me. In my poem "testimony" there is a part which goes:

> where the oxalis hides
> under streaked clouds
> that's where to find your voice
> silent one
>
> where the herb smell
> permeates your clothes
> when the earth is bare
> and nothing flows
> that's when your voice calls
> silent one

You're now putting together an anthology of poems from your ten years of editing New Coin. Do you have any plans to continue as a poetry editor?

No. Editing has been a long detour. I learned a lot, both about poetry and about South Africa. But it has been a detour. I need to get back to silence, to beginner's mind, and write.

I'm impressed by your sense of continuity.

Well I'm an African by now. Africa endures. We still help our neighbours, no matter how poor they are. We act communally. I can't see any of these things being destroyed. I'm putting myself with the poor people of Africa. We are going to survive.

Being a poet is only partly to do with language. The rest is about facing yourself, listening to yourself. When I'm not honest with myself my poetry is weakened and no amount of skill can rescue it. More and more I believe the only way to continue as a writer is to go with risky creative choices in your life as much as in your writing. They become one.

Interviewed by Joan Metelerkamp

ANGIFI PROCTOR DLADLA, also known as Muntu wa Bachaki, was born at
Wakkerstroom old location in 1950. He is a history and language teacher in Katlehong.
He wrote and produced the plays *Mene Tekel, Mistress Magumbo, Dennis the Goat on
Trial, Saragorah*, and other plays. For the past few years he has taught writing and
produced newspapers with inmates of Boksburg Prison and the youth in Katlehong.

Book of poems published:
The Girl Who Then Feared to Sleep (Deep South, 2001)

On a practical level, how do you write? Where and when you do it?

I write everywhere, anytime. That's why, when I go, I always carry a booklet and a
pen. If an image or anything flashes on me, I must be ready to jot it down, otherwise
I'll regret – it will never come back. Then at home I record that on the computer.

Do you do it in a disciplined way, every day? or once a week? do you have a rhythm?

Friday is my day – poetry day. During the course of the week, as I said, I record
sketches on the computer, allowing my mind to work on them. Then on Friday, I bring
things together. On Saturday I work on plays, because I'm also a playwright. But there
is flexibility. When a poem or a play shapes itself, it takes over – it becomes a
dictator, taking all my time – sometimes the whole night, sometimes many days. So
other work suffers! I want to be alone during this period, and my stamina is
incredible. If one can peep into my study, one would say "Disorder!" because things
are just scattered all over, even on the floor.

When I'm through, I'm filled with satisfaction. I want to go out somewhere where there
is noise, to a shebeen or tavern to talk and dance. Then as I am a teacher, during the
holidays, especially in December, I get enough time to polish my work.

*What is the relationship between writing drama and poetry? Do you see the two as
part of one enterprise, or are they divided?*

They're part of one enterprise. I let what has struck me settle in my mind, then the
genre will choose itself. Sometimes when I work on a poem, I feel I could explore
more and turn it into a play. Sometimes when I write a play, I steal something from it,
and transform it into a poem. When that relentless force takes over, the division no
longer exists. Though a play is different from a poem, they both deal with human life.

172

They influence each other : there is poetry in some of my plays and there is drama in some of my poems.

Like in the poem about the woman who drowned, "Remembering Zanyana after four decades" – that's complete drama! Do you have a sense of priority, that your plays are more important for this, or your poems more important for that?

A play gives me the feeling of how it is to be God, to be a Creator. I am a creator, creating worlds of my people including other creatures, the situations, and the atmosphere. This is exciting, especially the most difficult part – to be invisible as a creator!

But there's something unfair about a play. I tolerate the characters, but they do not tolerate me. As they go their own ways they become real human beings. I see them moving away from me like a growing child moving away from what the parents thought it would be. From the characters of the play I learn about human nature. Their independence frightens me, but at the same time it gives me pleasure and satisfaction. I hear their voices. That's why I want to be alone in this state, to talk and argue and laugh with these people.

With poetry it's more like crossing the borders. Poetry demands a search for the essence of things. The deeper I go, the more I'm sucked in and in and in. I become liberated from the physical world to the spiritual world! Take, for example, the poem "Rubbished". That was about a schoolchild who was shot and hacked and left to die at a rubbish dump in Katlehong. I wrote this poem the very day I saw the body. Then one day, after many years of seeing people dying and visiting the mortuaries to identify my relatives, I wrote "Ubuntu". This poem led me to go deeper, to write "At the government mortuary," "So turned a taxi", "Our bodies", "Rotting", "Bodies", "The dead". No matter how many corpses one sees, one cannot get used to them. I had questions!

Poems started to unfold as if a divine hand was working. My stepfather passed away one August. Then in August the following year he visited me. I wrote "Exposure" about that experience. Later I wrote another poem in Zulu, "Uhambo". It was when I was in hospital. While the doctors were busy with me, I left my body . . .

Your poems have a sense of objective observation at the same time as intense personal connection. How do plays differ?

My plays are not so personal. Characters are on their own living their own lives. But there is a new trend in my plays now – I share with the characters of my plays the great truths I gained from poetry.

I'm thinking of the title poem of your book: "The girl who then feared to sleep" – can you tell me a bit about that poem?

I won't go into detail, those memories . . . but she was afraid of death, she didn't want to sleep . . . Why? She thought if she fell into sleep, she would die.

There's something about the diction – the language is completely accessible. Do you read your poems aloud?

I read aloud what I write – lines, stanzas, and the whole poem. I want to hear the words, the lines! This helps in editing the work. That's why I want to be alone. Then I'll shelve the work for some months. When I return to it, it's a new thing. I read it, sometimes I change roles. Sometimes the people in my township ask me to write a poem for a certain event. The last poem in my collection, "song of the aged" is one of those. I was invited to an old age home in Katlehong.

How did that feel?

Inner joy and satisfaction. People themselves appreciated in wonder and awe. So engrossed were they that at the end of the poem they waited some seconds in disbelief, then they simultaneously ululated and clapped hands as if something pressed them. Again, I've got a lot of clocks at home, shirts, and other gifts presented by those who invited me to various events.

Which were you led to first – drama or poetry? or were you led to them simultaneously?

When I was a child, at the time I mastered reading, they hid all family letters, maybe because I used to read them aloud outside. That's when my aunt brought me comic magazines from where she worked. I started writing notes about my experiences, people I knew, places I visited. I was not aware that I was writing a diary! Nobody told me to do that. In that book there is a part where I wrote about my girlfriends, all of them: name, age, physique, personality. It's amazing! This diary is my treasure now, my mine!

When I was doing a teacher's course, we were compelled to take theory of music in the first year – staff notation and all that stuff. We students from Transvaal knew nothing about the theory of music. In Natal it seemed they were doing this even in the primary school. I was so frustrated, and our music master seemed to be amused when we struggled with these knobkerrie-like things. One day during the study period, as some students were composing their own songs, I wrote a poem in Zulu. My classmates praised me. That was the beginning . . .

What started you on the plays?

174

I guess it was the influence of radio plays and school sketches. At high school I had already started writing plays which were performed. One that I wrote at St. Chad's High changed my vision about plays. I was commissioned by one of the teachers to write it. We worked as a team – choristers, teachers, school clerks, villagers, local priest, the whole student body took part. The play became ours, not mine. It was one of the greatest moments in my life! Later I studied speech and drama. I had this vision of community involvement when I started the Akudlalwa Communal Theatre . . . We created a lot of plays with the nurses, social workers, students, church people, sangomas and the faith healers. Unfortunately the blood-letting of the 90s disrupted this vigorous community programme.

Was your reading of other poets an influence?

In those days, there was no 'poetry' in our midst except what we studied at school. The school did not regard community poetry as poetry because it was not in print. There was no soul of the community in the classroom. We were just forced to memorise poems in English, Afrikaans and Zulu. I first read a Zulu poetry book in Junior Secondary School. Even at the university I did not get a real sense of poetry. But I kept on writing. Then in the late 1970s Prof Zeke Mphahlele arrived from exile. I attended all his writing workshops. The hall was always full at first, but later we became very few. Those who remained are writers today.

Those workshops really opened me up. Mphahlele exposed us to African, Afro-American and Caribbean literature. It was my first time to hear of South African writers like Dennis Brutus, Mazisi Kunene, Keorapetse Kgositsile and others. He exposed us to strange names like Ngugi wa Thiong'o, Sembene Ousmane, Leopold Senghor, Antonio Jacinto, Frantz Fanon, Okot P'Bitek – names I couldn't even pronounce. I liked Okot P'Bitek's *Song of Lawino* and *Song of Ocol*. I still feel that one day I must dramatise this work.

And now? Do you read a lot?

Absolutely. A writer must read, must be knowledgeable about everything. I like ancient history and books on literary criticism and on spirituality.

What inspired you to teach writing?

It was Professor Zeke Mphahlele. From him I learnt that writing can be taught. In my school days, teachers used to say writing cannot be taught. A person must be gifted, that' s all! At the teachers' college we were just told that a composition must have a beginning, a body and an ending or conclusion. No details. This was troubling me. Then, from a certain book I learned about a topic sentence in each paragraph. I tried all this, but I was not satisfied. So, as a young writer, the school did not show me the way. Even as a teacher, it is obvious, I was stuck, I could not go further in really arming my students. For years I did what was expected – giving the kids topics and demanded work. I did not write with them; I was not exemplary!

I was a sole reader of their works. I was sort of a commander and a judge with a stick and a red pen, always finding faults, condemning the child to do corrections! The child gained nothing – but fear, frustration and the art of cheating for survival.

And the skills of teaching, where did you get them?

At (IAJ) the Institute for the Advancement of Journalism in South Africa and at the Poynter Institute, Florida, USA. Writing teachers such as Hugh Lewin, and Roy Peter Clark have really given me confidence with the writing process and everything concerning the teaching of writing. I am still learning . . .

Situations, incidents, are often a spur to your writing, aren't they? Like your poem, "An Intruder".

Oh yes. That was in 1979. I was a new teacher in Vosloorus. One day immediately after break, I was writing something on the board, and students were coming in. Then something came storming in. It was a wild man, kicking, punching, biting and scratching the hell out of me. Fortunately, the boys dragged and kicked him out. Girls were pleading to them he must not be killed "It is Mahlomola, the local madman."

I couldn't teach that day. Students and teachers were laughing at me, even the principal himself, though consoling me, was laughing in a way. I was not angry, I also laughed! After school at Moleba bus stop, there were students in groups. It was obvious they were talking about my misfortune and giggling. In the bus to Katlehong, same thing. At home I took my typewriter and worked on a poem . . .

In the morning, it was the same thing, even at the assembly. When students looked at me, they could not control themselves. Some were covering their mouths, others with tissue papers were wiping their eyes. My first period was in the same classroom where I was attacked. Laughter again! Smilingly I said, "I have a poem." All shushed one another. They collected themselves in that adolescent mischievous silence. I read the poem. "Encore, Meneer!" I read it again. Coins were tossed . . . "Read it again, Meneer!" That was the end of laughter . . .

At the end of my period the class did not want me to go. But I went out, some students following me. In the classes where I entered, I found one or two stanzas of the poem, though corrupted, already on the board. There was interception! They asked me to read. I read the poem several times even in the classes where I was not teaching. The headmaster said I should read the poem for the whole student body at once at the assembly. That was the end of laughter . . . Even today, when I meet my former students, they are oldsters now, some are in high positions . . . they all ask, "Meneer, where is 'The Intruder'?"

176

You often write directly in response to events, or even requests?

I was once persuaded by a friend of mine, Judas Mahlangu, the artist, to write poems on his artworks. He invited me while he was busy working on a fertility doll and other works. He wanted me to read them at the exhibition, to give dignity to the whole occasion. So I wrote a poem about the fertility doll; but unfortunately the exhibition did not happen . . . .

> call me between your tears and eyes;
> i'm the shadow, i won't drown.
> draw me between your pain and faith;
> i'm the shadow that leads.
> will me within your heart of hearts;
> i'm the energy that's divine.
> hug me with the arm of your heart;
> i'm reality, i am love . . .
> listen to the silence in silence –
> the dream materialising . . .

It's the voice of the fertility doll . . . the voice of our desires . . .

All the miracles are within us; we have a lot of power but we are not aware of the power we have. The fertility doll is a symbol of that – I'm meditating on how we work from within to make things happen

You're living in a spiritual reality, but at the same time you're looking out – grace and pain co-exist in your work. You manage to observe without being overwhelmed by the pain we inflict on one another. It's a quality of vision, an integration, which is very rare. It strikes me as the voice of wisdom.

Thank you, I was not aware of this. In the 1980s the scourge of the necklace took many lives in our country. The UDF used the youth to silence their opponents and to force people to join them. That agonised me. School kids would prowl around the township or schools and cause unspeakable havoc. They would burst into the classrooms and force others out to burn the shops, the houses, the vehicles and the people in the township as they wanted to make the country ungovernable. Teachers were damn scared of these 'comrades'. Even black journalists did not dare condemn them. They knew the scourge of the tyre! These boys and girls would disrupt even the funeral of their opponents, throwing away food and stoning the vehicles. Sometimes they would prevent the family from burying their loved one. They had an incredible urge for necklacing. If it happened that their 'enemy' was killed by other people, they would dig his body from the grave and necklace it there for their pleasure! In the 1980s Katlehong was one of the necklace champions.

Even though it was dangerous, you wrote about it . . .

Something said to me "Write a play. Write, write . . !" I wrote *Mene Tekel*. In this play I made the main character to be a powerful born-again Christian boy – these students who used to preach that "Si jola no Jesu, hhay abantu base zweni – We fall in love with Jesus, not lovers of this sinful world." In the play a powerful born-again girl was killed. Students suspected a notorious tsotsi. They toyi-toyied to necklace him. Later the detectives led to the arrest of the main character.

When it came to performing, I took for actors the very boys and girls who were the veterans of the necklace, to use their profession on stage. As we were rehearsing, teachers were afraid of coming nearer. They were afraid even of me. After three weeks of rehearsal, I invited the teachers, others from other schools, the parents, and some born-again people for a dress rehearsal at the school hall. Unfortunately the born-again people left during the play, shaking and visibly angry. When I pleaded with them to see the whole play and then we would discuss, they accused me of Satanism. They said I was inspired by the devil. I never saw them again, till to this day. But a certain pastor who saw the play several times encouraged me to continue with it. He sent his congregation to see the show and there were discussions.

Whenever we performed, we had our fanatics just like soccer fans – the halls were always full. The performance was ghastly. We used methylated spirits for the flame . . . And then – necklacing decreased in Katlehong! These kids, they changed!

That's an astonishing story!

Kids are kids, they like beauty, they like good things. It is easy to mould them. If you just work with their energy for a good cause, they'll follow you and do wonders. No wedge or threats can take them away from you. But don't take chances. Be professional. Nothing can beat honesty, truth, beauty and quality. Everybody wants to be praised for what is good and beautiful, no one wants to be praised or feared for being a monster.

It was interesting to see teachers mingling with the parents shaking hands with the performers. Imagine what happens to a child when a teacher asks: "How did you do that, you were so natural . . . you were crying, I saw your tears," or "You were a real pastor" or "You were a real tsotsi." Their parents invited me for lunch or supper, and asked: "How did you do that? SAP failed. SADF failed. But with you . . . these boys, they changed."

Your work in prisons, is it similar?

Ja, but there is a problem: a prison is a prison! Some people in power there are not yet ready, they are hampering the programme. But the parents of these inmates visit me and say, "Keep it up, these boys . . . their dreams now . . . their perception of the world now . . . is positive." This gives me strength that good will triumph. Even the prison bosses are also human beings, they do have human goodness. So, change they will!

Your experience suggests that art can be a powerful form for social healing.

No doubt about this. Experience has shown me that art is a shorthand for healing. For example, I used to have a terrible stutter. I am a sensitive person by nature, this stutter was embarrassing me. But strange, on stage there was no stutter, no stammer. Another example – some years ago I found out that my stepfather tried to poison me. I almost died a horrible death in a train to boarding school. This made me despondent and withdrawn. I trusted no one! I feared taking food or drinks from anyone. A year later I wrote a poem about my poison ordeal. I was literally crying as I was writing. But I was cured!

As a writing teacher, I encourage my students to write about their own lives, their own experiences – what they know best. Even with a play the actors or actresses, whether at school or in the prison, work from within, living their characters. It is taxing, but professional. I like the improvisation. We all contribute in making a play.

You have an amazing range of technique – many different voices and different forms. For example, in the fertility doll poem, you use a dramatic voice, the voice of the fertility doll that is quite close to another voice, the prophetic voice, which you also use. Then you have a narrative voice, a different mode; close to the dramatic, like in your tragi-comic poem "Remembering Zanyana".

Did you see the film *The Great Dance*? The Khoisan hunter says when he chases his prey he transforms himself into that animal. I also do that when I go deeper and deeper, I transmogrify myself into, for example, a fertility doll . . .

You are a history teacher. It is a crucial school subject. How can our children get any political or sociological perspective without it? and yet it isn't a priority in our schools. My daughter, for example, has to choose between science and history for matric.

All languages have past, present and the future tenses. For us to communicate we use these tenses; so does learning and teaching . . . so does this interview! For us to advance as a human race we need to remind ourselves of who we really are and thus we communicate and build on past achievements. Even ourselves, we are the products of history. The past exists in us – it is perceptible! South Africa is not Denmark because our history is different. History is crucial. Even the psychologists are aware of this – thus psychoanalysis. "Never Again" is the slogan of politicians in South Africa – never will we oppress another human being because of colour, gender, beliefs! And never will we misinterpret and distort historical facts to further our sectarian interests! The politicians look back and cry "Never Again." How can a child celebrate Human Rights Day if he or she is denied the history that led to this?

Our children must learn history whether they are interested in mathematics or physical science or economics or management. Our science students must know about Hiroshima and Nagasaki, Dr Wouter Basson and Dr Joseph Mengele, so that they will confidently sing a chorus, "Never Again will we invent a science of destruction!" How can economics students solve the problems of South Africa if they know nothing about the historical background? South Africa will never have geniuses if we run away from our history. We'll never be an inventive nation. Instead we will hire foreigners as consultants with foreign solutions to solve our problems.

Your historical awareness informs your poetics. Do you want to say something about your political beliefs? For example, in "When I was a child" and "From sunrise" you deliberately speak in terms of race. Why is this?

I am a Pan-Africanist. Robert Mangaliso Sobukwe, one of the shamefully marginalised giants, says, "There is only one race to which we all belong and that is the Human Race. In our vocabulary therefore, the word race, as applied to man, has no plural form." I am a Pan-Africanist, I belong to the Human Race! So are the Delits of India, the Australian Aborigines, the Gypsies of Europe, the Kurds of Iraq and Turkey and the native Americans.

But some human beings – the Hitlers of this world with their Herrenvolk sickness, because of their colour and shape of their noses feel superior to those with a different colour, different shape of nose. They regard them as things to be hunted, auctioned, owned, pressed, driven, operated and destroyed. As a Pan-Africanist I say I am not a thing, I am not a body – I am not what is bound by time, I am not what is disfigured by accidents and diseases, I am not what is aging and decaying. I am not a nose, you are not a hair! We all belong to the Human Race, even Hitler and his descendents. We can feed our bodies from sunrise to sunrise, but this is not our goal as a Human Race, we are not the stomachs. Though we are here, we are with the universe! Because of the Hitlers of this world and their segregation policies, we never lived side by side with those of a different skin colour . . .

Whites were a mystery to me, although I knew white police and white soldiers very well. I'm sure this made me fail to differentiate whites – they were all the same to me, as there are whites also who could not differentiate blacks. But again, this is a fact of history! My little boy does not fear the whites. When we are in town, at the mall, he stops and plays with them, he goes to a computer and plays games with them. He does not have a 'body mentality.' He does not see colour, he sees human beings. My son is a Pan-Africanist by nature, though I never talked with him about it.

It is true that our civilisation is highly advanced bodily, materially, but we lack the knowledge of why we are here. In South Africa bodies attract bodies – accumulation of weapons, money, Pajeros, Mercedes-Benzes (in Gauteng we call them Yengenis), mansions – these things all harmonize with those bodies in places of power. Where is love and compassion? I wonder what they think when their plane is about to land in Cape Town . . . down into an ocean of shacks, the constituencies of our leaders, singing after their names . . . I wonder . . . is this modern ubuntu or modern cannibalism?

It is our call as poets and learners to read the past, to work on the now, not for the future – but for eternity. Otherwise we'll be part of the Hitlers of this world, part of the 'bodyism' which is causing the destruction of our planet. So, it is clear in the poems, "When I was a child", and "From sunrise" and "Rotting" I am not dealing with race – but with humanity and with bodies. We are not just bodies!

You know people are always talking about the marginalisation of the poet, of poetry; but you seem to have a very different sense of poetry – does it worry you how the poet is looked at by other people?

But who is marginalising the poet?

Publishing houses, 'the market' – it's difficult to get poems published, as you know, you certainly don't have any institutional support if you're a poet. You can't make a living from poems . . .

Great teachers and poets in history did not make a living from their works. Socrates, Gala kaNodada and Mohlomi; Simon Kimbangu, Jesus of Nazareth or Simeon Toko; Fard Muhammed and Elijah Muhammed; Sobukwe, Tabata, Mothopeng, Lembede, Zulei and Biko; Arthur Nortje, Ingoapele Madingoane and many more. Apartheid made sure that nearly all publishing companies exist for schools. These companies won't publish anything that will hurt the politicians, otherwise their books won't be prescribed. Great poets are not cheap singers praising what is imperfect, disposable and dying. They praise only the universe . . . the Almighty God!

No, the market is there – we need only ideas to reach it. Jazz musicians in this country were or are in the same situation. Let's look at what they are doing . . . and take notes . . . Let's look also at those who came before us . . . History again!

You are suggesting that there are communities within communities that support poetry or who recognise a need for it . . .

Poems are with the people, they must remain there . . .

Is the support of poetry a community attitude, or is it your own attitude? Do you have a sense of yourself as a poet within a community? Or is it that the people amongst whom you live are receptive? How much do you have to make opportunities for yourself?

The people are important, not the publishing houses. The people regard poets in high esteem. In my community, for example, when there is a funeral, family members, either the kids or the adults, read poems they have written about the deceased.

Recently, a well-known businessman, but certainly not a poet – Mr Themba Mashinini – lost his wife. During the funeral, he let someone read a poem he wrote about his wife. At the lobola ceremonies, at the weddings, at parties for the initiates from the mountain school, at the school concerts and debates – poetry is there. Even at political rallies, poetry is there. This is our strength!